Pentecostalism

Pentecostalism

WOLFGANG VONDEY

B L O O M S B U R Y

LONDON • NEW DELHI • NEW YORK • SYDNEY

Bloomsbury T&T Clark
An imprint of Bloomsbury Publishing Plc

50 Bedford Square
London
WC1B 3DP
UK

175 Fifth Avenue
New York
NY 10010
USA

www.bloomsbury.com

First published 2013

British Library Cataloguing-in-Publication Data
A catalogue record for this book is available from the British Library.

ISBN: HB: 978-0-567-15460-6
PB: 978-0-567-2226-9

Typeset by Fakenham Preprss Solutions, Fakenham, Norfolk NR21 8NN
Printed and bound in Great Britain

To Noah Alexander

CONTENTS

ABBREVIATIONS

AE	American Ethnologist
AF	The Apostolic Faith
AJPS	Asian Journal of Pentecostal Studies
ASR	American Sociological Review
CPCR	Cyberjournal for Pentecostal-Charismatic Research
CT	Christianity Today
Digest	The Digest: Transdisciplinary Approaches to Foundational Questions
EI	Ecclesiological Investigations Series
ERT	Evangelical Review of Theology
IBMR	International Bulletin of Missionary Research
IRM	International Review of Mission
JASA	Journal of the American Scientific Affiliation
JEPTA	Journal of the European Pentecostal Theological Association
JES	Journal of Ecumenical Studies
JMER	Exchange: Journal for Missiological and Ecumenical Research
JPST	Journal of Psychology and Theology
JPT	Journal of Pentecostal Theology
JPTSup	Journal of Pentecostal Theology, Supplement Series

JRitS	Journal of Ritual Studies
JRT	Journal of Religious Thought
JSSR	Journal for the Scientific Study of Religion
MF	Ministerial Formation
MIR	Missiology: An International Review
NIDPCM	The New International Dictionary of Pentecostal and Charismatic Movements
PM	Pentecostal Manifestos Series
Pneuma	Pneuma: The Journal of the Society for Pentecostal Studies
PS	PentecoStudies
Rel	Religion
RevRR	Review of Religious Research
SGC	Studies in Global Christianity Series
SIE	Studies in Evangelicalism Series
SOR	Sociology of Religion
TS	Theological Studies
TTod	Theology Today
WeslTJ	Wesleyan Theological Journal
Zygon	Zygon: The Journal of Religion and Science

INTRODUCTION

Pentecostalism is a perplexing phenomenon. Beginning as a fringe movement at a marginal position in the Christian world, the modern-day Pentecostal movement has become one of the fastest-growing religious movements of the twenty-first century. Today's Pentecostalism is a global phenomenon, an ecumenical melting pot, a theological puzzle consisting of a multiplicity of voices and positions, and a major factor in the shaping of late modern Christianity. Among other things, Pentecostalism has been called a church, a religious faction, a sect, a doctrine, a spirituality, a revival, a fanatic stream, a schism, a renewal movement, an event, and an experience. While Pentecostals have traditionally understood themselves as a movement from God in the last days, outsiders have often denounced the movement as anti-Christian or at the very least located at a position far removed from the Christian mainstream. Advocates of Pentecostalism portray the movement as an ambassador for Christian unity and highlight its pathos of liberation, its vision of restoration, and its emphasis on personal relationships, human transformation, and ethnic reconciliation. In contrast, the anti-Pentecostal sentiment ranges from accusations of excessive emotionalism or eccentric but harmless ideology to harmful teaching and outright heresy. The unprecedented growth of Pentecostalism in all its diversity has led to characterizations ripe with platitudes, stereotypes, and misrepresentations. The opinions about Pentecostalism are at least as perplexing as the movement itself.

Global Pentecostalism is a movement in transition. Since the widely recognized revivals that mark the historical origins of classical Pentecostalism in different parts of the world at the beginning of the twentieth century, the movement has endured unprecedented changes in its global representation, doctrinal composition, ecumenical participation, organizational structures, liturgical make-up, religious ethos, socio-cultural significance, and political participation. These changes make it difficult for many to identify the complex composition of worldwide Pentecostalism. Observers struggle with the correct terminology: Some have suggested to speak of 'Pentecostalisms' in the plural rather than the singular; others use the word 'Pentecostal' as a blanket term that covers all movements that emphasize the work of the Holy Spirit, while again others prefer to distinguish the 'Pentecostal Movement' from the so-called 'Charismatic Movement' in the traditional churches. The result of these conflicting attempts to define the essence of Pentecostalism has been a myriad of arguments and studies on various elements of the Pentecostal movement albeit without an overarching theory of Pentecostal identity. The student of Pentecostalism is left with a choice to either produce a homogeneous image of the movement from the different accounts or to choose between one or the other element of Pentecostalism – either choice does not fit the global reality of the movement.

This Guide for the Perplexed is an invitation to engage the diversity of Pentecostalism without reducing the movement to one of its elements or distorting the image with a homogeneous account that does not reflect the movement's perplexing reality of often conflicting beliefs and practices. While this intention implies to a certain extent a phenomenological approach to Pentecostalism, the underlying goal of this introduction is to gain a general understanding of the identity of Pentecostalism as a whole. Consequently, this volume is not a historical introduction to Pentecostalism or a survey of the global dimensions of the movement, although both elements are present, nor is the intention to offer an account of Pentecostal distinctives or a characterization of Pentecostalism that would fit the movement exactly into the Christian landscape. On the contrary, this introduction to Pentecostalism concentrates on the tensions existing within the movement between its orthodox and radical elements. Rather than eschewing certain unwanted features or attempting to provide a homogeneous image of the complex movement, these perhaps irreconcilable struggles are presented as the hallmark of the Pentecostal movement worldwide. Moreover, what may be identified more readily as contrasts and controversies within Pentecostalism are in fact only the more visible tremors of a Christian world in transition. Pentecostalism exists amidst such tensions representative of a global shift of the Christian faith in the twenty-first century.

More precisely, this Guide for the Perplexed is based on the rationale that the bewildering elements that make Pentecostalism difficult to grasp are precisely the elements that best describe the character of the movement. Seven key themes are explored to illustrate this thesis: the tension between the local roots and global pluralism of Pentecostals, the tension between the Pentecostal emphasis on holistic spirituality and the excessive display of charismatic manifestations, the tension between a divisive denominationalism and the ecumenical ethos of Pentecostalism, the tension between orthodox doctrine and the sectarian rejection of the Christian tradition by some Pentecostals, the tension between social engagement and triumphalism, the tension between democratic egalitarian ideals and the divisive effects of institutionalism, and the tension between Pentecostal scholarship and the prevalent anti-intellectualism of the movement. These tensions are representative not of the anomalies but of the struggles of Pentecostalism within the emergence of a global Christianity. Simply put, understanding Pentecostalism provides a means to understanding the changing face of the Christian world.

The objective of this introduction is to embrace the tensions inherent in Pentecostalism as part of the self-understanding of the movement. Rather than simply contrasting two sides of the movement, each chapter expands the horizon of what is meant by 'Pentecostalism' and takes the reader to a broader appreciation of its diverse range and transitions by bringing the different positions into dialogue. The goal is to dismantle existing stereotypes, to guide the reader away from internal debates, oversimplifications, a one-sided focus on Christianity in the West, or an idealist, romantic image of Pentecostalism. The conclusions reached by this text are that the restrictive, parochial, extremist, and fundamentalist tendencies of Pentecostalism are confronted by the alternative ecumenical, global, interdisciplinary, and progressive nature of a movement representative of a Christian world in transition.

The first chapter provides the context and background to the study of global Pentecostalism and charismatic Christianity in all its diversity. The student unfamiliar with Pentecostalism can begin here with historical, theological, and sociological material that helps situate the study of Pentecostalism in the broader context of the history of Christian thought. The chapter focuses on the shifting emphasis of global Christianity from the West to the East and the southern hemisphere and places worldwide Pentecostalism in contrast to so-called classical Pentecostalism in North America, thereby preparing the foundation for understanding the perplexing nature of the Pentecostal movement in its diverse contexts. This framework emphasizes the significance of understanding Pentecostalism both as a local and a global phenomenon, which explains in part the tensions inherent in existing accounts of Pentecostalism. This explanation is illustrated by the tension between grassroots communities and mega-churches that characterize the Pentecostal landscape both locally and globally. The distinction between local and global, in terms of both location and membership distribution, is a hallmark of the discussion on contemporary Pentecostalism. All subsequent explanations always depend on this necessary dynamic and must be seen in light of both local and global developments of the movement. This approach allows for a clarification of the diverse terminology applied to definitions of Pentecostal groups worldwide. The results of this interdisciplinary overview provide the basis for a conceptual understanding of the difficulties associated with Pentecostalism as they are presented in the subsequent chapters.

In light of the foundational tension outlined in the first chapter, the second chapter tackles one of the most bewildering elements of Pentecostalism in its local and global manifestations: the emphasis on the reality of the spiritual dimension of life and on holistic spirituality, on the one hand, and the public scandals surrounding the excessive display of charismatic gifts, the exploitation of the miraculous, and the apparent lack of attentiveness to spiritual matters by Pentecostal leaders, on the other hand. This tension is well portrayed in the historical anti-Pentecostal argument that describes Pentecostals as devilish, demonic, and insane, while Pentecostals understood themselves as a movement from God and their actions as divinely inspired. The chapter introduces the dimensions of the spirit-driven reality among Pentecostals and brings both extremes into dialogue for a better understanding of the bandwidth of the charismatic life that characterizes Pentecostal practices. The underlying argument of this chapter is that the spiritual dimension of life is the most fundamental aspect of Pentecostalism, experientially, socially, intellectually, and theologically. All other explanations of the perplexities within the Pentecostal movement both locally and globally depend on the understanding of the tensions inherent in the spirit-oriented life. The goal is to outline these tensions as necessary components of a spirit-driven imagination that is potentially open to all forms of manifestations of the charismatic life while intended to remain subject to the sanctifying work of the Holy Spirit.

The third chapter examines the ecclesiastical tensions of the Pentecostal movement. The chapter addresses the particular difficulties associated with situating Pentecostalism among the Christian churches. On the one hand, Pentecostalism is portrayed as a Free Church movement characterized by rampant denominationalism, non-denominational splinter-groups, as well as internal and external tendencies toward segregation. On the other hand, Pentecostals have become a driving force in the ecumenical movement since the late twentieth century. The chapter traces the development of ecumenical attitudes among Pentecostals worldwide and brings into dialogue the tensions between separatist tendencies and the pursuit of Christian unity. The intention of this chapter is to explain the various factors that have contributed to the confusing ecumenical identity of Pentecostals. Emphasis is placed on the effects of restorationist criticism, persecution and rejection, internal divisions, as well as organizational demands and institutionalization. At the same time, the chapter also portrays the current shift in attitude among Pentecostals toward the ecumenical movement and outlines the active participation and leadership of Pentecostal groups in bilateral dialogues and ecumenical conversations. The goal of this chapter is to characterize the nature of the ecumenical mindset among Pentecostals and to reflect critically on the possibility to reconcile the current state of affairs with the ecclesiology and ecumenical attitude of Pentecostalism at large.

Chapter Four introduces the longstanding theological division among Pentecostals between advocates of an orthodox trinitarian theology and the so-called Oneness Pentecostals. The latter group rejects the trinitarian theology that developed as a result of the Nicene-Constantinopolitan Creed as a de-facto tritheism; the trinitarian camp views the Oneness camp as perpetuating a sectarian form of modalistic monarchianism. Accusations of heresy are found on both sides. The perplexities of this controversy are explained by bringing both sides into dialogue on the manner and method in which Pentecostals formulate and communicate the doctrine of God. The chief argument of the chapter is that the divisions are based on structural and methodological concerns rather than the content of orthodox doctrinal confessions. This argument is illustrated with the recent Oneness-Trinitarian Pentecostal dialogue. The impasse in the debate between both sides is explained as a confrontation of the two most challenging elements of trinitarian doctrine: divine personhood and the eternal processions. The intention of this chapter is to portray the difficulties inherent in these ideas as not unique to Pentecostalism but as representative of the development of Christian doctrine in general. The goal is to allow other ecumenical traditions to identify with the struggle for the doctrine of God as it is represented in the Pentecostal movement. The two sides thus emerge not as mutually exclusive positions but as representative of the efforts within a maturing global movement to come to terms with the classical formulations of Christian doctrine.

Chapter Five compares and contrasts two distinct ways of Pentecostal upward social mobility: social engagement, exemplified in programmatic and long-term expressions of Pentecostal social activism and political and socio-cultural involvement, and triumphalism, or social passivism, exemplified in the preaching of the health and wealth gospel. The former proposes active participation and leadership in the struggle against poverty, deprivation, and oppression; the latter withdraws into a sectarian mindset, individualism, and triumphalism. On a socio-cultural level, this discrepancy brings into dialogue the tension between poverty and prosperity as well as between the affluent Pentecostal groups of the West and the impoverished Pentecostals in the global South. On a theological level, this comparison joins the concerns of political theology and economic justice by focusing both on the liberating aspects as well as the problematic elements of Pentecostal theology in different cultural and socio-economic environments. The goal of this chapter is a comparison that offers both critical and therapeutic insights into the tensions resulting from the expansion of the Pentecostal movement to global proportions and the challenges inherent in its confrontation with diverse socio-economic, cultural, and political contexts. Pentecostalism is here portrayed as a mirror of unavoidable global and local dynamics that define its social ethics and character as a religious movement.

Chapter Six engages the tensions between Pentecostalism as an egalitarian movement and its growing institutionalism, exemplified in the debates about race and gender. Any attempt to come to terms with the perplexity of Pentecostalism cannot neglect the exorbitant tensions across all streams of the movement with regard to the authority of women in ministry or the divisions between black Pentecostalism and white congregations found in different configurations across the world. Existing stereotypes portray Pentecostalism, on the one hand, either as a movement of liberation and reconciliation or, on the other hand, as a bigoted, chauvinist, and racist movement that postpones the promises of full equality to the time of a new creation while holding on to established institutional patterns. Reasons for these tensions are complex, often depending on the heritage, social context, and history of particular Pentecostal groups. The chapter presents the divisions over the representation and authority of Pentecostals across the lines of gender and race in sharp contrast to the movement's emphasis on the priesthood and prophethood of all believers. These tensions have permeated the movement worldwide and have brought many Pentecostal denominations and churches to the brink of separation. The goal of this chapter is to present the tensions between egalitarianism and institutionalism in the context of race and gender in order to explain the underlying motivation and persistence of both streams among Pentecostals today.

Chapter Seven addresses the divide between anti-intellectualism and the emergence of Pentecostal scholarship in modern-day Pentecostalism. This chapter addresses the intellectual dimension of the movement: Pentecostal attitudes toward education, pedagogy, and the academy, the development of Pentecostal scholarship, and the stereotypes and tensions inherent in the expanding field of Pentecostal studies. The social face and perception of the movement is shaped by both an alleged anti-intellectualism as well as a rising Pentecostal scholarship. On the one hand, Pentecostals are seen as outsiders to the intellectual history of the twentieth century with no apparent theological tradition, no underlying intellectual system, and no interest in developing and formulating an intellectual structure. On the other hand, Pentecostal scholarship seems poised to become a central player in the theological academy. The goal of this chapter is to confront the contrast of scholarship and anti-intellectualism by defining the anti-intellectual attitude and its motivations among classical Pentecostals and introducing the still largely uncharted territory of Pentecostal scholarship, its development and current state of affairs. The tensions of anti-intellectualism and scholarship are brought into dialogue in a conversation about the future of Pentecostal studies. This conversation suggests that Pentecostals are shaping the movement into an intellectual tradition that is likely to play a central role in the telling of the intellectual history of the twenty-first century.

A conclusion would be inappropriate for this study of Pentecostalism. It might give the impression that the Pentecostal movement stands at the end rather than the beginning of its development. Instead, a brief epilogue summarizes what has been clarified in the previous chapters as the struggle of a worldwide movement to identify its place and character in the global Christian landscape. The perplexing tensions presented throughout are seen as symptomatic for the changing face of Christianity in general. Pentecostalism is merely a major representative of the dynamics of the Christian social, cultural, and religious milieu that is in transition since at least the twentieth century. These developments are shown to far exceed the realm of religion and to expand ultimately into all dimensions of life. In turn, this characterization also explains much of the bewildering character of the movement and suggests that the immediate future of Pentecostalism may show an even greater variety of perplexities.

CHAPTER ONE

Local roots and global pluralism

A first glance at Pentecostalism worldwide immediately reveals the sheer size and complexity of the movement. Widely used statistics (particularly by Pentecostals) suggest that there are over 500 million Pentecostal and Charismatic Christians in the world today.[1] A 10-country survey conducted by the Pew Forum on Religion and Public Life in 2006 began using the term 'Renewalist' as a catch-all category to refer to Pentecostals and Charismatics as a group and estimated their number as at least a quarter of the world's two billion Christians.[2] The World Christian Database, adopting the same terminology, speaks of 560 million Renewalists in 2010 with an annual growth rate by some Pentecostal denominations of an unusually high 15 per cent.[3] These surveys also emphasize that the number and composition of Pentecostal groups differ considerably from country to country, ranging from a minimal percentage to a large majority of the population. The Center for the Study of Global Christianity locates a large portion of the membership of Pentecostal groups in a new ecclesiastical 'megabloc' of 369 million 'Independents'.[4] Another recent statistic emphasizes 'Pentecostals' and 'Charismatics' as even more sizeable movements that transcend Christian megablocs, denominations, and ecclesiastical networks.[5] The considerably large numbers in these statistics, coupled with the new interpretative terminology, often gives the impression that Pentecostalism is a mega-movement consisting of large groups with significant numerical representation among the global Christian population. Despite these often overwhelming numbers, Pentecostalism cannot simply be described from the outset as a global movement.

On the other side of the Christian landscape, at a micro-vision so to speak, Pentecostalism must be characterized as a thoroughly local phenomenon. Any exclusive emphasis on the global nature of Pentecostalism may downplay the extent to which 'locality' (particularly local history, local culture, and local interests) play a critical role in the emergence and development of Pentecostalism as well as in the engagement of any particular group of Pentecostals in matters of global concern. In the contexts of the local and the global, Pentecostalism certainly exhibits traits of both sides.[6] However, the connection between the global character of Pentecostalism and its local representation is not easily defined in the simple terms of the globalization of a local phenomenon. At the very least, the idea of a homogenous globalization of Pentecostalism that is more or less identical with a 'pentecostalization' of Christianity is too simplistic to account for the global trends and local particularities of the Pentecostal landscape.[7]

This chapter introduces the relationship between Pentecostalism as a local and global phenomenon. The diversity of Pentecostals worldwide is best understood when we consider Pentecostalism as both a local and global culture while allowing any characterization of Pentecostalism to transcend the dialectic of local and global and the debate that tends to see the emergence of the movement as either a homogenous or heterogeneous phenomenon. The chapter begins with a description of Pentecostalism as a grassroots movement, followed by a section defining the global character of Pentecostalism. The final section examines the 'glocalization' of the movement, a term that combines the emphasis of local and global without bias to either side by explaining the phenomenon of its global pluralism on the very basis of the movement's local embed-dedness. In so doing, the chapter sets the tone for the rest of this guide by locating the diverse tensions within the movement in the diversity of its local phenomena set within the expanding character of the global Pentecostal movement.

Grassroots Pentecostalism

The Pentecostal movement today takes its name and identity from the events on the day of Pentecost recorded in the New Testament. The Acts of the Apostles portrays these events as originating in a local scenario, a room of gathered disciples upon whom the Holy Spirit rests and who, filled with the Spirit, begin to speak in other tongues (Acts 2.1–4). Limited initially to a small group assembled for prayer, the observer is quickly confronted with the fact that this event occurred not only in the midst of Jerusalem but on a crowded feast day. Large groups of people soon gather and are identified as residents of various nations (vv. 9–11). To these people, the apostle Peter interprets the event in even broader terms as promissory of a global outpouring of the Holy Spirit that involves not only the people present but also their children, families, servants, and 'all who are far away' (v. 39). At the end of the day, the small group of the upper room had grown to three thousand people who became part of the life of the first Christian communities. What began as an isolated local phenomenon took on international proportions overnight, reflecting the commission given by Jesus to his disciples at the beginning of the book to be 'witnesses in Jerusalem, in all Judea and Samaria, and to the ends of the earth' (Acts 1.8).

Modern-day Pentecostalism in many ways reflects the biblical events. From the outset, Pentecostalism was born as a grassroots movement in particular locations across the world. The growth of Pentecostalism can be attributed to both the emergence of new local pockets and the expansion of local groups to international proportions. Nevertheless, conversations about Pentecostalism as a global culture are premature if the local particularities of the Pentecostal movement are neglected.

North American roots

Historically, modern-day Pentecostalism is widely portrayed as a movement originating in the twentieth century. Although the role of the Holy Spirit and the exercise of spiritual gifts can be traced throughout Christian history, affecting individuals and groups at random across Christian traditions, the phenomenon of spontaneous revivals that lead to semi-organized and eventually

institutionalized movements, all of which claim a filling with the
Holy Spirit and a shared charismatic experience, is unique to the
early twentieth century. Contemporary literature has focused
primarily on the development of Pentecostalism in North America,
often associating the historical origins of the movement with a
number of local revivals in Cherokee County, North Carolina
(1886), Topeka, Kansas (1901), and at the Azusa Street Mission
in Los Angeles (1906–9). While these revivals are responsible for
the rapid spread of Pentecostalism in the United States and the
expansion of the movement beyond North American borders,
more recent histories of Pentecostalism point to the presence of
similar revivals in Wales in 1904–5, India in 1905–6, Korea in
1907–8, and a host of other revival movements in Africa, Asia,
and Latin America.[8] The origins of many of these local manifestations of Pentecostalism cannot easily be traced back to Pentecostals
of North America, but are instead the result of unexpected and
unpredictable events in a variety of distinct locations. What characterizes the history of origins of these diverse pockets of revivals
and awakenings is not the immediate rapid expansion of the
event from individuals to large groups and eventually organized
movements and denominations but the particular local character
of the Pentecostal pioneers as they persevered throughout this
entire development. In other words, portraying the local qualities
of Pentecostalism requires historical and ethnographic as well as
journalistic qualities.[9] It is as much a character study as it is a
collection of snapshots of moments in ongoing development.

The earliest snapshots of Pentecostalism in North America
show little of the mass movement that it is today. As Walter J.
Hollenweger, the father of the study of modern-day Pentecostalism,
puts it: 'For the earliest Pentecostals it was more important to
pray than to organize.'[10] Pentecostal groups typically emerged
from spontaneous revivals at the hands of individuals, often
preachers and missionaries, who brought with them nothing but an
experience of God and a desire to encounter God in a manner and
fullness yet unattained. In many instances, these groups were ostracized from the established Christian churches, frequently isolated,
and sometimes violently persecuted. The 'Christian Union', one of
the earliest Pentecostal formations in the United States, began with
a handful of individuals in search of a revived and united church.[11]
The origins of the revival in Topeka, Kansas, considered by many

the beginning of the modern Pentecostal movement in America, can be traced back to a small group of students seeking the baptism of the Holy Spirit accompanied by the unexpected event of one student speaking in a foreign tongue.[12] The Azusa Street revival in Los Angeles, seen by most as the occasion that put Pentecostalism on the international map, began not with the thousands of people that eventually attended the revival but with a small local congregation that emerged from a cottage prayer meeting.[13] Small Pentecostal groups emerged in the North American context from a diverse background of plantation prayer grounds and the camp meetings of the American South and were eventually carried to the cities, where Pentecostalism was reshaped by the social, cultural, and religious conditions of the urban environment.[14] From these local contexts, individuals and sometimes small groups set out as evangelists and missionaries to spread Pentecostalism worldwide.

Pentecostal roots worldwide

The rise of Pentecostalism in other countries reflects similar local origins as in North America, always tied closely to the grassroots of a particular culture. The influential Welsh revival originated in a series of small awakenings in a Welsh-speaking mining community that observed the particular cultural forms of the Welsh population.[15] The earliest Pentecostal revivals in India occurred among tribal peoples in the Khasi-Jainia Hills and isolated mission stations.[16] The beginning of the Pentecostal movement in Korea is found among a small group of Methodist missionaries restricted to the Wonsan area.[17] The local foundations of these widely-cited revivals are an important indication for understanding Pentecostalism on a global scale.

In Africa, the contemporary centre of gravity of global Christianity, the story of Pentecostalism is equally tied to diverse local phenomena that exhibit considerable variety on a small scale. Pockets of Pentecostal groups erupted during the twentieth century in response to both Western missionary efforts and a number of indigenous prophetic figures across the African continent, leading to a complex mix of African-initiated churches, missionary Pentecostal communities, and new independent churches.[18] The roots of Pentecostalism on the African continent are found in the rural regions and townships, many without their own church buildings. Charismatic forms of revitalization erupted first among numerous small groups that made little impact on the national scene until the charismatic revivals across Africa in the 1970s.[19] Character studies of these groups reveal significant differences between missionary Pentecostal communities operating in Africa and African-initiated churches in theological perspectives, rites and practices, as well as the appreciation of African indigenous religions and cultures.[20] Grassroots Pentecostalism in Africa exhibits a mixture and fusion of local characteristics symptomatic for Pentecostal origins worldwide.

Much like the African landscape, Pentecostalism in Latin America has been called 'a mosaic within a mosaic', a 'spontaneous combustion', an 'immense laboratory', or a 'bricolage under construction'.[21] According to Leonardo Boff, the continent is experiencing the building of a living church, an 'ecclesiogenesis', from a multiplicity of church base communities.[22] These small communities exist in a cultural and ecclesiastical melting pot both within and in contrast to the established churches. A vibrant dimension of Roman Catholicism in Latin America, the base communities often differ from the identity of the mother church and result in 'as many ecclesiologies as there are basic ecclesial structures'.[23] For the Pentecostal communities on the ground, a similar diversity is typically reflected in small communities and fragmented groups that combine different elements autochthonous to particular regions. Small pockets of Pentecostal revivals erupted almost simultaneously in the early decades of the twentieth century in a number of Latin American countries, often in denominational groupings that already existed or as a result of immigrated churches or foreign missionary endeavours.[24] It is this fragmentation that characterizes the image of grassroots Pentecostalism across the continent even beyond the rise of national Charismatic revivals.

The picture of Pentecostalism at the grassroots is similar in Asia, where Christianity is still a sizeable minority, and a national Pentecostal movement either does not yet exist or is suppressed by religious and political forces. The remarkable growth of Pentecostalism in China is attributed largely to the prominence of small independent house churches under often severe opposition and in isolation from one another and the rest of Christianity.[25]

The Pentecostal movement in Japan emerged almost entirely from small Western missionary efforts that still have hardly exceeded the grassroots level even with the rise of larger independent church movements after World War II.[26] In South-East Asia, Pentecostalism in Thailand, Malaysia, Singapore, Indonesia, and the Philippines is largely the result of Pentecostal missionaries working together with local preachers and evangelists.[27] Similar small origins and local communities characterized Pentecostals in Australia and the Pacific before the arrival of large-scale meetings in the 1920s.

Snapshots of the countries on the European continent show a widespread dispersion of Pentecostal groups that have remained active mainly in local areas and are less developed on a national level. Apart from the impact of the Welsh revival, Pentecostal groups have mobilized only 'a minority of people at the varied margins of that world'.[28] Most Pentecostals are still engaged in establishing social and cultural respect and stability in the local communities in which they were established – a development that is by some viewed as a ghetto while others see this 'invisibility' as a passing stage in the growth of the movement.[29] Others began as small revival fellowships in the existing churches before forming independent organizations.[30] Although most of these groups are now organized on the national level, they grow slowly and remain outside of the mainstream religious traditions. Central and Eastern Europe has also been a mission field for Pentecostals, but religious restrictions and persecutions from Communist governments and state churches have often forced Pentecostals underground.[31] The roots of European Pentecostalism are in the independent grassroots revivals and movements from which Pentecostal groups emerged and in which they are still very much embedded.

These snapshots of Pentecostalism on the ground emphasize the importance of understanding the Pentecostal phenomenon always within the particularities of local discourses, contexts, and perspectives. The images of the Charismatic Movement in the mainline churches differ little in their emphasis on the importance of local, small group and individual efforts in the shaping of modern-day Pentecostalism.[32] The same image also characterizes the independent Pentecostal churches, or Free Churches, which rarely form large-scale organizations or denominations, as well as the large number of individuals who do not belong to a Pentecostal organization but nonetheless exhibit Pentecostal or Charismatic elements in their experiences and practices.[33] This diversity at the grassroots makes it difficult to affirm large-scale characterizations of Pentecostalism that are accurate for the movement as a whole. Put differently, the image of Pentecostalism requires always an additional identification so that we speak not simply of the Pentecostal movement in general but always also of Pentecostalism in particular cultures (e.g. Pentecostalism in Latin America), countries (e.g. Pentecostalism in Brazil or Argentina), and other more particular localizations of the movement (e.g. classical Pentecostalism). Pentecostalism has remained in all its global manifestations a movement at the grassroots.

Global Pentecostalism

The shift from a view at Pentecostalism on the ground to the world at large requires a change of lens from a micro- to a macro-vision. At the heart of this transition stands the question of what exactly identifies Pentecostalism as a 'global' phenomenon. The most immediate answer given is typically a reference to the increasing size and pluralism of the movement. Modern-day Pentecostalism readily facilitates a 'big' perspective in its staggering numbers and worldwide expansion. A key characteristic of Pentecostalism are the large camp meetings, national revivals, and mega-churches. The sizeable number of Pentecostals worldwide is often used to emphasize the significance of Pentecostalism, to point to a certain homogeneity among Pentecostal beliefs and practices, and to allow for interpretations of the movement that are not bound to isolated phenomena. In other words, by using the word 'global' to identify the Pentecostal movement, we are looking for a certain redundancy in observing Pentecostalism worldwide in order to arrive at a definition of the term 'Pentecostal' that applies as a common denominator to all variations of the movement.

The numerical growth and worldwide expansion of Pentecostalism has made it necessary to distinguish between different types of Pentecostalism on a large scale. The most common distinction is between the so-called classical Pentecostals connected with the revival at the Azusa Street Mission in Los Angeles (1906–9), the members of the so-called Charismatic Movements in the established

Roman Catholic, Protestant, and Orthodox churches that surfaced in North America during the 1960s, and so-called neocharismatic groups, 'a catch-all category that comprises 18,810 independent, indigenous, postdenominational denominations and groups that cannot be classified as either Pentecostal or charismatic but share a common emphasis on the Holy Spirit, spiritual gifts, Pentecostal-like experiences (*not* Pentecostal terminology), signs and wonders, and power encounters'.[34] The distinctions made here on a global level reveal the dominance of North American Pentecostalism, particularly in the United States, in terms of its international influence, and the impact of Pentecostal and Pentecostal-like phenomena in the established churches as well as in the post-denominational and non-denominational terrains of Christianity worldwide.[35] The different streams of Pentecostalism portray the movement as a cross-cultural, cross-denominational movement that seemingly transcends localities, religions, nations, ethnicities, and ideologies. The following characteristics help identify the global make-up of the three dominant streams of Pentecostalism worldwide.

Classical Pentecostalism

Classical Pentecostalism is one of the most influential streams of the global Pentecostal movement. The influence of the Azusa Street revival is readily apparent in the almost immediate attempts to engage in an evangelization of the North American continent and a worldwide missionary programme. The Azusa Street Mission appointed and supported large numbers of evangelists who travelled westward across the country and spread the movement.[36] Former participants in the Los Angeles revival travelled extensively, testified fervently of the Pentecostal outpouring, organized meetings in churches, preached, made converts, and formed new congregations. Periodicals and newspapers established by the young Pentecostal movement advertised the revival, and the movement spread rapidly across the social, denominational, cultural, and racial spectrum of North America and beyond. The expansion of classical Pentecostalism is evidence of the global temperament of the movement that can be identified by a number of interrelated dimensions.

As a unique American phenomenon, the global identity of classical Pentecostalism must first be seen in its revivalistic origins that expanded the identity of American religion rapidly across local and regional boundaries and became representative of much of Western Christianity since the eighteenth century.[37] Pentecostal revivalism (the use of techniques in order to perform and sustain the original manifestations of the revival) was an effective tool in expanding Pentecostal thought and practice particularly with regard to certain theological and religious issues.[38] This dimension forms the broad base for the global temperament of classical Pentecostalism.

A second dimension, intimately connected with the first, is the association of Pentecostalism with the socially marginalized and disenfranchised as well as other social classes, a unique characteristic in American religion.[39] The presence and appeal that characterizes Pentecostalism among all social strata today has become largely synonymous with the idea of the global appeal of any religion and forms a large element of Pentecostalism's global attraction.

A third dimension of the global character of the movement is its expansive missionary programme, motivated by the revivalistic and eschatological ideals of the movement. Since the early revivals, Pentecostalism emerged as a mission movement that comprised both veteran missionaries and novices who often went without any training into all areas of the world and despite frequent failures left an unprecedented history of Pentecostalism around the globe.[40] Classical Pentecostalism combines a focus on conversion and revival with a sense of urgency and pragmatism that ultimately has made it the most significant global missionary movement in the twentieth century.[41]

A fourth dimension is the multicultural and multiracial character of North American Pentecostalism that pushed the movement to the crossroads of American, African, European, Hispanic, and other cultures.[42] The rootedness in African American liturgy and the camp meeting culture of the South as well as engagement in the civil rights movement dramatically increased the global reach of Pentecostalism even if such efforts were not greeted with enthusiasm by all.[43]

Finally, the global temperament can be seen in the foundational position of classical Pentecostalism as a catalyst for changes in worship, liturgical practices, and particularly the kinesthetic and spiritual elements of the Christian life.[44] The array of 'typical'

Pentecostal practices, among them dancing, jumping, waving, clapping, shouting, and swaying, express not merely the particular spirituality of a group but have come to represent a broadly accepted and replicated understanding of Christian worship in interaction with God and with one another. Classical Pentecostalism is global in terms of its charismatic, cross-social, multicultural, trans-ethnic, evangelistic, and missionary character.

The Charismatic Movements

The Charismatic Movements add a number of different components to the global character of Pentecostalism. The major difference to classical Pentecostals is the ecclesial rootedness of the charismatic renewal in the established churches (theologically, liturgically, and institutionally). Beginning in the mainline Protestant traditions and in the Roman Catholic Church in the 1960s, the charismatic movement immediately grasped the attention of the Christian world. While most of the early classical Pentecostal leaders did not intend to leave their churches but to revitalize the experiences and practices surrounding the Holy Spirit, many found themselves isolated and ostracized and, under the pressures of organization, institutionalization, and doctrinal conformity formed new churches and denominations.[45] The Charismatic Movements, on the other hand, remained intimately connected with their ecclesiastical origins and with them possessed an immediate network of global recognition.

As a worldwide phenomenon not restricted to North America, the Charismatic Movements add a number of important dimensions to the global temperament of Pentecostalism. The most significant among them is the ecclesial connectedness of the movement that integrates Pentecostal spirituality and practices in the liturgical and ecumenical contexts of the established traditions. The influences are reciprocal: Pentecostalism has been broadened in its ritual and sacramental practices while the Charismatic Movements have become a modifier of the mainline traditions rather than an isolated subculture.[46]

A second dimension is the widespread social acceptance of Pentecostal and charismatic spirituality often connected with church leaders, councils, well-known personalities, and representatives of the intellectual elite. The Jesus People movement counted 300,000 young people among its adherents by the early 1970s.[47] Popular writings, such as *The Cross and the Switchblade*, as well as newly established publications of the movement, such as the magazine *New Covenant*, captured the imagination of large audiences across the world.[48] Well-known personalities in entertainment and TV evangelism quickly expanded the charismatic ministry to massive proportions. Influential church leaders connected the Charismatic Movements internationally and helped spread this new form of Pentecostalism throughout established churches, networks, and organizations.

A third element of the global character of the Charismatic Movements is their intellectual and academic dimension. Whereas many classical Pentecostals traditionally emphasized faith and spirituality over intellectualism and education, espousing at times a radical anti-intellectualism, the charismatic movements embrace the educational elite and academia. The intellectual climate among Pentecostals has opened up to academic theology and scholarship and contributed to a uniquely Pentecostal pedagogy that affirms the epistemological importance of the Holy Spirit while challenging conventional forms of theological education.

Fourth, Pentecostalism has taken on a global character also in its theological dimensions. The Charismatic Movements initiated a globally oriented theological awareness among Pentecostals, nurturing the formulation of Pentecostal theology in a more systematic and analytical manner and gradually exposing Pentecostal thought to the established theological traditions. Pentecostal and charismatic theology today is at the forefront of engaging the opportunities and challenges of global Christian thought.[49] The result is a cross-fertilization in which Pentecostal theology is often formulated in the framework of traditional theological categories while the established theological traditions are beginning to reflect on their own formulations as a result of the global impact of the charismatic renewal.

Finally, the Charismatic Movements have significantly expanded the ecumenical sensitivities of Pentecostals. The ecumenical involvement of the Charismatic Movements contributes significantly to the recognition of Pentecostalism and its participation in international dialogues and conversations.[50] Although many classical Pentecostals continue to resist official ecumenical relationships, the emergence of the ecumenical movement and the charismatic renewal in the established churches is responsible for an entirely new set of global connections.[51] As a result, Pentecostal concerns, theology, and practices have entered ecumenical discussions and expanded Pentecostal language and perspectives. From the perspective of the Charismatic Movements, Pentecostalism is global in terms of its diverse ecclesial, liturgical, intellectual, theological, and ecumenical character.

Neo-Pentecostalism

The third stream of Pentecostals, the so-called neo-charismatic or neo-Pentecostal groups, have further advanced the global identity of Pentecostalism in distinct ways. The immense amount of independent, postdenominational, and nondenominational groups form a stark ecclesiastical contrast to the rootedness of the Charismatic Movements in the established churches. The most immediate dimension of the global character exhibited by these groups is their unprecedented cultural exposure. Far exceeding the evangelistic and missionary presence of classical Pentecostals in many parts of the world and the establishment of the Charismatic Movement across the established Christian traditions, the neo-Pentecostal groups have added a myriad of autochthonous churches and congregations indigenous to cultures with little or no historical contact to Christianity. The result has been a wedding of Pentecostalism with native spiritualities, religions, and cultures in a process of constant disconnecting and recombining that is widely responsible for the success of Pentecostalism worldwide and has come to closely define the idea of the globalization of Pentecostalism.[52] This process of hybridization has not only expanded the religious base of the Pentecostal movement but interchanged patterns and vehicles of transmission of the religious, cultural, political, and economic heritage of various local, national, and international sources.

Another dimension neo-Pentecostalism has added to the global character of the Pentecostal movement is the deliberate engagement with the masses. The most tangible form of this aspect are the mega-churches that have begun to appear particularly in the urban centres of Asia, Latin America, and North America. The half-a-million members of Yoido Full Gospel Church in Seoul, Korea, for example, the Universal Church of the Kingdom of God in São Paulo, Brazil, or City Harvest in Singapore, have redefined both the face of modern-day Pentecostalism and the visible expression of contemporary Christianity.[53] The enormous organizations, like most of their kind, are based on myriads of cell-based groups that facilitate the administration, communication, and fellowship of their communities. The chief character of these mega-churches is their diversified and stratified representation of ministries under a single organizational umbrella exhibiting an exceptionally wide range of physical space, facilities, organizational and regional outreach, and social ministries.[54]

Finally, the neo-Pentecostal movements have added a range of independent churches, assemblies, fellowships, and loosely defined ecclesiastical groups that have come to shape the face of charismatic Christianity in what many see as representative of the postmodern and pluralistic elements of the late modern world. While this group is equally as diversified as the mega-churches, the ministries are divided among autonomous organizations, often occupied with single forms of social ministries and particular audiences. Captured under the umbrella term 'neo-Pentecostalism', the range of different groups has added a unique element of mobility, independence, and innovation to the global temperament of the Pentecostal identity.[55] From the perspective of neo-Pentecostalism, the Pentecostal movement is global in terms of its cross-cultural, diversified, independent, variable, and progressive character.

The various dimensions of the global temperament of Pentecostalism should not be seen in isolation. Elements of classical Pentecostalism, the Charismatic Movements, and neo-Pentecostalism often form a blend of practices and beliefs that make it easier to speak of Pentecostalism, in general, than to identify the particular shape of what defines Pentecostalism in each location and situation. Global Pentecostalism represents a microclimate of global Christianity. The various dimensions that define the global character of the main streams of Pentecostalism are also representative of the emergence of global Christianity in the late modern world, yet few of these characteristics are found together to the same extent in any other Christian tradition. Briefly put, Pentecostalism is a key representative of global Christianity in development. A definition of this movement requires attention not only to the global and the local but also to the relationship that connects both worlds.

Pentecostalism and globalization

The assessment of the global pluralism of the Pentecostal movement in all its diverse manifestations frequently overwhelms the focus of Pentecostal communities on the ground. Neither the micro- nor the macro-vision is a realistic perspective of the Pentecostal world if maintained exclusively in the long-run. What characterizes the identity of the Pentecostal movement is both its local roots and global temperament. Elemental to this existence in the big *and* the small is not only the recognizable reach beyond the local but the insistence that the global dimensions of Pentecostalism cannot be understood apart from the movement's local existence. We might say that Pentecostalism is 'a religion made to travel'[56] between the local and the global. The most dominant theory to explain these interdependencies is the idea of globalization.

The globalization of Pentecostalism

The most basic model of globalization explains Pentecostalism as a movement that transitions from the local to the global. Globalization is seen in the growth of numbers (members, churches, and converts), geographic expansion (regional, national, and global), and the development of a global consciousness (subjectively and objectively) coupled with the emergence and formation of an increasingly larger and diversified infrastructure that adapts to the conditions of the world as a whole.[57] Two different interpretations of globalization have emerged from this broad perspective, one that emphasizes the homogeneity and the other pointing to the heterogeneous nature of the development. The emphasis on a homogeneous globalization frequently ties together Pentecostalism and modernity, pointing to the fact that numerical growth and geographical expansion has always been a feature of Pentecostalism (and of modernity) and that it is difficult to define at what level we begin to speak of the movement as global and no longer as a local phenomenon. Similarly, a global consciousness can be said to have accompanied Pentecostalism (and modernity) from the beginning, especially in its eschatological form and perception of the world, and thus is present in all streams of the movement.[58] From this perspective, Pentecostals as representative of a general temperament of modernity were always globally oriented and continue to see the local as a starting point and significant representation of the global. If Pentecostalism has always grown, expanded, and developed, then we can apply the term 'global' to the movement without reservation. The homogenous perspective understands globalization as an inherent tendency of modern-day Pentecostalism.

On the other side, there are some who resist the application of the term 'Pentecostalism' as a generic identifier of the movement. At least during the twentieth century, in the widespread internal attempts by Pentecostals to define the distinctives of the movement, the term 'global' does not appear.[59] The emphasis on heterogeneity speaks of the success of Pentecostalism in reverse terms and understands the movement from the outset as a global phenomenon that exists as always adapting localizations 'that reach across national boundaries, take on local color, and move on again'.[60] This perspective emphasizes significant differences in religiosity, spirituality, morality, social engagement, as well as political and economic participation among Pentecostals in East and West, the northern and southern hemispheres, Europe and the USA.[61] Others highlight the racial, social, and linguistic diversities of Pentecostal groups even on the regional level.[62] Globalization therefore refers to cultural discontinuities and contradictions, including irreconcilable differences in theology and worship that divide not only the global space but also the history of the Pentecostal traditions. This heterogeneity questions the ability to capture the empirical reality of Pentecostalism as a global community.[63] In its place, the heterogeneous viewpoint advocates that 'localization' and 'deglobalization' are proper terms that identify the Pentecostal movement worldwide. This characterization is frequently associated with postmodern sensitivities.

The conflicting interpretations necessitate a theory that can explain the relationship between local and global Pentecostalism without reverting exclusively to one side or the other. Theories that depend fundamentally on one dimension are no longer able to offer explanations of the range of Pentecostal and Pentecostal-like communities and their development worldwide. The global

character of the Pentecostal movement is a historically and socio-
logically late phenomenon that requires for its explanation reference
to the origins in and continuing dependence on the local beyond
the confines of the modern or postmodern. This interdependence
can be described with the term 'glocalization' – the elimination of
'distance' between the local and the global that ultimately finds the
global *in* the local and vice versa.[64] Instead of proposing the globalization *of* local Pentecostalism and thereby effectively juxtaposing
the global *against* the local, the understanding of Pentecostalism as
a glocal phenomenon embraces the relationship between the local
and the global because Pentecostalism as a whole depends on both
realities.

The glocalization of Pentecostalism

Roland Robertson introduced the concept of glocalization in the
1990s to overcome the problematic juxtaposition of local and
global.[65] Adopting his perspective advocates the essential proposal
that the reality we label 'Pentecostal' is dependent upon both its
local and global manifestations. Pentecostalism, when seen as a
glocal phenomenon, is not defined in terms of either its local or
global characteristics but in terms of its actual contribution to
the structuration of the world in both dimensions.[66] Glocalization
applied to Pentecostalism rejects a simplistic theory that equates
the dynamics of Pentecostalism with either those of a globalizing
modernity or its postmodern counterpart.[67] There is no global
mass-culture that can be labelled 'Pentecostalism' without identifying simultaneously the local roots or localized representations of
what we term 'Pentecostal'. On the contrary, the globalization of
Pentecostalism consists of the production and reproduction of the
local in the global and the global in the local, the mediation, or
more precisely, the encoding and decoding of local distinctiveness
and global generality.[68] This mediation finds its most tangible
expression in the remarkable mobility and migration of what is
after all popularly called the Pentecostal *movement*.

Pentecostalism as a movement has never been stationary.
Physical and geographical, as well as in a metaphorical sense,
social, cultural, and theological mobility are the hallmark of
Pentecostalism. Simply put, we must speak not only of the

existence or presence of Pentecostalism in the local and the global
but of Pentecostalism as a movement in glocal transition. The
evangelistic and missionary temperament of Pentecostalism forms
only one component of the mobility of the movement. Apparent in
Pentecostalism is also the migration and importation of 'foreign'
cultural and religious identities and the consequent adoption of
transnational identities, the penetration of and association with
established churches and traditions, the building of formal and
informal networks across and beyond local boundaries, the forming
of transnational spaces, the deterritorialization of particular local
or national identities and cultures, including the phenomenon
of reverse mission, and a general trend toward upward social
mobility.[69] The dialectic process of localization and delocalization,
globalization and deglobalization is accompanied by tensions and
conflicts that do not lie either in the local *or* the global but in the
fusion of both dimensions.[70] Consequently, it is the combination
of the tensions inherent in a dedication to both the local and the
global that forms the heart of Pentecostalism.[71] What is taking
place among Pentecostals worldwide is an ongoing 'reconfiguration
of Pentecost'[72] that involves the simultaneity and interpenetration
of the local and the global, sometimes in response to the other,
sometimes in opposition, but never with the ability to escape either
dimension. This perspective has significant implications for the
actual reality we call 'Pentecostalism' and for the way we understand this reality in its various dimensions.

The notion of Pentecostalism as a glocal phenomenon marks a
pattern for the further examination of the movement in this volume.
Glocal Pentecostalism is defined both by a search for Pentecostal
distinctives, a discussion that favours the local viewpoint and
particular identity of Pentecostals, and a search for fundamentals,
a conversation that privileges the global perspective.[73] In other
words, Pentecostalism is both fundamentalist and experientialist
without confining either characteristic to the global or the local.[74]
Pentecostalism is both a contextual and intercultural religious
movement. It can be identified on a global scale as Spirit-oriented
without neglecting the very corporeal nature of Pentecostal life and
worship on the ground. Pentecostalism is as much a recovery of
primal piety as it is the progressive face of global Christianity. Only
a limited number of these identifiers can be produced without losing
the integrity of the whole attempt to come to terms with a general

definition of Pentecostalism. Ultimately, Pentecostalism exists on the most visible level as both a local and global phenomenon in a dynamic transition of its various features. This description provides a foundational explanation for the multifarious nature of the Pentecostal movement.

CHAPTER TWO

Holistic spirituality and charismatic extremism

A holistic spirituality forms the heartbeat of Pentecostal thought and practice. From the beginning of the modern-day Pentecostal movement, the Holy Spirit, spiritual gifts, charismatic manifestations, and spiritual discernment have been the hallmark of Pentecostal preaching, teaching, revivals, ecumenical conversations, and eventually scholarly works. These elements generally form also the most immediate seedbed for confrontation, propaganda, polemics, misunderstandings, and stereotypes. The seemingly singular emphasis on a life centred around the Holy Spirit is host to some of the most bewildering tensions in Pentecostalism: the emphasis on the reality of the spiritual dimension of life and on the need for discernment of the intermingled realities of the human spirit, the divine Spirit, and demonic spirits, on the one hand, and the public scandals surrounding the excessive display of charismatic gifts, the exploitation of the miraculous, and the apparent lack of spiritual etiquette by Pentecostals, on the other hand. The present chapter introduces the dimensions of Pentecostal spirituality and worldview and brings the extremes into dialogue for a better understanding of the bandwidth of the charismatic manifestations that characterize the Pentecostal movement in its local and global dimensions.

The spiritual dimension of life forms the tangible reality where the diverse local and the global realities of Pentecostalism come to life. The emphasis on the Holy Spirit defines the different streams of Pentecostalism experientially, socially, intellectually, and theologically; other explanations of the perplexities within the Pentecostal movement depend on the understanding of the tensions inherent in the Spirit-filled life. It is the goal of this chapter to outline the tensions inherent in the Pentecostal spirituality and worldview and to present them as the unavoidable elements of an imagination that is potentially open to all forms of charismatic manifestations while submitting to the sanctifying work of the Holy Spirit that draws all matters of faith and praxis to the gospel of Jesus Christ. A description of the Spirit-filled life comprises the first part of the chapter. The second part traces the extent of excessive charismatic practices in the various streams of the Pentecostal movement. This contrast is brought into dialogue in a concluding outline of the pneumatic, pneumatological, and charismatic elements that together form the Pentecostal imagination.

Holistic spirituality

Adherents and critics of the movement have often described Pentecostalism as a form of spirituality. For Pentecostals, this designation indicates that being Pentecostal is not synonymous with membership in a particular denomination or tradition; doctrines and beliefs are not the only elements that shape the Christian life. For their critics, the description often denotes the more pejorative idea of a movement that lacks the elements commonly attributed to the Christian mainstream. While for Pentecostals, spirituality elevates the movement beyond the denominational, doctrinal, and liturgical patterns of the churches to a movement of universal significance, others see in this designation a lack of behavioural consistency, institutional accountability, and ecclesiastical reputation. In the most basic sense, the tensions surrounding the different perceptions of Pentecostalism are concentrated in two distinct elements: the worldview and spirituality of the charismatic life.

Pentecostal worldview

The worldview of modern-day Pentecostals crystallizes most clearly from their reading of those biblical texts that emphasize the work of the Holy Spirit. Classical Pentecostals have typically interpreted the biblical records with particular focus on Luke-Acts, often to explain, justify, and affirm their doctrines and practices but also to come to a self-understanding of the particular features that identify them as Pentecostals in the first place.[1] The Pentecostal reading of the New Testament emphasizes the Spirit-filled life of Jesus and its implications for the Christian life in the form of the so-called fivefold or full gospel that heralds Jesus as saviour, sanctifier, Spirit-baptizer, healer, and coming king.[2] In the devotional life and piety as well as theological statements of Pentecostal groups, Jesus is clearly the predominant figure. Yet, while Christ is central to the proclamation of the fivefold gospel, its organizing motif is the work of the Holy Spirit. The events of Pentecost are interpreted through this lens as the instatement of Jesus as the one who baptizes with the Spirit. The entire Christian existence is seen as a consequence of this interpretation and described as a Spirit-baptized life. The worldview of Pentecostals depends overwhelmingly on a recognition of the Spirit's activity in the world.

The worldview of the Spirit-baptized life embraced by Pentecostals works itself from the centrality of Christ outwards to the church and the world.[3] At Pentecost, Jesus Christ, the messiah anointed with the Holy Spirit, poured out the gift of his Spirit upon all flesh. Luke's theology of the Spirit in the messianic age is seen as heir to the charismatic theology of the Old Testament while transcending it clearly with the identification of the Spirit itself as the gift of God accompanied by charismatic manifestations.[4] Classical Pentecostals typically identify three primary implications of this outpouring, though not always in the same breath: power, mission, and holiness.[5] The detailed formulation of how these matters are connected is the subject of wide-ranging discussions, often cast in the language of a 'Spirit baptism' with the evidence of speaking in tongues. At the base of this language is the particular image of the Spirit's universal outpouring in the form of charismatic manifestations that occupies the central position in the Pentecostal worldview.

Speaking of Spirit baptism as an *image* of the Pentecostal worldview has several advantages. First and foremost, the notion of a theological image emphasizes the absence of any propositional statement (in the established traditions as well as among Pentecostal pioneers) that would have identified theologically what was happening in modern-day Pentecostalism. Even the biblical records provide no exhaustive data, which allow for congruent formulations that are universally accepted among Pentecostals.[6] Moreover, the idea of Spirit baptism as an image is consistent with the fact that the pneumatological perspective among Pentecostals is a worldview rather than an isolated theological idea. The image of the Spirit-filled life takes the Pentecostal worldview beyond any particular doctrine or theological focus. As an image, Spirit baptism serves as the precognitive motivation for verbal formulations and propositional statements of Pentecostal beliefs.[7] Even in the face of disagreeing interpretations, the original image can maintain its motivational power. In this way, Spirit baptism can be seen as the inspiration for a Pentecostal worldview that is still very much in development.

Pentecostal accounts of the world often employ the contrasting language of the natural and supernatural or the ordinary and the miraculous. With this language, Pentecostals draw clear distinctions between the human and the spiritual, the spirit and the flesh, as well as between spirits, human and divine, holy and demonic.[8] While the lines are clearly drawn between these identities, the realms in which they are to be found often overlap. The different streams of Pentecostalism frequently preserve native cosmologies that inspire a rather complex image of the world as a realm where spiritual forces, principalities, and powers are in constant confrontation. The human being is found between Satan and his evil spirits and demons, on the one hand, and the Holy Spirit and angelic forces, on the other hand.[9] While good and evil are fundamentally opposed to one another, human beings are subject to the influence of both realms and can, at times, manipulate evil spirits for their purposes.[10] Signs and wonders are immediate representations of the meeting of different realms and signal the spiritual dynamic of the world. For Pentecostals, the baptism in the Spirit stands midway as the meeting of the divine and the human, the immanent and the transcendent, the world and the kingdom of God as it confronts the dominion of Satan. The bursting forth in tongues of thanksgiving, praise, prophecy, or judgment symbolizes the human self-transcendence and bridge-crossing in a spirit-filled worldview.[11] The reality of a life in the Spirit therefore necessitates the practice of spiritual discernment.[12] The Pentecostal view of the cosmos is not only a worldview; it is a spirituality.

Pentecostal spirituality

Worldview and spirituality are intimately connected. Yet, the two realms can be related in different ways. In the case of Pentecostalism, to speak of the Pentecostal view of the Spirit-filled life as spirituality is to say that the image of the outpouring of the Holy Spirit is distributed affectively. The affections inform, shape, and direct the Pentecostal worldview as not merely an objective understanding of the world but as active involvement in the world's transformation. Pentecostal spirituality represents not merely a reflective worldview but an active participation in the Spirit who provides the gratitude, compassion, and courage necessary to engage the world in worship, witness, and prayer.[13] From this perspective, a holistic spirituality is seen as a way of relating the Christian being-in-the-world to their knowledge of the world and their actions for the world. Pentecostal spirituality thus brings the Spirit to the centre of understanding human existence.

The Pentecostal view of human existence relates our entire being, knowing, and doing to the presence, power, and person of the Holy Spirit.[14] This holistic spirituality unfolds on three inter-related levels. At its base, the Spirit-filled life is always *pneumatic*; it is an existence imbued with the person of the Holy Spirit. At this primary level, Pentecostal spirituality is above all experiential, often preceding theoretical and theological reflection. On a second level, the knowledge and interpretation of this experiential existence proceeds *pneumatologically*; it is always a reflection that pursues an understanding of the world in terms of the work of the Holy Spirit. Participation in the Spirit's transformation of the world is the inevitable consequence of a pneumatic and pneumatological spirituality. On a third level, this participation is always *charismatic*; it is carried out by the Spirit's distribution of spiritual gifts. The charismata are the corporeal manifestations of the experiential and theological affirmation that life always involves the all-encompassing reality of God's Spirit. The gifts of the Spirit typically serve as 'evidence' of a theological reflection on pneumatic encounters and experiences with the Spirit of God. Ontologically, epistemologically, and existentially, Pentecostalism is defined by a Spirit-centred spirituality.

The charismatic and neo-Pentecostal movements in the global contexts create a particularly vivid picture of a Spirit-centred spirituality. In the charismatic movements of the established Christian traditions, the Pentecostal emphasis on the Spirit-filled life has found deep connections with the mystical and pietistic traditions.[15] In the neo-charismatic and neo-Pentecostal communities, Pentecostal spirituality reflects a Spirit-oriented worldview already explicit in most societies. Particularly in Africa, Asia, and Latin America, where these streams of Pentecostalism are the most prevalent, the emphasis on a holistic spirituality is firmly established in every aspect of personal, communal, cultural, and religious life.[16] Pentecostal spirituality in these contexts is perhaps best described as an emphasis on encounter.[17] The predominance of the human encounter with God has revitalized the spiritual teachings and experiential emphasis of the established Christian traditions and shaped the image of the church as a charismatic fellowship. In the global contexts of the many independent and indigenous churches, this emphasis has left many of the already existing spiritual traditions and practices intact albeit now redirected through its emphasis on the Holy Spirit to the centrality of Jesus Christ. The meeting of different spiritual traditions is manifested in the variety of manifestations of the Spirit-filled life. While a holistic spirituality forms the necessary response to the Pentecostal worldview, it is the charismatic life where both realms meet.

The charismatic life

Pentecostal worldview and spirituality should not be seen as isolated from each other. The interpretation of the world as a spiritual realm bears immediate consequences for human participation in this reality. For Pentecostals, the Christian life in a world occupied by satanic and demonic principalities and powers exhibits in sharp contrast the character of a life redeemed by Christ and empowered by the Spirit of God. In this cosmological framework, Pentecostal spirituality directs a person from mere interpretation of the world to participation in the world. More precisely, the purpose of the Christian life is a participation in God's transformation of the world through the outpouring of his Spirit. Above all, Pentecostals stress the significance in this process of the Spirit's self-bestowal on the believer that is evident in the manifestation of spiritual gifts.

The elevation of spiritual gifts by Pentecostals in the twentieth century came at a time of widespread cessationism – the notion that spiritual gifts were limited to the age of the earliest Christians and thereafter ceased to exist.[18] In contrast, Pentecostals lament that cessationism has led to an abandonment of a holistic spirituality and the suppression of the charismata. The consequences are evident in a dramatic decline of spirituality in its pneumatic, pneumatological, and charismatic dimensions of Christian spirituality. While Pentecostals may not see charismatic manifestations as a measurement directly reflecting a person's spirituality, they would emphasize that it is precisely in the exercise of spiritual gifts that the transformation of the world occurs.[19] The gifts of the Spirit serve the edification of the church, the proclamation of the gospel, and the exaltation of Jesus Christ. The bestowal of these gifts is not seen as unique to the biblical Pentecostal community or to modern-day Pentecostals but rather as a normal and normative element of the Christian life endowed with the Holy Spirit. Christian beliefs and practices are transformed by the presence and activity of the Spirit and thereby more deliberately and actively participate in the story of God in the last days.[20]

Most Pentecostal accounts of spiritual gifts point to the nine charismata listed in 1 Cor. 12.4–11, wisdom, knowledge, faith, healing, mighty deeds, prophecy, discernment of spirits, tongues, and the interpretation of tongues. Other treatments include Rom. 12.6-8 and its emphasis on prophecy, ministry, teaching, exhortation, generosity, diligence, mercy, and cheerfulness as well as the institutional gifts of apostles, prophets, evangelists, pastors, and teachers noted in Eph. 4.11.[21] Few Pentecostals would see these lists as exhaustive of the charismata active in the church today but rather as representative of any number of other potential manifestations of the interpenetration of the divine and the created realms.[22] The exercise of spiritual gifts ultimately emerges from the fusion of the worldview and spirituality that form their root and motivation. As a result, the practice of spiritual gifts differs widely in the various streams of Pentecostalism. Nonetheless, the image of Spirit baptism at the juncture of understanding and participating in the world marks the core event of experiencing the Holy Spirit that moves the believer into charismatic manifestations. Although the exercise of spiritual gifts can be cultivated, the number and occasion of these gifts is attributed to the sovereign direction of the

Spirit in the particular community or context for which they are intended.[23] The charismata are the gifts of the kingdom of God – different gifts from the same Spirit, different forms of service under the same Lord, different works but from the same God for the benefit of all (1 Cor. 12.4–7). Heralding the coming of the kingdom of God, the charismatic manifestations in the realm of the already approaching but not yet fully realized kingdom are limited only by the extent to which the divine reign is not yet completely realized in the world. In the worldview of Pentecostalism, the potential for the manifestations of the charismatic life is thus practically limitless.

Charismatic extremism

The charismatic manifestations and display of spiritual gifts among modern-day Pentecostals has always been subject to severe criticism. From the beginning of the movement, Pentecostals were recognized primarily for their outward display of physical manifestations. The neglect of the charismatic life in the established churches quickly painted the Pentecostal movement in the colours of an extremist religious sect. In most quarters, the Pentecostal movement was virtually synonymous with the so-called 'tongues movement'.[24] Glossolalia, divine healing, prophecy, and exorcism are among the most prominent elements labelled as extremes. Contemporary observations and evaluations of the movement have focused almost exclusively on these outward manners and charismatic practices and therein quickly found examples of excessive behaviour often interpreted as the radical, spurious, and unorthodox examples of a misguided religious group.

The disapproval of dancing, jumping, shouting, and other emotional outbursts that accompanied the revivalism of previous centuries are today often in the same tone also applied to the activities and practices of modern-day Pentecostals.[25] In many parts of the world, individuals, groups, and churches of the emergent Pentecostal movement were at times violently persecuted by other Christians and non-Christians, while the criticism in the Western world today tends to be carried out largely on verbal and intellectual terms.[26] The immediate strong reactions to the birth of classical Pentecostalism subsided somewhat as Pentecostals began to move into more prominent roles in the West, yet criticism has exploded again with the rise of the Charismatic Movements and the neo-Pentecostal groups since the second half of the twentieth century. Many of the concerns come from outsiders of the movements, who observe Pentecostals with particular interest in the ritual, spiritual, and psychological dimensions of the charismatic life. At the same time, varied practices as well as new and unusual forms of charismatic manifestations have also caused divisions within Pentecostal groups. The results are twofold: most visibly, the Charismatic renewal in the Roman Catholic Church shed its original designation as 'Catholic Pentecostals' in favour of 'Charismatic Movement'. This division was accompanied by similar criticism among many classical Pentecostals who often reject the beliefs, practices, rituals, and manifestations attributed to the new revivals in the established mainstream traditions as aberrations of the movement's origins. Less visible is also the group of former adherents to the various streams of Pentecostalism who left the movement disappointed, hurt, or confused. The external critique and internal divisions shed clear light on the excessive charismatic manifestations that some attribute without exception to all parts of the Pentecostal movement.

External critique

Sustained observations and substantive criticism of the Pentecostal manifestation of charismata comes predominantly from other Christian groups. With the rise of modern-day Pentecostalism, the movement was quickly nicknamed 'tongue talkers' and 'holy rollers' or in sharper terms identified as heretical, regressive, divisive, escapist, deranged, and demonized.[27] Pentecostal services were described as a 'pandemonium' and 'madhouse' of the psychologically unstable.[28] Many labelled the movement as inhabited by a 'spirit of confusion' resulting from fundamentalist attitudes, rampant sectarianism, anti-intellectualism, cultural opposition, and its lower-working-class environment.[29] Some identified Pentecostalism more sharply as 'the handmaiden of apostasy and the servant of the Antichrist'[30] blamed on a false interpretation of history, a weakness of human experience, and a departure from divine revelation. Others have attacked the character of the Pentecostal revivals in general and identified them as counterfeits, fabrications, lies, fantasies, hypnotism, and fraud.[31] Few of these accusations engage directly with Pentecostal worldview or spirituality, but most if not all draw implications for both realms from the observations of the movement's charismatic manifestations.

A popular study of excessive Pentecostal practices labelled the movement a 'charismatic chaos'[32] characterized by the ostensibly undirected, disorganized, misinformed, and undisciplined practices of spiritual gifts. This unfriendly assessment derives from an accumulation of numerous case studies of often bizarre and scurrilous events attributed to the various streams of Pentecostalism, particularly the Charismatic Movement and the 'third-wave' neo-Pentecostal groups. These accounts portray Pentecostals as aggressively pursuing 'ecstatic experiences, mystical phenomena, miraculous powers, and supernatural wonders – while tending to under-emphasize the traditional means of spiritual growth'.[33] During the first half of the twentieth century, speaking in tongues almost always occupied the centre of attention, and the so-called 'gibberish' was widely heralded as a result of various degrees of mental instability ranging from mob psychology to hypnotism and demon-possession.[34] Since then, interest in the manifestation of glossolalia has ebbed in many circles, and other more spectacular events have come to represent Pentecostalism in popular perception.

Popular illustrations of Pentecostal extremism include the so-called laughing revivals of Pensacola, Florida, or Toronto, Canada, which exhibited unusual physical manifestations such as falling to the ground, uncontrollable loud laughter, intense weeping, and even animal sounds, as well as spiritual 'drunkenness' often resulting in uncontrolled movements, intense shaking, jerking, and rolling on the floor.[35] Critics view these displays less as a manifestation of spiritual gifts than of spiritual delusion and desperation manifested in a contradiction of biblical patterns and resistance to biblical scrutiny, bewilderment, lack of control, inebriation, irreverence, indecency, false teachings, women in leadership, and ecumenical zeal.[36] Even the more conservative treatments of these revivals describe the more spectacular elements as a mixed blessing and a subtle shift away from sound doctrine, an emphasis on manifestations of the Spirit rather than the centrality of Christ.[37]

External criticism has generally described Pentecostalism as a 'charismatic calamity' readily seen at the meetings of 'wild-eyed fanatics screaming and shouting', people falling to the ground 'struck by the Spirit', with faces in 'frenzied agony', and all in all 'skipping the basics' of proper Christian behaviour.[38] 'Confusion' is the general trademark of Pentecostalism resulting almost exclusively from what is seen as erroneous and misplaced charismatic practices and beliefs.[39] Although the charismatic life is considered a significant component of contemporary Christianity by all but the most stringent cessationists, Pentecostals provide numerous popular examples of an obsession with the spiritual, miraculous, and sensational that stand in sharp contrast to the expectations and established practices of the mainstream Christian traditions. In these highly visible areas of the Christian life, the reconciliation of Pentecostalism with orthodox Christianity seems virtually impossible.

Internal controversy

Pentecostals have also been plagued by internal divisions and controversy over charismatic manifestations. While many of the debates can be cast in the form of theological disputes, the controversies typically emerged primarily from different practices and interpretations of the charismatic life. After all, it was the common experience of speaking in tongues that bound the early Pentecostals together and allowed them to identify with each other as a larger religious movement. However, the emphasis on speaking in tongues differs among Pentecostal groups, and the addition of different streams of the movement has contributed to a diversity of practices that has led to an atmosphere of suspicion. Criticism arose early between members of the same stream, for example on the question of the relationship of tongues and Spirit baptism among classical Pentecostals, and between the adherents of different streams, particularly between classical Pentecostals and later Charismatic and neo-Pentecostal forms of the movement.

Among the pioneers of classical Pentecostalism, a practice soon developed that identified the speaking in tongues and its interpretation as 'messages' that could be utilized to receive personal and communal guidance. This practice was widely known as 'inquiring of the Lord' and served as means to affirm or discourage directions but in some groups was also used to legitimize particular teachings and actions.[40] In these factions, the speaking in tongues and especially the much rarer gift of interpretation became professionalized, reproduced, and routinized at the hands of some individuals and groups seeking authority by appealing to divine revelation. In response, the practice of tongues and interpretation as the preferred means for teaching and discernment was rejected by other Pentecostal leaders.[41] The abuse of these practices has caused division and strife between leaders and congregations and has divided the movement along the lines of factions that either endorse or reject the practice of speaking in tongues as primary means of decision-making.

The internal critique of excessive use of some spiritual gifts has surfaced among Pentecostals most prominently in the form of the debate about tongues as the so-called 'initial evidence' of Spirit baptism. While this teaching emerged as early as 1901 among the revivals that marked the beginning of classical Pentecostalism, the debate has continued throughout the movement and gained new impetus with the emergence of neo-Pentecostals, or 'Third Wavers', many of which refuse to even adopt the label 'Pentecostal'.[42] This stream of the movement rejects the classical Pentecostal position of tongues as the biblical evidence that initially accompanies the post-conversion experience of the baptism with the Holy Spirit. In turn, classical Pentecostals criticize the lack of emphasis on glossolalia as a reduction of the charismatic manifestations to a mere potential openness that robs the Christian life of the assurance of divine power.[43] To each side, the other represents an excessive position, whether overemphasis or neglect, on the role of the charismatic manifestations.

For the one side, the emphasis on tongues as the initial evidence of Spirit baptism easily leads to abuse in granting glossolalia a privileged place among the charismata that cannot be generalized for all Christians. Examples of this position include the countless seekers who never find the ability to speak in tongues, despite earnestly desiring the gift, or the superficial practice of repetitively speaking in syllables of a made-up language and accepting it as divine speech. The routinization of spiritual gifts in the Charismatic Movement has been attributed to the influence of hierarchical leadership, liturgical patterns of the mother church, and the widely disseminated patterns of do-it-yourself charismatic practices.[44] For the other side, the neglect of tongues leads to an equation of Spirit baptism with conversion and effectively obliterates the experiential dimension of the central Pentecostal conviction from the Christian life. Classical Pentecostals remain sceptical of associating Spirit baptism too closely with the sacramental life instead of a second and definitive crisis moment following conversion, and fault the Charismatic Movements for the neglect of glossolalia among many new Pentecostal streams.[45]

Overall, what some Pentecostals understand as normative manifestations of charismata others have described as a 'charismania'.[46] The amount or intensity of the display of spiritual gifts is certainly a chief concern among Pentecostals. On the other hand, similar controversies have emerged where charismatic practices engage native spiritualities in forms that are perceived by some as syncretistic behaviours. These controversies are particularly loud in Asian, African, and Latin American Pentecostalism. The so-called Spirit churches in Africa, for example, represent to many adherents of the older Pentecostal churches the character of a religion unduly penetrated by expressions of the spirit world that are more reminiscent of African spirituality than of Christianity.[47] Many practices of Pentecostal groups in Africa are seen as a mere reflection of traditional anti-witchcraft movements, spirit-possession cults, and demonic-deliverance mechanisms.[48] Similar criticism appears throughout Asia particularly at the less nuanced forms of syncretism; for example, the slaughter of animals at religious ceremonies, prayer to ancestral spirits, or pagan dance rituals, are practised by some Pentecostal groups in the Philippines.[49] The influence of shamanism on parts of Korean Pentecostalism has led for some to a confusion of shamanic ideas of spirit possession and the Pentecostal notion of Spirit baptism.[50] Pentecostal groups in Japan have been accused of adapting Pentecostal charismatic practices to Japanese folk religion and ancestral cult.[51] These examples illustrate the tensions inherent in Pentecostalism and its diverse representations as a global and historical movement. Internal controversies tend to connect charismatic practices more immediately with Pentecostal beliefs, worldview, and doctrine. Nonetheless, the extreme positions emphasize the importance of spirituality and worldview in the same breath with the experiential and corporeal nature of the Christian life. While these dimensions may not be easily reconciled, they form the unavoidable dimensions of a complex imagination unique to the Pentecostal movement.

The Pentecostal imagination

The characterization of certain manifestations of the charismatic life as 'excessive' should not give the impression that these manifestations are to be excluded from the image of modern-day Pentecostalism, that they are unwarranted surplus of a movement that otherwise could be classified as 'moderate'. Excessive practice can be seen in both too much and too little emphasis on the charismatic life, depending on one's point of view. Removing these realities as simply disproportionate from the characterization of Pentecostalism would paint a picture of the movement that is unrealistic, at best, and misleading, at worst. Unlike most other Christian traditions that exist on a narrower range of 'orthodox' beliefs and practices, the experiential orientation of Pentecostalism locates the movement on a much broader playing field.[52] The breadth of charismatic experiences among Pentecostals is typically attributed to particular psychological characteristics. The psychology of religion has followed modern-day Pentecostalism and paints an insightful picture of contrasting interpretations of the movement that underscore the need for a comprehensive and unbiased picture of the charismatic life.

Psychology of religion

The approach to Pentecostalism from the psychology of religion demonstrates the difficulty of attempting to characterize the movement in any unilateral manner that too easily dismisses the excessive elements. Psychological research at the beginning of modern-day Pentecostalism can be readily identified as hostile to the movement.[53] During this phase, charismatic manifestations among Pentecostals were viewed as abnormal behaviour and expressions of pathological phenomena and mental disorders such as schizophrenia, hysteria, neuroticism, regression, or emotional instability.[54] The chief object of these assessments was clearly the phenomenon of speaking in tongues.[55] Many studies of this phase were not substantiated by empirical data; nonetheless they created lasting stereotypes.[56] Casting Pentecostalism under the dominance of abnormal psychology, the entire movement was generally dismissed as excessive.[57]

However, in the 1960s, a friendlier period emerged that virtually overturned the results of the hostile phase. Pentecostals were now portrayed as psychologically stable, in many regards more so than the general population, with lower values in hostility, psychoticism, depression, submissiveness, and self-esteem.[58] Explicit use of data now showed Pentecostals in a much more favourable light, and what was initially dismissed as excessive must now be considered essential to the dynamics and structures of Pentecostal religiosity. What is overshadowed by the initial reductive approach to Pentecostalism is the foundational question of what exactly constitutes the inherent motivation of the Pentecostal understanding of and participation in the world. The stimulus of Pentecostal spirituality and worldview was either dismissed or neglected.

The history of approaches to Pentecostalism from the psychology of religion shows that value judgments based on exogenous causes and consequences have influenced the interpretation of the movement in a far less objective and unbiased manner.[59] In addition, the predominant occupation with exogenous psychological factors has largely suppressed the investigation of endogenous psychological structures and dynamics.[60] A fruitful but hitherto largely unexplored venue exists in examining Pentecostalism precisely in the core dimensions of religiosity: Pentecostal ideology, intellect, experience, public and private practices.[61] These dimensions seek to understand Pentecostalism from the content of the movement itself and open the field to other disciplines of study. In this young and promising approach to discover the heart of what motivates Pentecostals, the emphasis on the Holy Spirit remains the most central explanatory element.

Identifying the Holy Spirit as the central motivation of Pentecostals is perhaps the most basic feature of endogenous Pentecostal dynamics, but it is also the most contested feature and offers little explanatory power for the divergent range of charismatic manifestations and their interpretations. Nonetheless, the emphasis on the Spirit suggests that operative within Pentecostals is a fundamental engagement of the world that can best be described as an orientation toward the Spirit.[62] This orientation derives fundamentally from Pentecostal worldview and spirituality. Rather than constituting a certain knowledge or understanding of the world, Pentecostalism purports a spirituality – an affective disposition, an aesthetic, and a way of experiencing the world

– that is derived from and oriented toward the Spirit in often pre-cognitive, inarticulate, and unstructured ways.[63] In short, the most basic endogenous feature of Pentecostalism is a Spirit-driven imagination.

The Pentecostal imagination

The notion of Spirit baptism is the typical formulation given by Pentecostals to describe their Spirit-driven imagination. This image points to the centrality of the Spirit in any attempt to comprehend the range of the Spirit-filled life and its outward manifestations. The Spirit-driven imagination among Pentecostals operates on the three interrelated dimensions of pneumatic activity, pneumatological reflection, and charismatic practice. These dimensions form the foundation for understanding the significant breadth of manifestations of the Spirit-filled life among Pentecostals. While the Pentecostal imagination operates always on all three dimensions, a closer look at each dynamic offers further explanation of the diverse range of expressions and charismatic manifestations among the movement worldwide.

The Pentecostal imagination is pneumatic in the sense that it originates from specific encounters with the Holy Spirit.[64] Such encounters, traditionally captured by the Pentecostal notion of Spirit baptism, are responsible for directing a person toward greater sensitivity for the spiritual dimension of life. The result is an awareness of the various 'spirits' operating in the world – divine, human, natural, demonic, or other powers, forces, and energies – a recognition of the influence these spirits have on all things, and a sensitivity for the intricate relationship of spiritual powers and forces in which human beings find themselves in the world.[65] The pneumatic dimension sets the Pentecostal imagination immediately in the framework of *participation* in the reality of the diverse spiritual powers that precedes deliberate reflection and can subject a person not only to the divine but also the demonic or other influences.[66] Pentecostals have variously described participation in the pneumatic reality in terms of the militaristic language of 'spiritual warfare' and more recently as 'power encounters.'[67] The Spirit-driven imagination points to the necessity of confrontation with the spiritual world through engagement in spiritual discernment, deliverance, and exorcism. Originating as a pneumatic activity, Pentecostal spirituality highlights the demand for immediate pneumatological reflection. The potential distance between participation and reflection opens up the Christian life to the contrasting range of influence of spiritual forces and powers.

The Pentecostal imagination is pneumatological in the sense that it is an 'action-reflection in the Spirit'.[68] Derived from the challenges of immediate participation, the desire for a genuine experience of the divine elevates attention to the Holy Spirit to the inescapable condition for a sensitivity to all spiritual powers and forces. The pneumatological dimension combines participation with *perception* on the two fundamental levels of discernment and engagement of the world and transcends a mere 'worldviewing' reflection toward a 'worldmaking' activity.[69] This action-reflection means that the perception of the spiritual world is always a rigorous and challenging engagement of the diverse manifestations of that reality.[70] Pentecostals often attend in a common-sense oriented way to questions of character, communication, and content, relying on Scripture, hierarchical structures of authority, and social context for discerning spiritual phenomena.[71] At the same time, the pneumatological imagination proceeds also in transrational ways that have not been charted clearly.[72] It is perhaps more accurate to speak of the perception of spirits as also a penetration of spiritual powers and forces. This interpenetration exposes a person not only to the contrast of the radical otherness of the self and the demonic or divine but also to the radical engagement in these pneumatic dimensions.[73] Even on this level, the Pentecostal imagination remains largely experiential and affective in its intention to grasp the divine reality and its counterparts. The ongoing demand of this dynamic but fragmentary procedure leads, naturally, to questions of the endowment or ability of a person to engage in such action-reflection. In other words, the Pentecostal imagination is also a charismatic activity.

The Pentecostal imagination is charismatic in the sense that it is a spiritual activity of human and divine co-operation mediated through the gifts of the Spirit. Participation in and perception of the spiritual dimensions of life are both a human ability and a divine gift that are manifested in concrete events. Put differently, as charismatic activity the Pentecostal imagination is always the *practice* of participating in and perceiving the Spirit-filled life.

Originating from specific encounters with the Holy Spirit, the
Pentecostal life is practised explicitly through the gifts of the Spirit.
Speaking in tongues, prophecy, divine healing, exorcism, interpretation of tongues, words of wisdom and knowledge, and the less
spectacular charismata of teaching, leadership, ministry, exhortation, and others are the concrete practices of the Spirit in and
through individuals and communities that are intended to bring
about discernment, correction, reconciliation, and healing. The
charismatic dimension is not simply a performance of the imagination but the occasion where a person engaged in the spiritual life
is transformed by the divine power of the Spirit to disengage from
the demonic and to participate in the divine.[74]

As participation in the divine, spiritual gifts are the immediate,
often pre-cognitive, pneumatic manifestations of the power of the
Spirit. At the same time, the manifestation of the charismata also
serves the perception of the divine presence and activity in the
world. In other words, the Pentecostal imagination is perceptive
of the spiritual reality while it participates in the spiritual life.
However, as a spiritual practice, the manifestation of the charismata
is also cultivated and preserved in a variety of micro- and macro-
rituals among Pentecostal groups.[75] This cultivation of charismatic
rites both confirms and invites the participation in the divine nature.
Yet, the liturgical sensibilities among Pentecostals are less perform-
ative, institutional, and structural than in the established liturgical
traditions and tend toward a more playful character marked by
the freedom and enthusiasm of the moment.[76] In this way, the
charismatic practice can in turn influence the pneumatological
perception of the spiritual dimensions of life and one's participation
in the spiritual powers and forces. The result is a further expansion
of the range of endogenous structures and dynamics that explain
exogenous causes and consequences even if they do not justify them.

This interpenetration of participation, perception, and practice
characterizes the Pentecostal imagination as that inherent
motivation that is largely responsible for the wide range of charismatic expressions among Pentecostal groups. For Pentecostals, the
charismata are essential and not accidental to the Spirit-filled life.
To limit the range of charismatic expressions would inherently alter
the character of Pentecostalism. Put differently, the Pentecostal
movement *is* the tension between holistic spirituality and the range
of its charismatic manifestations.

The range of spiritual gifts and their expressions in the public and private life cannot be compromised when we talk about modern-day Pentecostalism. Excessive charismatic manifestations are the unavoidable characteristics of a movement that is limitless in its worldview and spirituality and that pursues the Spirit-driven life with all the powers of the imagination.

CHAPTER THREE

Ecumenical ethos and denominationalism

The Pentecostal movement is not easily placed among the Christian churches. On the one hand, Pentecostalism is often seen as a Free Church movement characterized by rampant denomination-alism, non-denominational splinter-groups, as well as internal and external tendencies toward segregation. Concerns for the unity of the Christian household and the fellowship of the churches – an ambition summarized in the terms 'ecumenism' or 'ecumenical' – are difficult topics among Pentecostals.[1] On the other hand, Pentecostals have become a driving force in the ecumenical movement since, at least, the late twentieth century. Unlike many existing churches and denominations that originated in deliberate response to splits and separations resulting from doctrinal and practical differences, Pentecostal communities worldwide often did not organize or institutionalize in deliberate patterns. Instead, Pentecostal churches, assemblies, fellowships, and smaller groups have emerged in both continuity and discontinuity with various existing doctrines, practices, rituals, disciplines, spiritualities, and institutions. The resulting character of Pentecostalism does not readily form a homogeneous ecumenical picture. The Pentecostal movement is an ecumenical melting pot.[2]

The present chapter traces the development of ecumenical attitudes among Pentecostals worldwide and brings into dialogue the tensions between the ecumenical ethos and denominationalism among Pentecostals. The task of this chapter is to explain the various factors that have contributed to the confusing ecumenical identity of Pentecostals and to portray the current shift in attitude among Pentecostals toward the pursuit of Christian unity. The goal of this chapter is to outline a way in which Pentecostalism can be understood amidst the landscape of churches and denominations today. The most promising path in this situation remains the characterization of Pentecostalism as a 'movement'. In order to outline this path, the first section provides a brief history of Pentecostal endeavours to establish and maintain Christian unity. The second section paints in broad strokes the denominational picture of Pentecostal divisions and offers a characterization of the divisive elements of the movement. In the final section, the identification of Pentecostalism as a movement is upheld as a fruitful way to speak of the unity of Pentecostals worldwide amidst the tensions Pentecostals bring to the ecumenical life of the churches.

Pentecostals and Christian unity

The first major study and still the standard of research on the modern-day Pentecostal movement surprised with the assessment that ecumenical endeavours form a central 'root' of Pentecostalism.[3] The shared experience of the Holy Spirit among Pentecostals pioneers motivated an ecumenical optimism, which saw the Pentecostal movement as participating in God's activity in the last days that would bring unity to the churches. Popular labels for the movement, such as 'Pentecostal', 'Apostolic Faith', or 'Latter Rain', were seen as ecumenical titles commonly used by the groups to express their continuity with the history and mission of the church and their eschatological expectation of a forthcoming universal restoration of God's people.[4] The diverse Pentecostal groups are linked together by a central emphasis on the events of the day of Pentecost that ultimately point forward to the unity of all believers in the kingdom of God.

Pentecostal pioneers across the globe reflected this ecumenical hope from the beginning in often pragmatic ways. In North America, one of the earliest Pentecostal groups was named 'Christian Union' to reflect the true intention of the revival.[5] In the influential paper of the Azusa Street Mission, *The Apostolic Faith*, pastor William J. Seymour declared that the Pentecostal movement stood clearly for 'Christian Unity everywhere'.[6] Frank Bartleman, a similarly important figure of early Pentecostal history in North America, declared unambiguously, 'There can be no divisions in a true Pentecost. To formulate a separate body is but to advertise our failure as a people of God.'[7] Thomas B. Barratt, who carried the Pentecostal revival to several Scandinavian countries, envisioned Pentecostalism as the 'Very Revival Christ had in His mind when He prayed that *all His disciples might be one*.'[8] Gerrit R. Polman, a pioneer of the Dutch Pentecostal movement, admonished sternly: 'The purpose of the Pentecostal revival is not to build up a church, but to build up all churches.'[9] Ecumenical conversations were encouraged by well-known Pentecostal leaders in the Netherlands, Great Britain, France, Belgium, Germany, and other nations.[10] While the body of opinion in the Pentecostal movement included also frequent ambivalence and opposition to ecumenical ties with existing churches,[11] Pentecostals saw themselves overwhelmingly as an ecumenical movement.

The force of these ecumenical convictions is closely related to the revivals that occurred in broad ecumenical contexts during the late nineteenth and early twentieth century in Europe. The rise of the ecumenical movement since the World Missionary Conference in 1910 and the ecumenical embeddedness of the charismatic renewal in the established churches contributed significantly to Pentecostal participation in ecumenical affairs. Across the European continent, and later also in Latin America, Africa, and Asia, positive ecumenical attitudes frequently resulted from the encouragement of foreign missionaries and the international and interdenominational origins of the Pentecostal pioneers themselves. The Pentecostal movement emerged as an ecumenical melting pot of existing doctrinal traditions, organizational structures, liturgical practices, national and local ecclesiastical cultures, and spiritualities. Today's ecumenical landscape shows with clarity that the ecumenical root of Pentecostalism produced significant fruit throughout the movement. A brief survey shows the extent of Pentecostal participation in ecumenical conversations.

Global ecumenical conversations

Pentecostals are participating in a variety of ecumenical conversations, often on the grassroots level but also in regional, national, and international contexts. In many places across the global South, Pentecostalism represents a particular challenge to the older historic churches.[12] Ecumenical conversations in these countries often result from co-operation with existing national forums and organizations but also depend on the personal commitment of pastors and ministers.[13] In the West, the dominant form of ecumenical relations is conciliar institutional dialogue, and Pentecostals have entered into several official discussions with the Roman Catholic Church, the World Council of Churches, the World Communion of Reformed Churches, the Lutheran World Fellowship, the Baptist World Alliance, and other Protestant organizations.

A particularly strong ecumenical commitment among Latin American Pentecostal churches since the 1960s has contributed to the formation of significant ecumenical institutions such as the Latin American Council of Churches (CLAI), the all-Latin American Pentecostal Encounters (EPLA), and the Latin American Evangelical Pentecostal Commission (CEPLA). Many Pentecostals are active participants in the Evangelical Service for Ecumenical Development (SEPADE), the Evangelical Union of Latin America (UNELAM), the Evangelical Christian Aid (ACE), and other ecumenical organizations. Several of these fellowships have organized or assisted Pentecostal meetings at the national level in countries across Central and South America. Pentecostal consultations have also been convened by the World Council of Churches in various Latin American countries.[14] Nonetheless, these national organizations have not always been successful in bringing Pentecostals across the continent to the ecumenical table. Pentecostal participation still depends heavily on grassroots efforts. This scenario is symptomatic for other parts of the ecumenical world.

National conversations and ecumenical organizations have undergone a number of transitions especially in North America and Europe. In order to bridge the divisions between churches historically associated with the National Council of Churches and communities not so aligned, Pentecostals have led the formation of the joint fellowship of Christian Churches Together in the USA in 2001.[15] The first Pentecostal church became a member of the

European Council of Churches in 1984. Three years later the Pentecostal European Fellowship was established. The significant growth and expansion of the charismatic movement has further contributed to a number of national dialogues involving Pentecostal churches throughout Europe.[16] The initially racially and doctrinally exclusive Pentecostal Fellowship of North America was replaced in 1994 by Pentecostal/Charismatic Churches of North America, which includes African American Pentecostals.[17] Black Pentecostals and churches have gradually entered the ecumenical landscape, although many of them do not yet visibly participate in established conciliar dialogues.[18] Similar efforts to engage in ecumenical endeavours are undertaken in Africa and Asia, particularly in countries that increasingly serve as the host of international ecumenical dialogues.[19]

The extent of ecumenical co-operation among Pentecostals is still virtually unknown in many circles in and beyond the Pentecostal movement. The heart of these activities is often found among individuals and small groups dedicated to the ecumenical and Pentecostal ethos. Ecumenical conversations originate mostly on an informal level and often remain undeveloped, since official ecumenical dialogues demand institutional, administrative, financial, and logistic resources that the Pentecostal movement does not yet possess.[20] Official ecumenical dialogues form the more visible side of Pentecostal participation in establishing and maintaining Christian unity. Nonetheless, the diverse character of the Pentecostal movement points increasingly in a direction of personal and informal conversations as a means to increase global participation in the ecumenical life.

International ecumenical dialogues

Pentecostals are participating in a small but significant number of official ecumenical dialogues. The most significant long-term commitment is doubtlessly the international Roman Catholic-Pentecostal dialogue. The renewal of the Roman Catholic Church since Vatican II, strong institutional support for ecumenical dialogue, the rise of the Charismatic Movement, and the increasing visibility of Pentecostalism worldwide have led to consistent meetings since 1972. The make-up of the Pentecostal community has changed

dramatically over the course of the conversations that address a
large number of topics of mutual concern such as Spirit baptism
and spiritual gifts, Christian initiation, and worship, Scripture and
tradition, faith and reason, speaking in tongues, divine healing, the
role of Mary, the church, the sacraments, the communion of saints,
evangelization, proselytism, common witness, and most recently
conversations on faith and Christian initiation, Christian formation
and discipleship, as well as experience and spirituality.[21] Although
these conversations have been met with criticism and scepticism on
both sides, the meetings and reports have significantly strengthened
the ties between Pentecostals and Catholics.[22] Most significantly,
the fellowship has helped Pentecostals understand their own
identity, sharpening and reaffirming their ecumenical commitment,
and leading to dialogue with other churches.

Similarly influential and controversial has been the increasing
involvement of Pentecostal groups in the World Council of
Churches. Since the 1970s Pentecostalism has moved into the
field of vision of many member churches, and the Consultation
on the Significance of the Charismatic Renewal for the Churches
brought Pentecostal concerns to the centre floor of discussion.
Concentrated efforts to involve Pentecostals in the work of the
Council have significantly advanced mutual co-operation, although
most Pentecostal churches are not holding official membership
status.[23] Today, Pentecostals have been fully integrated in the
work of the Commission on Faith and Order and participate
in national and international meetings and conferences. A Joint
Consultative Group with Pentecostals has contributed further to
establishing close ties. Pentecostals participate in more than 40
national councils of churches.[24] These visible forms of ecumenical
co-operation gradually overcome existing stereotypes and help
build an ecumenical infrastructure for Pentecostal participation.
Nonetheless, the interaction between the diverse constituencies
continues to present various complicated challenges to both sides.

Mutual efforts to strengthen ecumenical ties with other traditions have also led to official dialogue between Pentecostals and
the World Council of Reformed Churches since 1996. With the
experience gained from the Pentecostal-Roman Catholic dialogue,
these new conversations quickly focused on mature theological
themes such as the relationship between the Word and the Holy
Spirit, the church and the world, worship, discipleship, community,

and justice.[25] Similar conversations with the Lutheran World Federation since 2005 have led to official discussions on encountering Christ in the churches. In contrast to other dialogues, conversations are less concerned with discussions of doctrine than with allowing space for a genuine expression of faith, a form of conversation more genuine to Pentecostal experience. The interaction with concerns of Christian experience have allowed for genuine explorations of an encounter with Christ in worship, proclamation, sacraments, and spiritual gifts.[26] Initial stages of informal conversations not yet fully developed also exist between Pentecostals and the Ecumenical Patriarchate of Constantinople, the Mennonite World Conference, and the Salvation Army.

While formal conversations and institutional dialogues continue to develop, much of the ecumenical atmosphere increasingly draws attention to informal and personal meetings that are perceived as less invasive and more genuine to the practices and sensitivities of the participating traditions. The most recent among those initiatives is the Global Christian Forum, an ecumenical gathering originating in 1998 and striking a chord rapidly among all Christian traditions, including Pentecostals. Unlike established formally organized conciliar dialogues, these conversations consist of a sharing of testimonies and establishing personal relationships.[27] Doctrinal agreement and organizational unity are not in the immediate purview of the forum. Rather more modest goals exist to contribute to mutual understanding, to encourage communication, to overcome existing stereotypes, and to build up ecumenical communion. Pentecostal participation in the forum and its leadership is forming a new kind of ecumenical environment that challenges the format of traditional bilateral conversations and the lack of informal opportunities for intimate ecumenical relationships. The international make-up of the forum parallels the dramatic shift of the centre of Christianity worldwide toward the East and the global South. The informal environment and testimonial conversations are more consistent with Pentecostal forms of self-expression and promise to engage a greater Pentecostal constituency in the future. While Pentecostalism has from the outset been an ecumenical movement, the contours, organizational and institutional shape of ecumenical fellowship with Pentecostals is still very much in development.

Denominationalism and separatism

Conflict and dissension belong to the ecumenical picture of the history of the church. Neither biblical texts nor historical records show evidence of a 'clean' ecumenism – a unity of the churches that exists without dispute and disagreement. Christian unity exists always amidst the struggle for fellowship and communion. The modern-day Pentecostal movement is no exception. Hence, the ecumenical efforts among Pentecostals are overshadowed by concerns for organization and structure, and it is difficult to speak in ecumenical perspective of a single, unified Pentecostal movement. Attempts to identify and categorize the churches, assemblies, fellowships, communities, societies, alliances, associations, missions, crusades, conferences, and other bodies generally identified as 'Pentecostal' face the uneasy task of dealing with the distinctions made among Pentecostals between classical Pentecostal groups, the Charismatic Movement, and neo-Pentecostalism, as well as the broader distinctions between Pentecostals that have formed denominational patterns similar to other Protestant traditions and the overwhelming number of independent congregations.[28] The number of independent fellowships is particularly staggering in the developing countries of the global South.[29] The World Christian Database lists almost 2,500 denominations as 'Pentecostal' and often associates these groups with different headings in different countries, categorizing some as Protestant in North America but as Independent in Africa or Latin America.[30] Many Pentecostal groups carry the same name, featuring with particular prominence the title 'Assemblies of God', 'Church of God', or a variation of the term 'Pentecostal' – despite often considerable differences in doctrine and practice. The still largely uncharted terrain of Pentecostal denominationalism has contributed to stereotyping the Pentecostal movement as inherently divisive and opposed to efforts that establish and maintain the unity of the churches.

Ecumenical exclusivism and anonymous ecumenism

The reasons for denominationalism and separatism among Pentecostals are complex. The worldwide expansion and growth of the Pentecostal movement quickly led to concerns for the coherence and preservation of the movement itself that overshadowed interests in ecumenical relations. Organizational patterns and institutional examples were readily found in other Christian traditions but were often viewed with scepticism or outright rejection by those who had been former members. The rise of the charismatic and neo-Pentecostal groups further adds to debates about the nature and purpose of the movement worldwide. The result is a focus on matters of self-interest and essential concerns for the organization and structural composition of Pentecostalism, or rather of particular Pentecostal groups, that suppress active participation in matters of Christian unity.

The popular perception of ecumenical practices held by many Pentecostals is characterized by frequent ambivalence.[31] Responsible for this attitude is a widespread misunderstanding of the goals and intentions of ecumenism, a lack of awareness of the ecumenical heritage among Pentecostals, low participation of Pentecostal leadership in official ecumenical endeavours, organizational disadvantages of the diverse and pluralistic landscape of Pentecostal churches, the absence of institutional support and umbrella organizations to initiate and sustain ecumenical activities, and a consequential lack of resources for ecumenical formation.[32] On the other hand, obstacles to further ecumenical growth are also brought to Pentecostals from the outside. Many non-Pentecostal traditions display unfamiliarity with and scepticism toward ecumenical relations.[33] Accusations of a lack of theological depth, overzealous emotionalism, aggressive evangelism, proselytism, liturgical impoverishment, institutional ineffectiveness, and unorthodox doctrines are just a few of the stereotypes that prevent the development of a more positive ecumenical climate. As a result, much of ecumenical groundwork is spent in repairing damaged relations, dismantling stereotypes, and establishing personal relationships. Even so, the conversations, dialogues, and official reports that result from endeavours in Christian unity are virtually unacknowledged among most Pentecostals.

Underlying these visible issues that hinder a more comprehensive engagement in ecumenism are a number of theological presuppositions that affect the ecumenical attitude among classical Pentecostals. A dominant mindset confronting ecumenical participation is the primitivist or restorationist impulse among Pentecostals. This mindset is based on a critical evaluation of the contemporary church and is particularly visible in the frequent demand for a return to the practices of the apostolic community.[34] Pentecostals argue that the established churches have altered the original forms of Christianity, de-emphasized the work of the Holy Spirit, and stifled spiritual growth.[35] Consequently, a restoration of apostolic faith and practices is seen as a necessary, primary objective of restoring the church. This pervasive attitude in classical Pentecostalism and many of the independent Pentecostal groups often creates a rather sharp contrast to ecumenical fellowship with precisely those groups that Pentecostals hold responsible for the problems. In turn, hostility toward Pentecostals has dampened many ecumenical ambitions on both the grassroots level and among the denominational leadership. In response, the isolation of Pentecostals has invigorated the restorationist mindset, created new prejudices, and led much of the Pentecostal movement into a realm of ecumenical anonymity.[36]

In addition, the ecumenical investment among Pentecostals suffers under internal debates and divisions particularly over disagreements on doctrine, church politics, personalities, and practices.[37] Not least, Pentecostals are divided over the extent of their ecumenical engagement in general, a problem that concerns not only their relations with other churches but also internal associations among Pentecostal groups. The global Pentecostal movement has become a composition of different branches of Pentecostal bodies that sometimes look with suspicion at other parts of the movement. Closer alignment with denominations and institutions critical of the ecumenical movement has forced many Pentecostals to forsake the ecumenical conversations in which they had participated.[38] Others grant higher priority to internal relations among Pentecostals, such as the Pentecostal World Fellowship, and ecumenical associations with non-Pentecostals have been either neglected or remained undeveloped. The repercussions of such decisions are only gradually repaired and demand more concentrated efforts in understanding the nature and identity of the Pentecostal movement and its position and function in (or apart from) the body of Christ.

Isolation from the Church

Ecumenical exclusivism and separatism show the symptoms but reveal little of the inherent problems responsible for the ambiguity and divisiveness among Pentecostals. On a more substantive level, the ecumenical mindset of Pentecostals is deeply restricted by the absence of a comprehensive Pentecostal ecclesiology. The movement has neither formulated a theology of the church nor situated itself consistently in any existing proposals. It is unclear whether communion with Pentecostals implies structural and institutional union or if such forms of reconciliation can even be entertained in the first place. The most persistent label for modern-day Pentecostalism is without doubt the description as a 'movement'. However, this designation bears significant consequences for Pentecostal self-understanding and the possibility of ecumenical relations with Pentecostals.

Historically, classical Pentecostalism emerged from ecclesiastical roots that were already commonly designated as 'movements' within Christianity, such as the Holiness Movement and the Apostolic Faith Movement, and the application to Pentecostals seemed appropriate. However, the designation of Pentecostalism as a 'movement' by Pentecostals is often a critical, even countercultural choice that expresses the contrast to what Pentecostals frequently describe as the 'stagnation' and 'institutionalism' of the so-called 'old churches'.[39] Pentecostals understand their own identity in often radical opposition to the historical consciousness of the established churches; many see in the existing use of the term 'church' itself a sectarian designation. The distinction of Pentecostalism as a 'movement' from the broader, established notion of 'church' highlights the difficulty and resistance of fitting Pentecostals into established classifications.

Attempts to categorize and incorporate Pentecostalism among the churches have generally located the movement at the margins. Pentecostalism is identified less in terms of 'church' than of 'sect' or 'faction' or 'stream'. In most cases understood as a temporary extreme element, Pentecostalism is seen as an afterthought to the landscape of church history, an addition at the end of tables and diagrams, an outgrowth of existing streams and developments, a mere example or the most recent expression of developments in already existing traditions.[40] Thus added to the established Christian landscape, Pentecostalism is widely perceived as a temporary renewal or revival movement much like others that have appeared (and disappeared) throughout church history. Pentecostals have been hesitant to understand themselves as any more permanent and have readily used the designation as a movement to distinguish themselves from other particular groups as well as from the entire arena of mainstream Christian churches.

Pentecostal groups have understood themselves fundamentally as a missionary movement of the Holy Spirit. This perspective derives essentially from the idea of the Great Commission centrally placed within the evangelistic and eschatological life of the church.[41] In simple terms, Pentecostals understand themselves as the realization of the biblical promise of the outpouring of the Holy Spirit on all flesh, a movement in and beyond the churches – but not a church in itself. Put differently, many Pentecostals possess a sense for what the church is *not* rather than for what the church actually is. In its most basic form, the church remains essentially identical with the kingdom of God as an ideal yet to be reached but not a reality already attained. Pentecostalism in this sense is a movement becoming the church, a transformation of existing traditions into one movement toward the church.[42] This rejection of the designation 'church' has made co-operation with Pentecostals difficult on many levels. A remedy for this dilemma is not simply found in a revision of Pentecostal doctrine or ecumenical practices.

As Pentecostalism expanded to worldwide proportions, the movement began to suffer most visibly from disorganization and divisions among the missionary workers. Initially, Pentecostals saw themselves as a movement of the Spirit that swept across the existing denominations and that would soon usher in the kingdom of God. As the eschatological expectations failed to materialize, organizational instabilities, administrative weaknesses, and the absence of any clearly formulated theological understanding of the church soon caught up with the growth, stability, coherence, and unity of the movement.[43] The lack of planning, structure, formal

institutions, and networks severely hampered the growth and effectiveness of Pentecostals abroad. As a result, Pentecostals turned to
the existing visible structures of denominations surrounding them
and adopted the title 'church' as a means of self-designation.[44]
The establishment of effective missionary structures initiated a
widespread institutionalization and denominationalization among
Pentecostals that promised growth, stability, and survival – yet
still without formulating an accompanying theology. As a result,
missionary and evangelistic activities among Pentecostals have
become the formal endeavor of particular Pentecostal churches.
The unity of the church is no longer the final realization of
the contemporary Pentecostal movement; the church is already
located within today's Pentecostalism or, perhaps more pragmati-
cally, among the Pentecostal denominations.[45] This perspective has
served as implicit justification for establishing and maintaining
denominational structures without questioning if they are genuine
to the Pentecostal ethos. Denominations formed quickly and
spread rapidly throughout Pentecostalism and virtually eliminated
the original mindset of a 'movement'. Instead, Pentecostal denominations have entered a competitive mindset among themselves and
with others.[46]

A closer look reveals that Pentecostal groups have frequently
adopted the title 'church' not only for the local assembly but also
for the administrative group of churches that associate with one
another on a regional or national level. Internal dissention and
schisms hastened the process of institutionalization, including
groups who continue to reject any denominational designation
outright.[47] This shift to the realm of formal organization has
complicated the use of the designation 'church' and effectively
shut the door to a more pronounced ecumenical theology and
participation. The adoption of the traditional classification,
'church', inevitably led to confrontation internally as well as
with other churches and denominations. The Pentecostal self-
understanding today allows for the existence of multiple churches
and denominations, yet there has been no parallel development
to advance the communication and cooperation of churches in
and beyond the Pentecostal movement. Umbrella organizations,
such as the Pentecostal World Fellowship, do not represent a
decision-making body and hold no authority beyond the assemblies of particular Pentecostal denominations. Pentecostals have

become anonymous behind denominational structures that are not equipped for ecumenical conversations. Most visibly, this development has further consolidated an exclusivist attitude toward other non-Pentecostal communities.[48] No substantive theological formulations of the church and Christian unity are underlying these structures. Ecumenical documents with Pentecostal participation are rarely consulted by Pentecostal leadership. The choice to enter the competitive mindset of existing Christian denominations has effectively made Pentecostalism a movement isolated from the church.

Unity and diversity in the Pentecostal movement

Pentecostals have always looked at the book of Acts for biblical patterns of the church. The biblical narrative presents the church since the day of Pentecost as a group in constant transition. Pentecostals found that even the day of Pentecost itself does not mark a definite transformation of the Christian group, but that the expansion and rapid changes of the church demanded other 'Pentecosts' that allowed the church to move forward. Much of this transitional character is reflected in modern-day Pentecostalism, at times deliberately, but more often in ways embedded in the historical character of the movement that have not yet found a consistent and deliberative crystallization among the churches. The reconciliation of rampant denominationalism with the ecumenical attitudes among Pentecostals demands a closer look at the way Pentecostalism can be understood as an ecumenical movement that exhibits patterns of both unity and diversity.

Unity and diversity among Pentecostals

The tensions between ecumenical exclusivism and ecumenical participation among Pentecostals reflect the enormous changes that characterize the short history of the Pentecostal movement. The significant developments impacting modern-day Pentecostalism worldwide have confronted the movement with the question of its own identity among the churches amidst concerns for the global status of the movement.[49] Mixed attitudes toward Christian unity, both positive and negative, are not a unique feature of Pentecostals but reflect dominant global forces that have shaped the worldwide ecumenical agenda in general. The proper characterization of Pentecostalism among the churches acknowledges the coexistence of unity and diversity. Admittedly, the distance between the two may be greater among Pentecostals than among the established churches and seasoned ecumenical traditions. Nonetheless, Pentecostalism is recapitulating the history of the ecumenical movement at a much faster pace. The tensions of Pentecostal engagement in Christian unity reveal that not all attempts to understand a tradition's identity necessarily invite ecumenical participation, and that concerns for one's own tradition can unfold at the cost of visible Christian unity. In this sense, a more complete understanding of Pentecostalism demands a renewed understanding of both what it means to be 'Pentecostal' and how to pursue unity with the movement thus identified.

From a Pentecostal perspective, the intention to understand the movement itself and its ecumenical position among the churches faces at least two major challenges: First, there exists no consistent, historical definition of the term 'church' among Pentecostals worldwide. Whereas the established Christian traditions possess longstanding accounts of the nature and purpose of the church, Pentecostals do not share a common idea and theology of the body of Christ.[50] Second, the diversity of Pentecostal perspectives on the church allows at best for multiple theologies of the church that reflect both the tensions within the Pentecostal movement and the challenges of ecumenical reconciliation. Pentecostals have entered a phase of ecumenical pragmatism – an intermediate stage on the way to more genuine Pentecostal forms of participation.[51] Contemporary approaches to ecumenism slowly move beyond Anglo-European dominance to broader international participation and ecumenical organization that address the concerns of the broader Pentecostal community. Reasons that this development is filled with tensions should not be sought in the pluralistic image of Pentecostalism alone but rather in the absence of opportunities for Pentecostals to define themselves as Pentecostals among the churches.

The most celebrated attempt to identify an ecumenical Pentecostal self-description is found in the concept of *koinonia* – a

New Testament idea of the fellowship of believers rooted in the trinitarian communion of God.[52] Formulated not least in conversations between Pentecostal and Roman Catholics, ecumenical perspectives on *koinonia* have become a widely accepted and fruitful basis for approaching a shared understanding of the church.[53] For Pentecostals, the church already exists in *koinonia* due to the divine action manifested in the outpouring of the Holy Spirit. This pneumatological understanding of Christian unity implies for Pentecostals a shared life in the Spirit and a common manifestation of spiritual gifts that exists not merely in the abstract ideal but in the concrete historical reality of the Christian life.[54] The neglect of this emphasis in the churches catholic remains for many Pentecostals the strongest obstacle to ecumenical participation. The large majority of this sentiment stems from convictions generally uninformed by detailed ecumenical discussions. Pentecostals worldwide exhibit a rather weak ecumenical pedagogy, although they certainly are not alone in its tangible expressions.

There exist a variety of 'experiences' of *koinonia* among Pentecostals that are often determined by the level of submission to ecclesial authority, institutional communication and co-operation, existing church structures and processes.[55] On a more pragmatic level, ecumenical participation often depends on the negative or positive influences that have shaped a person's self-understanding. Pentecostals allow for change and transition between different perspectives and ecumenical attitudes as part of arriving at their own self-understanding that is still emerging.[56] For the larger ecumenical community, this fluctuation is sometimes perceived as an inherent instability that prevents concrete achievements and long-lasting relationships. This perspective runs the risk of divorcing Pentecostalism from the common endeavour for Christian unity. Isolated from the ecumenical movement, Pentecostals will not arrive at a consensus on the global Pentecostal identity.

Instead, Pentecostalism and ecumenism must be seen as two mutually interdependent movements. For many Pentecostals and non-Pentecostals alike, participation in both movements remains 'an exercise on the frontiers'.[57] The diversity of global Pentecostalism also reflects the diversity of the ecumenical movement worldwide. The tensions in the Pentecostal movement manifest in many ways the broader ecumenical temperament, which in turn has not reflected much on its own constituency as a movement.

Identified as 'movements' in the contemporary Christian landscape, Pentecostalism and ecumenism share in common a unique identity that includes a shared understanding of existing at the margins of what is called the 'church'.

The critical function of Pentecostalism

Pentecostalism understood as a movement that both confounds the ecumenical landscape while at the same time standing at the forefront of revitalizing Christian unity has dramatically changed the perception of denominationalism and ecumenism within the movement. The acceptance of denominational and ecumenical language among Pentecostals suggests that both concepts will continue to coexist despite the tensions. Classifying Pentecostalism as a 'movement' remains a significant label that does not flatten the image of Pentecostal diversity but instead upholds the tensions within Pentecostalism as representative of religious movements in general. At the same time, there exists no theology of the church as movement, no movement-ecclesiology, which could be applied to Pentecostalism. It is found rather in the Pentecostal beliefs and practices that define the movement's historical reality and that consequently demand closer attention.

An understanding of Pentecostalism as a movement begins with its global representation and the diverse streams of Pentecostal groups. Simply said, Pentecostalism is itself inherently in transition. This movement internal to Pentecostalism affects the self-understanding of Pentecostals among the churches. Among classical Pentecostals, the church traditionally stands for a self-governing, self-supporting, and self-propagating body that proclaims an unchanging gospel to all cultures and contexts.[58] The expansion of classical Pentecostalism and the rise of new Pentecostal streams have turned the focus to the further contextualization of the church on the grassroots level in order to remain relevant and meaningful. In contrast, the ecclesiology of the Charismatic Movement is largely shaped by the mother church in which it is able to unfold. The ethos of Pentecostalism as a movement is upheld in these contexts by relating the charismatic revival to the historical life of the church rather than its abstract essence. Put differently, Pentecostalism is understood as a new movement in the church or the church in movement but not as the church itself.[59] The neo-Pentecostal movement has shifted Pentecostal ecclesiology again into quite opposite directions and much closer to a Free Church theology.[60] The notion of movement is here synonymous with a diachronic plurality of the churches in a framework of ecclesial interdependence where churches operate under a universal outpouring of the Holy Spirit that changes and varies from congregation to congregation and is more closely aligned with a personal confession of faith.[61] Global Pentecostalism does not propose one particular structure of movement but suggests that 'church' is experienced in a diversity of rhythms, beliefs, and practices.

If Pentecostalism is understood as a movement in these diverse ways, then it is equally important to emphasize the historical character of this identification. In the most tangible way, denominations are the history books of the churches, the stage where ecumenical relations are applied, tested, and verified. This perspective is based on the assumption that denominations are temporary replacements of an eschatological movement becoming the church. The pragmatic side of this temporary concept of denominations is perhaps the most challenging feature of Pentecostal ecclesiology. While theologically the Pentecostal denominations are considered transitory because they represent the churches in history but not yet the church in eternity, the application of this theology is typically overshadowed by administrative, organizational, and institutional concerns that depend on the long-term stability of the denomination. Moreover, the distinction between the historical reality of Pentecostalism and the eternal unity of the church should not lead us to deny denominations any significance and simply hold that they will eventually be subsumed under the eternal kingdom of God. Pentecostals have emphasized that denominations exhibit a valuable critical function toward the established cultures and structures of the churches.[62] Pentecostals thus frequently identify with a particular denomination as it represents a sort of historical anti-structure to existing practices.[63] At the same time as the local assembly emulates the denominational patterns, the denomination itself moves toward its full realization in the eternal church. Denominationalism in the Pentecostal movement therefore exists amidst the tension between the local assembly and the whole church as a critical catalyst of the renewal and transformation of the whole church.

The critical function of denominations in the Pentecostal movement is important because it is exercised only in explicitly ecumenical contexts, since no single denomination represents the fullness of either the diversity of local assemblies or the eternal fulfilment of Christian unity. Put differently, denominations cannot exist in the singular. The denominational landscape among Pentecostals is not the result of an expansion of one particular form of Pentecostalism but the birth of genuine new communities from within different environments and as a result of particular developments. This diversity of history, manifested for Pentecostals in the outpouring of the Holy Spirit, is the soil in which denominations and the foundation for Pentecostal ecclesiology are planted.[64] The challenge of this reality is that the character of the denominations as the promissory note for the full unity of the one church can only be fulfilled in relations between the churches. Individual denominations are a partial, visible manifestation of this development but remain incomplete for any attempt to arrive at a Pentecostal theology of the church. From a denominational perspective, the church is never fully realized but remains always in movement. This is Pentecostal praxis par excellence.

The identification of Pentecostalism as a critical movement is neither synonymous with denominations nor opposed to their reality but points to a constant transformation of the historical reality of what we consider Pentecostalism today.[65] This element of transition is one of the most significant features of modern-day Pentecostalism and explains how different realities of the church can coexist in the same movement. It also represents the greatest challenge to ecumenical conversations – on the one hand, Pentecostals form a single entity that exists across a broad spectrum held together by a shared worldview and spirituality; on the other hand, the diverse, even contradicting practices and theologies among Pentecostals resist the identification as a single entity. The concept of 'the one and the many'[66] often used in traditional attempts to identify the church comes to a critical manifestation in the historical reality of Pentecostalism. As a result, the most immediate challenge remains the reconciliation of rampant denominationalism and uncritical adoption of a Free Church ethos with the worldview and spirituality of the Pentecostal movement. As the previous chapter has shown, the charismatic manifestations representative of this Pentecostal ethos show a wide spectrum of communion and fellowship in the Spirit that allows for contrasting experiences and convictions. This perspective does not justify the tensions between unity and diversity in the Pentecostal movement today, but it does suggest that to expect anything different leads to the portrayal of an unrealistic homogeneous image of Pentecostalism, which remains still in its most elementary forms a movement in transition.

CHAPTER FOUR

Orthodox doctrine and sectarianism

Some of the most visible tensions in the Pentecostal movement are found in divisions over doctrine. From the beginning of modern-day Pentecostalism, the movement exhibited a broad variety of beliefs that are not always readily summed up in doctrinal statements. The statements of faith and doctrinal teachings issued by particular Pentecostal groups do not easily apply to others within the movement. In addition, some Pentecostal teachings stand in rather sharp contrast to classical formulations of the Christian tradition and are considered heretical by many non-Pentecostals. The most significant among these tensions is the longstanding and often heated debate among Pentecostals between advocates of trinitarian theology and the so-called Oneness Pentecostals.[1] While the majority of Pentecostals have embraced the traditional Christian teaching of the doctrine of God, Oneness Pentecostalism has gained a large following throughout the world that rejects the creedal trinitarian tradition.

A general rejection of the creeds is a well-known trademark of Pentecostal history. Pentecostals frequently see in creedal formulations a limitation of spiritual freedom, a hastening of institutionalization and formalization of the Christian life.[2] Most Pentecostals, especially groups not closely associated with a mainline tradition, are less familiar with the actual wording of the creeds and hold no fundamental doctrinal opposition. Nonetheless, creeds are widely stereotyped as destructive to the unity of the church, a testing of allegiance that has relegated Pentecostals often to the margins of fellowship.[3] Oneness Pentecostals tend to sharply criticize the creedal statements over doctrinal disagreements that have ostracized them not only from other Pentecostal streams but from the mainline Christian traditions. This chapter presents these tensions between Oneness and trinitarian Pentecostals as representative of the struggle to conform to the teachings of Christian orthodoxy. The first part of the chapter outlines the traditional formulation of the doctrine of God among Pentecostals. The second part presents the contrasting position of Oneness Pentecostals. In the final part, these positions are brought into dialogue with particular focus on the factors responsible for the divisions. The goal of this chapter is to arrive at a closer understanding of the development of doctrine among the diverse adherents of the Pentecostal movement and their position in the landscape of Christian orthodoxy. A full reconciliation of the tensions and contrasting doctrines is unlikely. The considerable range of beliefs is an irrevocable feature of Pentecostal participation in the development of global Christianity.

Pentecostalism and the formulation of the doctrine of God

The narrative descriptions of the biblical texts have occupied a central place in directing the daily lives and doctrines of Pentecostals from the beginning.[4] Most Pentecostals find in Luke-Acts, in particular, an experiential pattern for the formulation of Christian beliefs that possesses a theological integrity in its own right and which is indicative of the development of Pentecostal doctrine. These narratives emphasize the importance of salvation as the key to understanding God's work in the world. Inside this narrative soteriology, Pentecostals have highlighted the centrality of Jesus Christ as the messiah anointed with the Holy Spirit. In turn, the outpouring of this Spirit on the world marks the proper frame for all subsequent formulations of Pentecostal doctrine. Together, these foundational elements offer insights into the general pattern of doctrinal articulation among Pentecostals today.

Narrative articulations of doctrine

Pentecostal theology is born out of the need to narrate the experiences of the salvific work of God in Christ and the Spirit and to do so in terms that do justice to their experiences rather than to official formulations of doctrine. Most Pentecostal groups are reluctant to formulate extensive systems of official doctrines. Classical Pentecostalism is representative of the larger Pentecostal constituency that has found it difficult to present doctrinal formulations without adopting them from other traditions and without thereby sacrificing the distinctive experiences that identify them in distinction to those traditions. The Charismatic Movement in the mainline churches has had its own challenges of remaining an integral part of their traditions without giving the impression of simply adding to it a doctrine of the Spirit. Neo-Pentecostal groups have added little significant texture to the actual formulation of Pentecostal doctrine, primarily because there is no magisterial theological guidance or official authoritative teaching for all groups. What ties the different streams of Pentecostalism together is a strong reliance on Scripture as a path to doctrinal formulations that support and direct the Pentecostal experiences.[5]

In Scripture, Pentecostals find a common emphasis on dreams, visions, prophecies, prayer, and worship that provide the foundation for articulating their own story. This articulation generally proceeds orally among Pentecostals, usually expressed in sermons, testimonies, and songs, and rarely in classical formulations of doctrine.[6] In trying to articulate their experiences, song, poetry, testimony, prophecy, and prayer seem the more appropriate media to Pentecostals than creedal formulations and doctrinal propositions. Theology is identified not primarily with creeds and doctrines but with a worshipful response to God's saving activity. While the experience of God's saving work forms the motivation for Pentecostal theology, it is the Pentecostal worldview and spirituality that inform the articulation and structure of that theology. Pentecostals have generally neglected to craft a formal doctrine of God. Instead, worship and prayer stand at the heart of a language evocative of the praise, petitions, lamentations, sighs, and groans Pentecostals find in the community of the New Testament.[7]

In their concept of doctrine, Pentecostals stand closer to the Roman Catholic idea of the development of doctrine than the Protestant understanding of doctrines as the unchangeable deposit of faith.[8] Formative in this understanding is the link between the authority of spirituality and the authority of doctrine (*lex orandi, lex credendi*).[9] Pentecostals can speak of spirituality *as* doctrine by locating the starting point for all doctrine in the human response to God. The response in immediate testimonies, visions, songs, tongues, or prayers is initially pre-cognitive, affective, and behavioural, or to put it differently, therapeutic and prophetic.[10] From there, a more articulate, scrutinized, and deliberative formulation of doctrine, such as creeds, dogmas, and official teachings are generally not attempted by Pentecostals. Nonetheless, most Pentecostals readily embrace formal articulations of doctrine from other traditions if these reflect their own spirituality and experiences.

The immediate link between spirituality and doctrine (and vice versa) among Pentecostals is formed by soteriology, or perhaps more accurately, the experience of salvation. We might say that salvation represents an epistemic and experiential commonality that informs all Pentecostal practices. Formulations of Pentecostal doctrine are ultimately rooted in the multidimensional character of salvation as it is observed and formulated among the Christian traditions.[11] This means that for Pentecostals all doctrine must remain verifiable in the concrete personal and communal experiences of God's redemptive activity.

This emphasis is clearly visible in the articulation of the so-called 'full' gospel – a theological formulation among classical Pentecostals that mediates between narrative account and formulaic expression. Two different theological accounts are in circulation among Pentecostals, the four-fold gospel of Jesus as saviour, Spirit baptizer, healer, and coming king, and the five-fold gospel that adds to this account the image of Jesus as sanctifier.[12] These articulations are guided by practical ambitions rather than structural concerns, biblical readings rather than doctrinal conventions. At the heart of the full gospel is the worshipping life of the community, both the affective disposition of individuals and the liturgy of the church, in which the gospel is not only proclaimed but exercised. Pentecostals continue to emphasize that any confession of faith remains primarily a form of spirituality. At the heart of articulating this spirituality among Pentecostals stands the central figure of Jesus Christ and the experience of the Holy Spirit.

The centrality of Jesus Christ

The Pentecostal full-gospel motif is centred on the person of Jesus. The core convictions of Pentecostals are not simply identified as salvation, Spirit baptism, healing, sanctification, and a strong eschatological orientation. Rather, it is the biblical picture of Jesus that dominates these theological formulations. Pentecostal piety has always been directed toward Jesus.[13] In other words, Pentecostal doctrine always expresses at heart a Christology. The central confession of Christ dominates doctrinal narratives among Pentecostals. The goal of these confessions is not primarily a teaching about Christ but a worshipful expression of faith and witness toward Christ. Pentecostal songs, testimonies, and sermons declare the centrality of Jesus for all proclamations of faith to God and to one another:

> We have heard a joyful sound, Jesus saves, Jesus saves;
> Spread the gladness all around, Jesus saves, Jesus saves;
> Bear the news to ev'ry land, climb the steeps and cross the waves,
> Onward, 'tis our Lord's command, Jesus saves, Jesus saves.[14]

In the Pentecostal narrative, Jesus is the central figure who makes possible the appropriation of and participation in the redeemed life. Pentecostal doctrine, in this sense, is both a confession that Jesus saves, baptizes, heals, sanctifies, and returns and that Jesus is the saviour, baptizer, healer, sanctifier, and soon-coming king. Pentecostal narratives describe this idea of salvation typically as an existential encounter with the person of Jesus:

> I have been to Jesus, he has cleansed my soul,
> I've been washed in the blood of the Lamb;
> By the precious fountain, I've been made whole,
> I've been washed by the blood of the Lamb.[15]

Salvation, sanctification, Spirit baptism, and other beliefs of Pentecostals are more than mere convictions of conversion, holiness, healing, or empowerment; they are seen as moments of the historical reality of Jesus in which Pentecostals continue to participate. Calvary is seen as the door where God opened his saving presence to the world once and for all. All moments in the life of Christ are thus reinterpreted as both historical events and testimony of the present-day where Jesus continues the saving work of God:

> He sweetly saves and sanctifies,
> The reign of sin is o'er;
> With holy fire he doth baptize,
> And seal forevermore.[16]

In Pentecostal piety, Jesus is thus clearly elevated to the model of Pentecostal spirituality and worldview. In the person of Jesus Christ, spirituality and doctrine meet, expressed in the often straightforward proclamations that we are redeemed by the blood of Jesus, healed by his stripes, lifted by his love, sanctified by his fire, equipped by his power, and comforted by his promises. These and other narratives of faith are the Pentecostal equivalent to the classical formulations of the creeds.

The pursuit of the Holy Spirit

The centrality of a personal relationship with Jesus at the heart of Pentecostal doctrine is not necessarily a feature that distinguishes Pentecostalism from other Christian traditions. More significant is the fact that the starting point for Pentecostal narratives of doctrine is a distinctive spirituality that focuses on the presence, manifestations, and power of the Holy Spirit. Only by the Spirit is Christ present to the believer, and only the spiritually responsive person is able to enter into this presence of God.[17] As Calvary represents the window for Christ to the salvation of the world, Pentecost is seen as the door for Christians to enter the anointed presence of Christ. For Pentecostals, the Spirit is 'God with us'[18] in palpable manifestations and personal experiences that always remain intimately related to the person of Jesus. In other words, Pentecostal doctrine and spirituality are never exclusively directed toward Christ or the Spirit; they always form a Spirit-Christology.[19]

Pentecostals find an explicit Spirit-Christology in the biblical witness of Luke-Acts to Jesus as the revelation of God anointed with the Holy Spirit and to the passing on of this anointing to a world in need of salvation. The Spirit is the presence of the resurrected Jesus in history, and this presence is manifested in the experiences lifted up by the narrative of the full gospel.[20] The Pentecostal longing for an experiential encounter with God's presence joins together both the doctrine of God and Pentecostal spirituality. The result is primarily a soteriological reflection on Christ typically expressed with focus on the Holy Spirit.

> Breathe upon us, Lord from heaven,
> Fill us with the Holy Ghost;
> Promise of the Father given,
> Send us now a Pentecost.[21]

On a theological level, one might argue that the Holy Spirit represents for most Pentecostals an experiential entrance point to the narrative of salvation. This theme is most explicit in the Pentecostal doctrine of Spirit baptism, where theology and spirituality meet deliberately. The presence of the Spirit and the presence of Christ are both identified and distinguished to the same extent as the presence of God unites with the Christian community but also remains beyond it.[22]

> Thou Christ of burning, cleansing flame,
> Send the fire, send the fire, send the fire!
> Look down and see this waiting host,
> Give us the promised Holy Ghost,
> We want another Pentecost,
> Send the fire, send the fire, send the fire![23]

The doctrine of Spirit baptism remains historically and theologically the most explicit formulation of the doctrine of God among Pentecostals – the kerygma of the full gospel. Spirit baptism, whether conceived as doctrine or spirituality, features at heart God's bestowal of the Holy Spirit. For the majority of Pentecostals, we might say that 'Spirit baptism brings the reign of the Father, the reign of the crucified and risen Christ, and the reign of the divine life to all creation through the indwelling of the Spirit.'[24]

Pentecostals readily find in the biblical texts the unrestrained bestowal of the Spirit by the Father on the Son, documented in the anointed life of Christ, and the outpouring of the Spirit on all flesh on the day of Pentecost, documented in the Spirit-filled life of believers. While formulations of this doctrine rarely depend on particular visions of the inner life of the triune God, the outpouring of the Holy Spirit is tied closely to the person of Jesus as the one who baptizes and is baptized with the Spirit of God. These confessions speak less of the Father or creation and more of the Word and the Spirit or regeneration and charismatic empowerment, often distinguishing between the work of the Spirit as the one who baptizes us into Christ and the work of Christ as the one who baptizes us in the Spirit.[25] This reciprocal emphasis contrasts with the frequent neglect of pneumatology in Western formulations of the doctrine of God. The Spirit-Christology eminent among Pentecostals favours a dynamic perspective of the person of Jesus that has only recently emerged among other Christian traditions. Nonetheless, few of these considerations make their way into formal articulations of doctrine. Above all, the close connection between the doctrine of God and the various moments of the Spirit-filled life in the Pentecostal worldview suggests that the Pentecostal doctrine of God remains at heart always a doxology.

Oneness Pentecostalism

The most far-reaching theological tension among contemporary Pentecostals is the division between trinitarian Pentecostals and the Oneness tradition. Recent estimates locate the number of Oneness Pentecostals in the world at 15–20 million, with more than 400 organizations, strong roots in the United States, Canada, India, Indonesia, Japan, and Russia, and a majority presence among Pentecostals in China, Mexico, Colombia, and Ethiopia.[26] Information on many groups beyond North America and Europe is sparse, but expanded global demographics suggest considerable diversity among the groups in both practice and doctrine.[27] The common denominator among these groups is the rejection of the doctrine of the Trinity and the consequential separation from the majority of trinitarian Pentecostals. In turn, Oneness Pentecostals often have been stereotyped as heretical by trinitarian Pentecostals and non-Pentecostals as well as former Oneness Pentecostals.[28] While trinitarian Pentecostals affirm the creedal tradition of the three divine persons, Oneness Pentecostals reject classical trinitarian formulations of the doctrine of God. This section details the motivations for rejecting the trinitarian creeds and highlights the centrality of Jesus and the experience of the Holy Spirit for a closer understanding of Oneness Pentecostal teaching.

The rejection of the trinitarian creeds

Tensions between Oneness Pentecostal teachings and traditional formulations of the doctrine of God are concentrated in the acceptance and application of the creeds. While many Pentecostals display an animosity toward creedal formulations of doctrine, Oneness Pentecostals reject the trinitarian teachings of the ecumenical councils outright. The council of Nicaea, in particular, represents the threshold between the Oneness and trinitarian Pentecostal groups.[29] David Bernard, senior theologian of the United Pentecostal Church International, the largest Oneness Pentecostal organization, emphasizes the lack of explicit trinitarian language until the fourth century and sees the primary reason for the dominance of trinitarian articulations in the necessary response to heresy.[30] Bernard faults the creed for failing to provide a trinitarian vocabulary, depending too strongly on a division of the confession of faith instead of its unity, and neglecting the notion of divine personhood.[31] For Oneness Pentecostals, the doctrine of God can be formulated apart from the traditional language of the creeds.

Advocating a non-traditional view of God, Oneness Pentecostals find in modalistic monarchianism of the fourth century a historical predecessor that affirmed the two central aspects of their own convictions: '(1) there is one indivisible God with no distinction of persons in God's eternal essence, and (2) Jesus Christ is the manifestation, human personification, or incarnation of the one God.'[32] At the centre of these convictions stands the concern for the administration of water baptism, or more precisely, the correct biblical paradigm for baptism, its interpretation, and application. In its doctrinal dimensions, the debate questions the correctness of the baptismal formula based either on the single name of Jesus (see

Acts 2.38) or the three titles 'Father', 'Son', and 'Holy Spirit' (see
Mt. 28.19). In practice, Oneness Pentecostals emphasize baptism
'in the name of Jesus Christ' as the original apostolic formula to
be seen as convocation of the grace of God that contains the grace
of the Father and the sanctification of the Holy Spirit.[33] Baptism
'in the name of the Father, and the Son, and the Holy Spirit' (Mt.
28.19) is therefore synonymous with the practice of 'one baptism'
(Eph. 4.5) without juxtaposing the oneness of God with the idea of
three divine persons.

Oneness Pentecostals view the Nicene-Constantinopolitan
Creed as the result of an inadmissible amalgamation of the radical
monotheism of the Old Testament and the redemptive manifesta-
tions of the Father, Son, and Holy Spirit in the New Testament.[34]
Held responsible for this confusion is a departure from the biblical
revelation and subjection of Scripture to philosophical reasoning.
While the biblical witness affirms the unity and diversity of the
Father, Son, and Holy Spirit in the work of salvation, Oneness
Pentecostals see neither a threefold division of works nor a
threefold division of persons in the doctrine of God.

In contrast to the creedal texts, Oneness Pentecostals attribute
the idea of personhood only to Jesus Christ. In this way, the group
seeks to avoid the apparent problem of trinitarian doctrine to
reconcile the singular being of God with the idea that this being
is shared by three persons without thereby dividing the deity
threefold and falling into the heresy of tritheism. While classical
trinitarian formulations speak of the interpenetration of the three
divine persons, Oneness Pentecostals consider the one God to
be one indivisible being in the single person of Jesus Christ who
encompasses in his person all three manifestations of the Father,
Son, and Holy Spirit.[35]

The emphasis on the single name of Jesus has earned Oneness
Pentecostals the misleading characterization of being a 'Jesus only'
movement. Although the singular emphasis on Jesus is typical for
the group, it should be understood as an emphasis on the 'name'
that replaces the traditional emphasis on the divine persons.[36]
Simply put, for Oneness Pentecostals, in God 'the name and the
person are synonymous'.[37] This identification avoids the univocal
use of the term 'person' for the Father, Son, and Holy Spirit.
Oneness Pentecostal doctrine replaces the idea of three 'persons'
with the concept of the single 'name' of God as it is revealed in

the person of Jesus Christ. In other words, from the Oneness Pentecostal perspective, the person of Jesus *is* the name of God. It is therefore both possible and necessary to confess faith in the Father, Son, and Holy Spirit among Oneness Pentecostals.[38] However, this seemingly triadic confession is actualized through water baptism 'in Jesus' name' so that practically and theologically Jesus Christ is proclaimed as the only personification of God.

The supremacy of the person of Jesus

The theological convictions and consequences of the Oneness Pentecostal view have only recently been formulated in an analytical manner that corresponds to the practices and experiences of the tradition. Oneness Pentecostals' Christology derives from a reinterpretation of the biblical words 'Father', 'Son', and 'Spirit', which rather than identifying three distinct divine persons, 'describe God's redemptive roles or revelations, but they do not reflect an essential threeness in His nature'.[39] For trinitarian Pentecostals, this identification means that when we speak of God as Father, Son, and Spirit, we highlight the necessary and coexistent redemptive roles of God in the work of salvation. In Oneness Pentecostal doctrine these functions of God are expressed in the terms of creator, saviour, and sanctifier and characterize the essential unity of God's being. The confession of this unity in being and function in salvation history is concentrated in the experience of Jesus Christ in a manner that reveals some foundational differences in Christology, that is, in the manner in which Christ is seen as the eternal God.

Oneness Pentecostals reject the trinitarian designation of Jesus solely in terms of the 'Son of God' and as the 'second' divine person.[40] In their place, Oneness Pentecostals state that 'Jesus is not the incarnation of one person of a trinity but the incarnation of all the identity, character, and personality of God.'[41] Contrary to traditional Christian teaching, Jesus is the eternal God – not the eternal second person – who became flesh. More precisely, Oneness Pentecostals speak of a 'begotten Sonship'[42] marked initially by the Incarnation as the starting point for the work of the Son, whose redeeming role will end when the present world ceases to exist. The same understanding of redemptive manifestations is attributed to the Holy Spirit, who as the Spirit of Jesus 'does not come as another person but comes in another form (in spirit instead of flesh) and another relationship ('in you' instead of 'with you')'.[43] The statement of faith of the United Pentecostal Church International summarizes this understanding of God succinctly:

> We believe in the one ever-living, eternal God: infinite in power, holy in nature, attributes and purpose; and possessing absolute, indivisible deity. This one true God has revealed Himself as Father; through His Son, in redemption; and as the Holy Spirit, by emanation.... Before the incarnation, this one true God manifested Himself in diverse ways. In the incarnation, He manifests Himself in the Son, who walked among men. As He works in the lives of believers, He manifests Himself as the Holy Spirit....[44]

The biblical terms 'Father', 'Son', and 'Spirit' are thus taken as redemptive titles indicative of the closeness of relationship between God and humanity. The title of Father indicates the transcendence of God, the title of Son the Incarnation, and the title of Spirit the indwelling of God in the believer. For Oneness Pentecostals, all of these roles are manifestations of the person of Jesus Christ.

The experience of the Holy Spirit

As for Pentecostal doctrine in general, the pneumatological perspective is highly significant for the articulation of the centrality of Christ in Oneness Pentecostal teaching. The experiential focus among Pentecostals guides much of the doctrinal formulations in this regard, and Oneness Pentecostals affirm strictly the experience of the one God as one Spirit: Pentecostals 'do not experience three personalities when they worship, nor do they receive three spirits, but they are in relationship with one personal spirit being'.[45] Therefore, the Spirit of God can be called 'simply God', 'God himself', or 'the one God'.[46] From this perspective, Oneness Pentecostals criticize the traditional distinction between understanding God in a self-contained manner and God's activity in the world. This characteristic distinction in trinitarian theology between immanent and economic Godhead is seen as overtly dependent upon philosophical identifications of substance and person that are foreign to the biblical texts. In their place, Oneness Pentecostals give priority to the biblical concept of 'spirit' that allows them to maintain a distinction of the manifestations of God while rejecting the idea that these manifestations are to be identified as three distinct persons.

> The Spirit of Jesus existed from all eternity because he is God Himself. However, the humanity of Jesus did not exist before the Incarnation, except as a plan in the mind of God. Therefore we can say that the Spirit of Jesus preexisted the Incarnation, but we cannot say the Son preexisted the Incarnation in any substantial sense.[47]

This Spirit-oriented perspective on the redemptive manifestations of God illustrates the important feature of Oneness Pentecostal doctrine to speak of the Father, Son, and Holy Spirit as simultaneous rather than successive manifestations. Whereas Pentecostals in general prefer to speak of the present time as the age of the Spirit, Oneness Pentecostals do not see this emphasis as representing a substantial distinction in God's being. The crucial trinitarian terminology of the 'procession' of the Son and the Spirit is interpreted as a 'sending' or 'appointment' in 'the supernatural plan and action of God'.[48] Any distinction of the divine substance or a pre-existence of the divine persons apart from the economy of salvation is consequently rejected. When applied to the Son, 'the sending ... emphasizes the humanity of the Son and the specific purpose for which the Son was born'.[49] In contrast to classical trinitarian formulations, the Son is not identified as Son because of his eternal procession from the Father but because he is begotten by the Spirit as the human manifestation of God. When applied to the Holy Spirit, the sending refers to the 'return ... of Jesus manifested in a new way'[50] after the glorification of the Son. In this manner, Oneness Pentecostal pneumatology consistently returns to the doctrine of Christ at the heart of the doctrine of God.

At the centre of the Oneness Pentecostal doctrine of God, the sending of the Son is a necessary presupposition for the sending of the Holy Spirit, since both are redemptive manifestations of the one God. Nevertheless, this perspective precludes the idea of the pre-existence of Christ as person before the Incarnation and grants this pre-existence only in the terms of the eternal Spirit.[51] Put differently, the Holy Spirit is the eternal being of God; the Word is the relation of this being to the world. In turn, the Spirit does not precede or follow the Word in any substantive or personal manner but remains identical in deity with them. In practice, the experience of the Spirit is the experience of the Son and the experience of the Father who are all simultaneous manifestations of the one being of God and ultimately reveal the one person of Jesus Christ. For Oneness Pentecostals, the person of Jesus remains the revelation of the single being of God who encompasses and supersedes the redemptive manifestations of the Father, Son, and Holy Spirit as the eternal Lord of glory.

Pentecostal theology and the development of doctrine

The Oneness-Trinitarian Pentecostal dialogue, although received with much optimism, reveals little alteration in either group's theological position.[52] While the vocabulary of 'orthodox' and 'heretical' has subsided and the conversation has become impartial and respectful, it is unlikely that the two opposing views on the doctrine of God will ever coalesce. A complete view of Pentecostalism can therefore not neglect the undeniable tensions that exist despite joint foundational commitments between both groups. The structure of the previous pages has indicated that at least three factors are responsible for the coexistence of these tensions: 1) the replacement of doctrine by an emphasis on experience; 2) foundational differences in Christology; 3) the focus on the Holy Spirit in all statements of faith. This concluding section highlights the significance of these factors for Pentecostal perspectives on the future development of Christian doctrine.

Replacing doctrine

Pentecostal theology is marked by an experience, not by a doctrine. This slogan may oversimplify the theological dynamics of the movement worldwide, but it serves as a helpful reminder that classical formulations of doctrine do not occupy a significant place in Pentecostal theology. The overwhelming emphasis on experience and spirituality outweighs contemplation on speculative elements of doctrine. We might say that experience replaces doctrine in Pentecostal faith and praxis. This perspective is particularly significant in the context of the doctrine of God that Pentecostals formulate primarily (if not exclusively) on the basis of a tangible encounter with God.[53]

The emphasis on the encounter with God translates theologically to an equation of the experienced God with the fullness of God's being (even if that cannot be experienced in its entirety). Where classical theism has drawn a distinction between God's self-sufficient being and God's involvement in the world, it can be argued that this distinction is not typically made by Pentecostals.[54] The emphasis on encounter focuses on the presence of God in the here and now, a pragmatic rather than dogmatic pursuit of the divine.[55] If there is a distinction between God-for-us and God-in-himself, this distinction is of little significance to the Pentecostal experience and formulation of doctrine. This insignificance allows room for both Oneness and trinitarian Pentecostals.

While doctrinal distinctions or historical precedence occupy less significant roles in Pentecostal theology, the importance of biblical support for the Pentecostal experiences cannot be underestimated. Theological explanations for a divine encounter that has been experienced but not understood are typically sought directly from the Scriptures. The call for a return to biblical Christianity and the reliance on Luke-Acts has been widely recognized among Pentecostals.[56] The significance of an experience-based interpretation of the Bible exposes that for Pentecostals there is no alternative to such interpretation (even if it exposes the lack of such specific experiences). Nonetheless, granting experience and spirituality a central place in theological hermeneutics allows Pentecostals to exercise a broad scale of interpretations ranging from those who look for repeatable patterns of divine activity throughout Scripture to those who elevate isolated passages to authoritative doctrinal status. At least among Pentecostals, the transition from experience to Scripture is less difficult than from the interpretation of Scripture to the formulation of doctrine.

The distance between experience and doctrine is particularly visible in the Pentecostal tensions surrounding the view of God. Oneness and trinitarian Pentecostals both uphold the authority of

Scripture for all matters of experience and practice.[57] Yet, while each side upholds the biblical support for their respective position, theologically both sides significantly overlap. Oneness Pentecostals exhibit an unexpected triadic element in their understanding of God, while trinitarian Pentecostals tend to collapse the experiential reality of the three divine persons into a central experience of Christ or the Holy Spirit. For both sides, it is the authority of spirituality that dictates the theological position. The lack of concurrent experience of all three divine persons, or to put it positively, the particular elevation of one person in worship and encounter suggests significant theological agreements among Pentecostals that face confrontation only in specific doctrinal formulations or practical applications. The most significant of these agreements is the quest for the centrality of Jesus.

The quest for the centrality of Jesus

The overwhelming emphasis on the person of Jesus shapes the content of a theology based on experience among both Oneness and trinitarian Pentecostals. In principle, the doctrinal emphasis on Jesus attributes all divine qualities and functions to Christ. What might therefore be called a 'Christological maximalism'[58] in the Pentecostal doctrine of God leads among Oneness Pentecostals to a factual substitution of the three divine persons with the single person of Jesus, while trinitarian Pentecostals typically elevate Christ from the 'second' person of the Trinity to the central figure of Christian faith and worship. This Christocentric formulation of doctrine is not unique to Pentecostals.[59] The Pietistic and Evangelical heritage of classical Pentecostalism, in particular, represents a seedbed for an experiential faith that is fundamentally Jesus-centred.[60] Pentecostal doctrine, however, fluctuates more broadly between classical formulations of theology and the demands of compatibility with their Pentecostal experiences.

No large-scale theological treatments of Christology among Pentecostals have yet been attempted. Scripting what might be called 'ordinary theology'[61] among Pentecostals, the oral and testimonial nature of Pentecostalism yields primarily a narrative account of Christology. The so-called 'full gospel' offers a broad pattern for a general narrative among Pentecostals, but concrete mechanisms of affirmation and reinforcement of such a pattern in everyday life are found primarily in the personal stories of experiences and encounters with Christ and the consequences of such events rather than in propositional statements of doctrine.[62] Ordinary Christology among Pentecostals, although essentially rooted in some form of confessing the full gospel, varies widely between personal stories of encounter with Christ, the particular congregational story of local groups, and the denominational story or larger public life of Pentecostal bodies in their respective socio-cultural, economic, political, and theological contexts. The glocalization of Pentecostalism, that is, the increasing interdependence of Pentecostalism on both local and global theology, is a significant phenomenon contributing to the reality that Christ is recognized in a particularly diverse variety of faces. Christology among Pentecostals is a quest for the glocal Jesus.

Christology from a Latino/a perspective illustrates this diversity with particular clarity by showing a dominating fluidity in the perception and proclamation of Jesus that is symptomatic for Pentecostalism. In the Latino/a Pentecostal experience, Jesus is the baptizer (or doctrinal Jesus), healer (or liberator Jesus), and coming King (or political Jesus).[63] Any particular emphasis is dictated by the cultural context and social location and may favour the divinity of Jesus, emphasizing his supernatural activity, or his humanity, focusing on how Jesus relates to the human situation. The doctrinal Jesus can serve as the standard of piety and spirituality, the liberator Jesus as the centre of faith, and the political Jesus as the motivation and goal of Christian living.[64] The ways these perspectives are represented in Latino/a Pentecostalism are not as strictly defined as these categories suggest. A relational Christology that manifests Jesus as companion in the concrete socio-economic situation of the believer is perhaps the most dominating element of what could be called a glocal Christology.[65] This can be illustrated further in the context of Pentecostal Christology in Africa.

Pentecostal Christology in Africa affirms the influence of glocalization in a theological environment shaped as much by traditional creedal models imported by missionaries as by the genuine language and symbolism developing in post-missionary Africa.[66] The prolonged impact of slavery and colonization and the current rediscovery of genuine African culture, language, and worldview have shaped the image of Christ as the healer of Africa.[67] The healing encounter with Christ is as much a personal as it is a public event that concerns the family, the church, and the marketplace. Christ is transforming the soul, liberating from evil, and empowering a godly life in which health and salvation refer as much to the body as to the political, economic, and natural world.[68] The strong emphasis on orality in African life is shaping a form of 'oral consensus' in the place of formal doctrinal agreement that is based primarily on the shared experience of Jesus Christ through the Holy Spirit.[69] Prayer, testimony, song, and dance create a diverse and living imagery of Jesus in terms of health, healing, and wholeness that extends as a life in the Spirit to the whole symbolic structure of the African universe while remaining grounded in the particular experiences of local Pentecostal faith.

The responsiveness of the image of Christ to the particularities of Pentecostal experiences at the local and global dimensions of the Christian life is a hallmark of Pentecostal theology and its formulation of doctrine. This responsiveness is primarily responsible for the differences between Oneness and trinitarian Pentecostals that find little or no reflection in classical formulations of doctrine. If Pentecostalism is representative of the development of glocal Christianity, then we can expect an increasing diversity in the doctrine of God and its formulations among Christians worldwide as it is already anticipated among Pentecostals. The pursuit of the Holy Spirit sketches out the more visible dimensions of this manifold and contrasting development of doctrine.

Cosmic pneumatology

The focus on the Holy Spirit penetrates all Pentecostal theology, even if this is not always explicit in the articulation of formal doctrines. Combined with the centrality of Christ, a foundational sensitivity to the Holy Spirit has led to a certain binitarianism, a neglect of the Father, that is not unique to Pentecostals.[70] To overstate the point, Spirit-Christology among Pentecostals overemphasizes the presence of Christ and the presence of the Spirit as the chief characteristics of participation in the life of God while neglecting to distinguish clearly between each presence.[71] Pneumatology necessarily extends the lines of Christology in order to explain the presence of the risen and exalted Christ among a creation not yet fully glorified.

Pentecostals accentuate the historical self-manifestation of God in the world through the Son and the Holy Spirit. This perspective reflects Irenaeus's classical image of the Son and the Spirit as the 'two hands of God'. However, while this image allows trinitarian Pentecostals to distinguish between the related yet distinct work of each person, Oneness Pentecostals can maintain that the work of each hand is factually always only the work of the one God. In either perspective, the formulation of doctrine is extended by the testimony of the Spirit.

The testimony of the Spirit inspires among Pentecostals what has been called a 'pneumatological imagination' as part of a theological hermeneutic that proceeds by way of Spirit and Word within a community of faith.[72] The goal of this hermeneutic is transformational rather than doctrinal interpretation. While classical articulations of doctrine certainly do not exclude trans-formation, theological interpretation for Pentecostals is more akin to 'a communal enterprise to discern the Spirit, to understand the Word, and to be transformed by the Spirit and the Word'.[73] In praxis, this means that the orientation toward the Spirit directs the Pentecostal interpretation of the world. The pneumatological imagination inspired by the outpouring of the Holy Spirit makes possible a receptivity towards the mission of the Spirit in the world in all its multifarious historical manifestations.[74] While the discernment of these manifestations is a difficult task, discerning the Spirit in the world is the central motif of Pentecostal doctrine responsible for a limitless albeit critical openness of all Pentecostal theology.

The openness of Pentecostal theology resulting from its pneuma-tological imagination extends to all matters of life. Pentecostals view in a very distinctive manner the church, society, and the world through the lens of the Spirit.[75] The diversity of experi-ences of the Spirit expands clearly beyond the confines of classical formulations of doctrine. This leads frequently to either resistance or incorporation of Pentecostal themes and traditional orienta-tions.[76] Pentecostals have noted that the focus on the Spirit creates particular tensions with the themes of Protestant scholasticism, feminist theology, theology of the religions, or the theology and science dialogue. While some may view these confrontations as irreconcilable differences, such evaluations offer little explan-atory power for understanding the doctrinal diversity among

Pentecostals. More helpful is the perspective that pneumatology as a foundational component of theological inquiry inevitably expands the purview of Christian doctrine.

This expansion of the purview of doctrine is particularly visible in the emphasis on discerning the Spirit in the world that has taken Pentecostals into dialogue with the sciences and the theology of creation.[77] While Pentecostals were traditionally suspicious that an engagement of the sciences would undermine belief in the Holy Spirit, the pneumatological imagination has kindled interest in the human, social, and behavioural sciences.[78] Hermeneutical sensibilities among Pentecostals derived from the biblical record of Pentecost have opened up space for a reading of nature that sustains interest in the natural sciences.[79] The emphasis on the Spirit is taking Pentecostals beyond their own methodological presuppositions (or prejudices), institutional arrangements (or absences), and particular socio-cultural practices (or stereotypes).

For many outsiders of the debate, the designation of Pentecostalism as either orthodox or sectarian in doctrine will likely remain an important characterization. For those participating in the dialogue, the joint pursuit of the Spirit may be able to overcome the glaring divisions between Oneness Pentecostal doctrine, a subtle binitarianism, and more fully developed trinitarian accounts of the doctrine of God.[80] At least, the pneumatological focus offers a plausible explanation for the existence of such diversity. If Pentecostal Christology is marked by a quest for Jesus in the local and the global experience of faith, then Pentecostal pneumatology is characterized by a quest for the Spirit of Christ in the human being, nature, and the cosmos. For Pentecostals, pneumatology is therefore the heartbeat of the development of doctrine.[81] The tensions between Oneness and trinitarian Pentecostals illustrate that this development is not exclusive to an abstract idea of doctrine, but that the church develops in the Spirit as part of the Christian story in ways not always conforming to orthodox standards. Pentecostalism embraces this non-conformance as a manifestation of the creative work of the Spirit that knows no boundaries but nonetheless strives toward the harmony and reconciliation of all creation in all its differences, strangeness, and seemingly irreconcilable otherness.

CHAPTER FIVE

Social engagement and triumphalism

Pentecostalism is a socially, economically, and politically diverse phenomenon. Sociological characterizations and theories of the movement have changed as Pentecostals expanded in size and scope worldwide. One of the most significant, and still dominant, theories described the emergence of classical Pentecostalism in North America during the twentieth century as the result of the distinct social roots of deprivation.[1] While such theories of social deprivation have been revised to account for the upward mobility of Pentecostals, recent observations continue to support the idea that Pentecostalism essentially flourishes as a religion of the poor while moving its appeal toward the masses.[2] Upward mobility in socio-economic terms has become a central element of modern-day Pentecostalism with regard to both the outward perception of the movement and the self-understanding of its followers. In the developed nations, Pentecostalism often elicits ideas of finding meaning and purpose in life including a more vibrant spirituality.[3] In developing countries, Pentecostalism speaks to the desires of the new middle classes to enter the modern world and its anticipated advantages.[4] In undeveloped countries, Pentecostalism is seen as a route of escape from poverty, corruption, and oppression toward affluence, consumption, prosperity, and freedom. Despite the first impression, these identifications are not tied to particular locations or cultures but exist around the world, often overlapping and not clearly distinguished. Common to all of these dynamics are explicit tensions in the scope of Pentecostal mobility and its implications for involvement of Pentecostals in the broad spectrum of society. Significant differences exist between the participation of Pentecostals in social struggles and concerns for social justice. The means of participation in social struggle have sharply divided global Pentecostalism.

The present chapter compares and contrasts two distinct ways of Pentecostal upward social mobility: social engagement, exemplified in programmatic and long-term expressions of social activism and Pentecostal political and socio-cultural involvement, and triumphalism, or social passivism, exemplified in the preaching of the health and wealth gospel. The former proposes active participation and leadership in the struggle against poverty, deprivation, and oppression; the latter withdraws into a sectarian mindset, individualism, and triumphalism. This chapter seeks a comparison of both sides that is critical and therapeutic, offering insights into the tensions resulting from the expansion of the Pentecostal movement to global proportions and the challenges inherent in its confrontation with diverse socio-economic, cultural, and political contexts. Pentecostalism is here portrayed as a mirror of unavoidable global and local dynamics that define its character. The first part of the chapter addresses the realm of social engagement among Pentecostals with focus on Asia, Africa, and Latin America. The second part presents the teaching of the health and wealth gospel as well as the influence and reception of prosperity preaching among Pentecostals in North America and elsewhere. In the final part, the two accounts are brought into dialogue through a conversation on the state of contemporary Pentecostal social ethics.

Social engagement in the Pentecostal movement

There exists among Pentecostals worldwide a large group that might be termed 'progressive Pentecostals' oriented toward social transformation.[5] The progressive groups often understand social engagement as a direct mandate from God, exemplified in the Scriptures, and a normative element of the Christian life. A significant characteristic of these groups is the personal experience of poverty, deprivation, oppression, and persecution or the identification with such underprivileged and marginalized people. In some cases, both elements together shape a highly activist, even revolutionary attitude against the status quo. This aspect demands closer examination before the motivation for and character of social engagement among Pentecostals can be identified more clearly.

Pentecostalism as a movement of social change

A global perspective on the worldwide distribution of Pentecostals shows the movement most dominantly among the undeveloped and developing nations; the largest growth of Pentecostals is found among the poor and in countries where the patterns of deprivation are multidimensional.[6] The multidimensional poverty index shows the centres of poverty reflecting acute deprivation in health, education, and standard of living concentrated in parts of Africa, South Asia, East Asia, and South American countries below the general threshold of Latin America and the Caribbean.[7] The significant presence of Pentecostals in these regions is well known, even though there exists no comprehensive study to date on the relationship of multidimensional poverty distribution and the worldwide growth of Pentecostalism.[8] At the very least, the similarities suggest that oppressive social, economic, and political patterns are able to encourage and solidify the presence of Pentecostalism.

Significant for understanding the closer relationship of social deprivation and social engagement is the growth of Pentecostalism in regions that experience multidimensional forms of poverty. The highest Christian growth rates expected by the year 2025 in developing regions of East and South-East Asia as well as across Africa suggest that religion, in general, and Christianity, in particular, serve as and are perceived as vehicles to escape deprivation.[9] The percentage of church growth experienced by Pentecostal denominations in these regions during the first decade of the twenty-first century is unusually high.[10] In contrast, the industrialized nations and regions with high human development often show stagnant or declining Christian growth and a comparatively low percentage of Pentecostals. While these developments cannot be generalized, and other factors influence the inception and growth of Pentecostalism worldwide, the prospect of escape from deprivation, oppression, and persecution, and the ideals of social welfare, human rights, and egalitarianism have shaped the new face of Christian social engagement in which Pentecostals occupy a significant position.[11]

Social deprivation theory has been among the first to explain the growth of Pentecostalism as a result of identification of the poor and disenfranchised with the movement. The earliest efforts to situate classical Pentecostalism in the social and cultural setting of the early twentieth century resulted in one of the most dominant historiographies of American Pentecostalism. Robert Mapes Anderson exemplifies this movement in his classic characterization of Pentecostalism as the direct result of economic, social, cultural, and physical displacement and deprivation.[12] However, Anderson's theory aimed primarily at explaining *why* Pentecostalism emerged without showing *that* Pentecostals actually identified with a reaction to the socio-cultural conditions and with no comprehensive examination of *how* the movement responded to such conditions. In fact, the identification of Pentecostalism with enthusiastic and ecstatic religion prohibited the portrayal of Pentecostals as concerned with social justice. As a consequence, Anderson explains Pentecostalism as a substitute for participation in the social struggle.[13] Instead of promoting social activism, deprivation theory suggests that Pentecostals turned 'inward' and 'upward' – concerned primarily with themselves and God – and failed to direct their attention to the struggle for social justice surrounding them.

While deprivation theories consequently have been rejected as a sole explanation for association with Pentecostalism, the significance of deprivation cannot be discredited entirely.[14] Deprivation theory fails to account fully for the appeal of Pentecostalism among all social classes. Nonetheless, Anderson correctly observed that the experience of, or identification with, social deprivation does not necessarily lead to social activism. This conclusion is supported by the fact that, for many years, classical Pentecostals have inadvertently nurtured the image of being oblivious to social justice.[15] In contrast, recently developed social-movement theories examine Pentecostalism as a phenomenon more closely related to upward social mobility among a broader spectrum of factors contributing to the conversion process.[16] While the general conditions of deprivation are not discredited, Pentecostalism is seen more broadly as a mechanism associated with social change across the entire range of socio-economic conditions.[17] Observations of the explosion of Pentecostalism in North and South America suggest that the movement in these contexts of unprecedented growth is perceived as active and participatory, voluntary, and transformative, directed toward egalitarian ideals.[18] Among the poor, Pentecostalism is seen as a form of religious participation in the socio-cultural reality that affords new and effective means to cope with and to overcome economic and political oppression. More stable and traditional environments may see Pentecostalism as a vehicle to address concerns of human development by those not immediately suffering from social, political, or economic oppression but identifying with a concern for the poor and the persecuted. At least in principle, a combination of these mechanisms forms the seedbed for social engagement among progressive Pentecostal groups worldwide.

Social engagement among progressive Pentecostals

The personal experience of devastating social, economic, and medical conditions in the developing nations have led to an emergent social form of Pentecostalism characterized by explicit social engagement in a variety of ministries, services, and programmes. Consistent models include emergency services (response to floods and earthquakes), medical assistance (including medical response to disasters, preventive care, drug rehabilitation programmes, psychological services, and establishing health and dental clinics), mercy ministries (such as homeless shelters, food banks, clothing services, and services to the elderly), educational programmes (especially day care and schools), counselling services (assisting cases of addiction, pregnancy, divorce, depression, or prison ministries), economic development (including job training, housing development, youth programmes, urban development programmes, housing programmes, and microenterprise loans), policy change (with focus on monitoring elections, opposing corruption, or advocating a living wage), and services in the arts (with training in music, drama, and dance).[19] Many of these programmes are specific to certain regions and their particular contexts and types of Pentecostalism.

One of the earliest examples of active social engagement among classical Pentecostals is Pandita Ramabai's Mukti mission in India in the early 1900s. Beginning as a revival among young Hindu women, Ramabai understood the events as the introduction of a uniquely Indian Christianity and interpreted them in the context of the unjust political, economic, and religious practices of the time.[20] Herself an orphan and widow, Ramabai set out to alleviate the particular issues confronting Hindu women and widows. She became known initially for establishing a mission to disposed women and children at Mukti in Maharastra State in western India. Presenting her case to the Indian Education Commission, Queen Victoria supported Ramabai's social efforts by establishing women's hospitals and schools for women and widows. An erudite scholar, Ramabai also worked on translating the Bible into popular Marathi, recommended the adoption of Hindi as the national language of India, and established missions, orphanages, and schools to realize a new social reality for the women of India.[21] Ramabai's social vision included preschool and elementary education, vocational and industrial services, health services, feeding and clothing ministries, and communities for children, widows, prostitutes, and the blind. Her ministry expanded to England, the United States, and Chile.[22] She represents a Pentecostal pioneer in the struggle for social justice. Pentecostal social activism in the tradition of Ramabai's social vision has slowly begun to shape a form of spiritual capital that has the potential for broad socio-cultural changes.[23]

Among the poverty-stricken and politically oppressed nations of the African continent, Pentecostals have also emerged at the forefront of various programmes of social action. Particularly in places ridden by hunger, disease, unemployment, indebtedness, and corruption, Pentecostals have provided an alternative community, morality, lifestyle, and spirituality.[24] South Africa, in particular, is representative of Pentecostal involvement in the social and economic affairs of the African continent. The famed conditions of Soweto, for example, including 80 per cent unemployment and a high rate of HIV/AIDS cases, also shows an astonishing growth rate of Pentecostal churches.[25] Located in the midst of deprivation, Pentecostals have shaped a new mindset of discipline, hard work, and self-reliance at the core of concrete poverty alleviation projects. Many of these ministries, services, and activities are carried out 'under the radar' of public knowledge despite unprecedented energy and entrepreneurship in South Africa.[26] Highlighting the intensity of spiritual engagement as a central feature of the movement in Africa, Pentecostals have helped inaugurate a new culture of self-confidence, self-esteem, personal agency, and determination.[27] Pentecostal churches have helped establish and maintain autonomous organizations among the poor and provide opportunities for entrepreneurship and social mobility. In and beyond South Africa, Pentecostals participate in rural health clinics, agricultural services, educational institutions, microenterprise loans, legal aid, HIV/AIDS awareness programmes, and other social ministries.[28] African Pentecostalism is emerging as a movement directed towards physical, psychological, spiritual, and material struggle of the individual and the community.[29] Overall, the Pentecostal movement has begun to occupy a difficult and transitional position in the redefinition of national and transnational identities among many African nations.

Contemporary Pentecostalism in Latin America shows a similar picture of active participation in social and economic development. In Brazil, Pentecostals are seen as interested in social welfare on a pragmatic level ranging from installing public utilities to building schools, establishing medical facilities, and participation in labour struggles.[30] Pentecostals in neighbourhood associations have instilled an image of trustworthiness and reliability that spans across towns. In most instances, Pentecostal congregations serve as mutual aid societies that function like crisis centres for health, family, and employment concerns.[31] Social activism is typically a small-group endeavour affecting individuals through motivational and cultural strategies that aim at engendering a cultural and political organization and autonomy among the poor.[32] In some cases, social activism has led to the emergence of a broader political culture among Pentecostal groups that has taken the movement from a sect mentality to the development of more effective institutional structures.[33]

In Chile, Pentecostals have more broadly participated in the country's social, political, and economic history. Particularly influential has become the so-called Protestant Development Service (SEPADE), a non-governmental organization that has taken on a leading role in community programmes and development, neighbourhood programmes, political mobilization, and various social participation programmes.[34] Emerging as one of the first non-governmental organizations of the country, SEPADE raised the socio-economic consciousness among Pentecostals, initially on a grassroots level, that eventually contributed significantly to the renewed democratization of the country.[35] With the help of international political and ecumenical development efforts during the Pinochet dictatorship, the organization set as its chief agenda the socio-economic development of the working classes.[36] Beginning with social services at the local, mostly rural neighbourhood level, SEPADE expanded to rural and urban community development, establishing soup kitchens, agricultural services, health organizations, community centres, educational and recreational programmes, child care, food aid, vocational training, trade unions, and a host of other activities.[37] SEPADE not only mobilized but integrated Pentecostals in broader Christian commitments to social engagement and helped shape a new social ethic in Chile.

The limited examples of the preceding survey should not give the impression that Pentecostals worldwide are generally found at the frontline of social transformation. The political, economic, and socio-cultural stance of Pentecostal groups remains highly diverse.[38] Similar forms of social engagement by Pentecostals can be found throughout South America, Central America, and North America.[39] At the same time, social activism among Pentecostals is less concentrated in the West and the northern hemisphere. In many cases, church-based activism is more frequently encountered than direct political participation.[40] Publicly recognized and more radical forms of political, social, and economic activism are located mostly in the hands of a progressive minority. Conservative and sectarian forms of Pentecostalism continue to coexist with Pentecostal groups that are deeply engaged in personal, communal, and humanitarian development.[41] Nonetheless, where Pentecostals have taken on the cause of the powerless, they often represent a liberator for those who have found no other help. Increasingly, Pentecostals are becoming attuned to the concerns of social justice and their own participation in the struggle for life, equality, and dignity.

Pentecostal triumphalism

In contrast to the preceding picture of social engagement among Pentecostals, observers of the movement can also find a more restrained, passive attitude and triumphalist behaviour in parts of the movement. This resistance to active participation in the struggle for broader economic, political, or socio-cultural improvements is exemplified in a complex phenomenon known in various terms as the 'health and wealth gospel', 'prosperity preaching', or 'word-faith theology'. These movements, though not dominant, represent a persistent phenomenon among Pentecostals. The triumphalism of these groups has been sharply criticized, even among Pentecostals.[42] Yet, the health and wealth gospel has nonetheless become widely established through the efficient use of mass media and has found a dedicated audience among a wide socio-economic spectrum of Pentecostals. This section introduces diverse representations of the health and wealth gospel among different Pentecostal groups worldwide in order to provide a sample of the diversity of the phenomenon. The initial overview is followed by a presentation of the theological underpinnings of the health and wealth gospel in contrast to the sources that lead to social engagement.

Diverse forms of the health and wealth gospel

The preponderance of social media in North America has made the health and wealth gospel particularly visible among African American Pentecostal and Charismatic Movements. Made popular by leading televangelists, a group of African-American Pentecostals have spread the healing and prosperity message among black churches and particularly the black Pentecostal community.[43] While it would be incorrect to portray the health and wealth gospel in North America as exclusively an Afro-Pentecostal movement, African American history and socio-economic status present a significant influence on its emergence. Beginning with the introduction of African slaves and their descendants, economic and material need have always formed a central concern of the black churches. The health and wealth gospel, however, has moved the concerns from the basic need of survival to the ideal of prosperity.[44] With a followership dominantly from the poor and working classes, the health and wealth gospel has redefined socio-economic participation among many Afro-Pentecostal groups.[45] In contrast to the countercultural attitude of social activists, the prosperity gospel locates these Pentecostals squarely in the stream of Christian capitalism. The emergence of mega-churches and the display of affluence in mass media have further shaped a new triumphant image of black Pentecostalism as a religion of the rich rather than the poor, a medium for upward social mobility rather than an identification with the socially and economically deprived.[46] This construction of a new identity has exerted a decisive influence on the spread of the health and wealth gospel.

Influenced by North American evangelistic campaigns, prosperity preaching has taken roots with particular fervour in many of the economically devastated environments of the African continent. The search for African national identity, economic stability, health, and social welfare has influenced African Pentecostal groups to adopt North American concerns for materialism and individualism.[47] As a result, the health and wealth gospel has transformed Pentecostal churches in many countries from conservative origins and advocacy for the poor to followers of the prosperity message.[48] In many African countries, this message is reshaping the image of the Christian into that of a culture-broker and affluent community leader who endorses the capacity of capitalism to produce autonomous, socially mobile citizens.[49] Not unlike traditional African religious leaders, prosperity preachers receive material gifts from their congregations as encouragement to intercede on behalf of the giver for health and material prosperity from God.[50] Reflecting the broader context of African cosmologies, the evils of poverty and sickness are attributed to the spiritual realm of devils and demons that are successfully confronted through exorcism and Christian faith.[51] However, this triumphalism directs Pentecostals away from active participation in social struggles. The prosperity of the church and the individual has assumed priority over the building of hospitals, medical facilities, counselling centres, soup kitchens, clothing ministries, vocational schools and other hands-on participation by those directly involved in socio-economic development. The strong social pressure across Africa directed at the redistributive accumulation of wealth has found in the health and wealth gospel a system of religious practices that seeks to overcome existing forms of corruption and inequality without engaging the ideas of public and civic service.[52]

A similar picture in Asia can be found in the Philippines, where the El Shaddai movement has become a popular representative of the health and wealth gospel, and in South Korea, where affluent mega-churches have come to dominate the image of Pentecostalism.

In the Philippines, the prosperity message has emerged specifically among the Charismatic Movement of the Roman Catholic
Church and is in the process of reshaping popular Catholic beliefs
and practices.[53] Popular among the Filipino urban poor and
aspiring middle classes, the movement's message not only promises
healing, prosperity, and employment but a reshaping of the social,
economic, and political environment, albeit not through critical or
countercultural involvement in the struggle against injustice.[54] El
Shaddai operates largely on the 'seed-faith' principle in the form of
gifts to the church in expectation for personal prosperity in return.
The broad mixing of religious sincerity, Catholic sacramental sensibilities, and materialism, and the failure to address the struggle for
social justice, have raised widespread criticism.[55]

Similar criticism has been directed at the health and wealth gospel
in South Korea, where Pentecostalism and prosperity preaching
have become synonymous for some with capitalism, commer-
cialization, this-worldly religion, and middle-class ambitions.[56]
Korean mega-churches have been criticized for a market- and
prosperity-driven form of 'McDonaldization' of Christianity that
appears to go hand-in-hand with the spread of Pentecostalism.[57]
This process exhibits a rationalization of social participation that
submits to the dominance of calculability, predictability, efficiency,
and control.[58] Marketability and success have taken the place
of a traditional theology of suffering (*minjung*) in Korea and its
customary participation in the relational dimensions of social and
cultural improvement.[59] In a nation where the churches helped to
provide food, clothing, shelter, and spiritual direction after the
devastations of the Korean War, the prospering mega-churches
are accused of abandoning the poor, the suffering, the elderly, the
widows and orphans, the socially disenfranchised and ostracized.[60]
The health and wealth gospel has contributed to the modernization
and revitalization of Korean society, albeit without mobilizing
explicit forms of social activism or awakening a moral social
consciousness.

In Latin America, the health and wealth gospel has also spread
widely among many poor and aspiring Pentecostals. The prosperity
message in the different socio-economic contexts of Brazil, for
example, has been successfully adapted to emphasize both economic
survival among the poor and economic success among the mobile
middle classes.[61] The Brazilian form of the health and wealth gospel

has gradually expanded to transnational organizations across Latin America.[62] Central to this successful ecclesiastical business model is the principle of successful reciprocity: the giving of money and tithes to the church in order to receive a response in kind from God.[63] This principle shapes not merely a triumphalist culture of giving and receiving but a global perspective on the integration of faith and economics in the Christian life.[64] The Universal Church of the Kingdom of God, the largest and most visible church of the prosperity movement in Brazil, has successfully expanded the reach of the health and wealth gospel and integrated the ideas of health and prosperity in the development of globalization.[65] While some perceive this growth as a transformation of the church into 'an enormous money machine',[66] others portray it as the unavoidable mechanisms of a Christian faith trying to reach the world for Jesus Christ.[67] The former lament the disengagement of these churches from issues of social justice, the latter insist that their intentions are just the opposite. This discrepancy warrants a closer look at the theological underpinnings of the prosperity message.

The theological message of the health and wealth gospel

The examples for the health and wealth gospel given above illustrate the diverse forms of practices and attitudes that characterize the prosperity movements. The proclamation of the health and wealth gospel proceeds in principle on the broad basis of three theological precepts: a reinterpretation of the doctrine of God, a contemporary view of humanity, and a word-of-faith mechanism interlinking both realities.

Foundational to the health and wealth gospel is a particular doctrine of God, a theological perspective, that is, rather than a socio-economic theory or business practice. Prosperity preaching depends upon identification with God and God's relationship to health and wealth. The roots of this interpretation can be found in the work of E. W. Kenyon (1867–1948), the grandfather of the health and wealth gospel.[68] A representative of quasi-Pentecostals during the early twentieth century (that is, exhibiting spiritual gifts while voicing criticism of the movement), Kenyon's basic theology shows the influence of the Holiness and healing Movements of the time on the perception of faith, health, sanctification, and the supernatural.[69] Not unlike Oneness Pentecostal beliefs, these influences display a central emphasis on the person of Jesus Christ, in whom the whole nature of God is personified. The cross represents the central place of the salvific work of God in terms of the forgiveness of sins as well as the redemption from sickness and poverty (placed on Christ and conquered through his death). Christ is therefore seen as the principal manifestation of the character of God, the author of a redeemed, successful, and abundant life in this world. Material prosperity and physical health are the promises of God fulfilled in Christ and given in the atonement.[70]

Intimately connected with this image of God in Christ is a particular image of the human being. Central to the anthropology of the health and wealth gospel is the 'law of identification' between the human person and Christ.[71] Extending from Christ's identification with humanity (marked by the Incarnation and the cross), humankind is automatically identified with Christ and participates in the fullness of Christ's victory. This fullness of identification includes the very real, material, and physical victory of the Spirit-filled believers who, in turn, have become 'the fullness of Christ', 'supermen indwelt by God', and 'spiritual giants'.[72] The image of Christ and the believer are bound together not in the image of poverty but prosperity, not emptiness but fullness, not defeat but triumph. This rhetoric is intended to support the practice that human beings not only possess the right and authority to the fullness of the Christian life but that they can claim all things in 'the wonderful name of Jesus'.[73] The law of identification is carried out by the believer's word of faith and in the promises of God made accessible through Christ.

The connecting element between humankind and God, or more precisely, between the human condition and the promises of God, is the emphasis on the word of faith. While the doctrine of God and the image of humanity are often quietly subsumed under the theology of the health and wealth gospel, the word-of-faith element constitutes its most visible and controversial aspect. Essential to this theology is the conviction that faith is an active practice rather than a spiritual attitude. In other words, the Christian does not *have* faith – faith is what is *done* by the believer.[74] The law of identification operates on the practice of faith by 'which believers exercise and by which they acquire for themselves the abundant benefits of redemption'.[75] At this point, Kenyon's basic teachings emerge with different emphases in various contexts. Nonetheless, there are certain mechanics of the word of faith that are common to the health and wealth gospel and that are subsumed under the principle of so-called 'positive confession'.

Positive confession is the idea that faith requires verbal declaration, and that the faithful receive what they claim by their vocal declaration of faith. This 'naming and claiming' of spiritual, physical, or material blessings generally proceeds in four stages: First, the believer locates the promises of what is sought in the biblical texts; second, the faithful assert that these promises are directed at them, and that they will receive them if they claim them. This step often includes the visualization of the desired objects and their anticipated reception. Third, the believer confesses this faith vocally and claims the results. Finally, the Christian proceeds immediately to live a life as if the promise had been received.[76] This central step of moving from 'naming' the desired result to 'claiming' it as one's own possession involves not merely hopeful expectation but the firm belief that the promises of God have been received through the act of the word of faith. Adversely, the absence of receiving the desired results is blamed on the absence of faith in the believer.[77] The health and wealth gospel is a proclamation of the triumphant Christian life that rejects negative confession, discouraging thoughts and practices, misdirected focus on one's condition, and acknowledgment of one's present struggle, in favour of positive assertion and the persistent pursuit of the abundant life.[78]

The anticipated (and claimed) result of positive confession is a life of health and wealth that reflects the abundance and prosperity of the eternal life of God. Divine healing provided in the atonement is a common teaching among Pentecostals.[79] Sickness and death are regarded as attributes of the work of Satan and the life of sin from which the believer has been redeemed through Christ. Prayer for healing, recovery, and even resurrection is therefore not uncommon among most Pentecostal groups. However, some health and wealth groups consequently reject the use of physicians, prescriptions, and medical science altogether, although the movement has become more moderate in recent years.[80] While prayer, anointing, and the laying on of hands are the general Pentecostal response to sickness, the health and wealth gospel encourages also unusual practices such as the purchase and use of handkerchiefs, aprons, and anointing oils to obtain health and prosperity. Special health and healing services are designed to demonstrate the power of faith and deliverance, often accompanied by numerous testimonies and – at least in the global South – often affirmed by physical evidence of healings widely labelled as miracles.[81] God and the believer are said to join in a covenantal exchange in which God's abundance is made available to the faithful. God's Word is guardian and assurance of the divine promises of prosperity and health accessible by all who claim them in faith.

Many of these theological underpinnings of the health and wealth gospel stand in contrast to traditional Christian teachings, in general, and active social engagement, in particular. Critics of the movement have pointed to a one-sided doctrine of God, an overemphasized Christology, an anthropocentric theology, including the deification of humanity, an altered doctrine of revelation, and a biased hermeneutics of Scripture.[82] A more nuanced overview of the movement than provided in this chapter would show a wide spectrum of beliefs and practices that at times can be identified closely with classical Pentecostalism while in other contexts lean more toward New Age thinking and mind science.[83] Yet even if we neglect the extremes of the prosperity movement, the health and wealth gospel has discouraged active participation in the struggle for social and economic justice in favour of the assurance of the triumphant life. The focus is placed on the instant changes made possible by the acquisition of wealth rather than the slow and demanding forms of social ministries, services, and programmes. Energy is invested in the individual's health and wealth rather than the healing and prosperity of the community. Solidarity with the poor and persecuted is executed largely on the basis of self-interest. Social and economic identification exists primarily on the basis of the prosperity of a particular group rather than society as a whole. As a result, the health and wealth gospel has divided Pentecostalism and the Evangelical and broader ecumenical traditions.[84] Social engagement and the prosperity movement stand on opposite ends of contemporary forms of Pentecostal social ethics.

Pentecostal social ethics

The undeniable tensions between traditional forms of social engagement, on the one hand, and the triumphalism of the health and wealth gospel, on the other hand, paint a clear picture of the wide range of social consciousness in the Pentecostal movement. Any attempt to construct a homogeneous image of Pentecostal social ethics inevitably results in the misleading assumption that either one side is dominant or that the tensions between both sides are negligible. Moreover, while the contrasting sides presented in this chapter offer a certain perspective on the global state of affairs, the local and particular forms of the movement typically contain Pentecostals that are neither socially active nor drawn to the health and wealth gospel. On the other hand, there are groups associated with the health and wealth gospel that show active social engagement and participation in civic and volunteer movements.[85] What we find among Pentecostals is not only a wide range of attitudes toward social engagement but also a social consciousness in transition that has become characteristic of the state of affairs of the young movement worldwide. A proper assessment of Pentecostalism therefore must take into account the dominant extremes as well as the position of ambivalence, ignorance, and shifting allegiances. This concluding section addresses these changing conditions with the aim of identifying proper labels for the social ethics existing among Pentecostals today.

Social consciousness in transition

The Pentecostal attitude toward engagement with social, economic, and political issues is not static. It is highly dependent on existing conditions, dominant cultural perspectives, economic developments, political leadership, religious examples and the corresponding desires for acceptance and effectiveness or reformation and change. Hence, Pentecostal groups exhibit sometimes a radical break and at other times a gradual shift in social consciousness. The confrontation of habits, values, and corresponding ethical responses is particularly evident in North America, where Pentecostalism has experienced some of the most dramatic socio-economic changes during the twentieth century. Although the beginnings of a similar development can be seen elsewhere, the highly visible complexity of the Pentecostal movement in the United States stands as representative for the broader patterns of emerging Pentecostal social ethics worldwide.

Classical Pentecostalism in the United States shows a shift regarding prosperity, consumerism, and capitalism soon after the first generation of the early twentieth century. Original anti-materialism dominated the eschatological mindset of Pentecostal pioneers, who had little time to engage in consumerism while expecting the imminent return of Christ.[86] Pentecostal leaders spoke out clearly against capitalism and materialism.[87] The missionary fervour of the early Pentecostals would have quickly made them averse to introducing imperialistic and capitalistic values alongside the gospel.[88] Theological convictions rather than economic theories dominated the mindset of classical Pentecostals. Prosperity preaching was the exception.

The second half of the twentieth century shows a significant shift in classical Pentecostal social ethics including the expansion of the health and wealth gospel. Shifting eschatological convictions placed more emphasis on the present socio-economic conditions and the demands of a growing movement than on divine judgment and evangelization.[89] Alignment with North American Evangelicalism led to identification with dominant middle-class ambitions rather than counter-cultural attitudes and changed the face of both Pentecostal and Evangelical Christianity. In addition, the use of mass media and technology significantly advanced the popularity of both Pentecostalism and the prosperity message. The growing acceptability and penetration of Pentecostalism among the more affluent social classes gradually eroded the original scepticism toward material possessions.[90] At the same time, the attraction of the American dream to immigrants seeking social, economic, and political stability, on the one hand, and the failure of the American dream among certain people groups have helped shape two very distinct forms of North American Pentecostalism and have redefined their attitude toward the health and wealth gospel: African American and Hispanic American Pentecostals.

The African American Pentecostal community has experienced the shift in social consciousness in both directions. Beginning perhaps as early as World War I, some black Holiness preachers, individuals, and churches, became leading social activists ahead of the Civil Rights Movement.[91] African American Pentecostalism became a movement within black civic society that challenged the established social values and norms and helped construct a new African American identity.[92] This movement, however, also led many black Pentecostal churches to a life in exile rather than inside the mainstream of American religion and culture.[93] In response, during the latter half of the twentieth century, many African American Pentecostals turned increasingly to the ideas of cultural integration, upward social mobility, and prosperity.[94] The health and wealth gospel was perceived as a form of constructing society primarily directed at the betterment of the individual situation. At the same time, the historical approaches to moral agency among black churches, including testimony, protest, uplift, co-operation, achievement, and remoralization, moved into the background.[95] At the turn to the twenty-first century, a reversal has been observed toward the resurgence of a 'new' black Pentecostal activism.[96] Today's engagement in social transformation includes traditional forms influenced by the civil rights and the black power movements as well as distribution of social services and more indirect ritual activities.[97] While the influence of the health and wealth gospel persists, many black Pentecostal communities have returned to the social activism that characterized their past.

Hispanic American Pentecostals experienced a similar transition of socio-economic values, political behaviour, religious affiliation, and Latina/o Pentecostal public voice.[98] Unlike African American Pentecostals, the Hispanic community is much more diverse, covering a vast array of a population tied together by common but broad heritage, language, and cultural traits. The twentieth century shows not only a dramatic increase of the Hispanic American population but also of Hispanic Pentecostalism, accompanied by significant upward social mobility and the far-reaching reorganization of Hispanic Pentecostal churches after World War II.[99] The initial picture of Hispanic Pentecostalism at the beginning of the twentieth century presents itself not unlike the image of Latinos in general at the time, that is, as less proactive than whites and blacks in social engagement, and at times as passively enduring the conditions of depravity and oppression as a minority in the country.[100] Hispanic social consciousness was aimed primarily at overcoming economic depression, educational disadvantages, immigration issues, and other circumstances related to the individual. Pentecostal churches represented a welcome communal support system, but the concentration of Hispanics in a few metropolitan areas and the lack of resources among most Pentecostals did not encourage broad socio-political engagement.[101] However, the subsequent increase of the Hispanic community also impacted the growth and spread of Hispanic Pentecostalism and its image of faith-based political and social action. By the end of the twentieth century, a national survey of the Hispanic Churches in American Public Life revealed that Latina/o Pentecostals had become just as involved as other religious organisations and in fact reported the highest involvement in all measures of social and political activism.[102] Latina/o clergy, churches, and religious organizations today have emerged as general and civic leaders involved in educational, social, and political issues frequently aimed at improving the conditions of the Hispanic community.[103]

This image of an apparently simple increase or change from sectarianism to social engagement demands a thicker description and expansion of the paradigm by which Latina/o Pentecostal faith is counted as a motivating factor.[104] The growth of the Hispanic Pentecostal community after World War II also shows widespread tendencies toward fragmentation of Latino denominations often resulting from divisions between new immigrants and established generations. While the former continue to be on the average younger, poorer, and less educated, the latter have adapted to American culture and found new social identity and economic stability. As a result, involvement in social and political action has become closely tied to the experience of socio-economic deprivation, particularly factors of income, immigration, education, and religious participation.[105] These and other factors continue to shape the Hispanic Pentecostal community and its social consciousness in North America.

These changes in social, economic, and political consciousness are symptomatic for broader shifts in classical Pentecostalism in other areas, for example, alcohol consumption, dress code, attending of theatre, and attitudes toward pacifism and war.[106] Toward the end of the twentieth century, classical Pentecostals adopted the principal values of American society.[107] This espousal of the dominant value system includes substantive changes in the Pentecostal social consciousness that have made Pentecostals less distinguishable from society and other religious groups. At the same time, Pentecostals have also maintained and rediscovered some of their own values that they believe American society should hold.[108] These conclusions are applicable to Pentecostalism worldwide and mark it as a phenomenon with social values highly dependent on the contextual history and development of social, economic, and political circumstances.

Ambivalent social ethics

Pentecostal involvement in social, economic, and political issues can be stereotyped as active or passive, progressive or regressive, accommodative or counter-cultural. A one-sided perspective of the movement's social engagement will likely capture a large portion of the Pentecostal social ethos. However, neglect of the tangible differences and shifts in the movement's social consciousness fails to account for both the oppositional forces present among Pentecostals as well as the diverse range of socio-economic and political modalities among Pentecostals worldwide. A view inclusive of the tensions does not have the luxury to speak of a single Pentecostal social consciousness. Instead, three necessary and complementary labels present themselves in the characterization of social ethics among Pentecostals today: contradictory, ambiguous, and multifarious.

The characterization of Pentecostal social ethics as contradictory is a helpful starting point to identify the existing tensions. The young Pentecostal movement, still in its infant stages, does not possess a single, global or local, social consciousness. As a movement closely tied to the local state of affairs, Pentecostalism is highly volatile and dependent on cultural, social, economic, and political developments in their particular contexts. That the response to these circumstances can be identified as contradictory does not discredit the movement or its social ethics. Rather, the reality of contradiction in the same movement points to the transitional nature of the global Pentecostal movement as a whole. Pentecostals are, so to speak, on the way of finding and defining themselves in the midst of the socio-cultural, economic, and political circumstances that are still shaping the movement. It is often assumed that the established Christian traditions have long completed this initial stage of ethical development and possess a firmly established stance. Yet the emergence of dominant ethical controversies that have divided Christianity during the twentieth century, including the debates on abortion, apartheid, capital punishment, contraception, genetic engineering, homosexuality, or pacifism, to name but a few, indicates that Pentecostalism may only be more expressive and extraverted than the established traditions in the display of inherently contradictory ethical positions.[109]

The characterization of Pentecostalism as an ambiguous social movement overlaps this perspective of inherent contradictions.[110] Ambiguity identifies a certain lack of clarity, both for Pentecostalism itself and its observers, without immediately juxtaposing certain positions or excluding others. When we speak of Pentecostalism as ambiguous, we mean not a lack of decision by Pentecostals but the absence of direction for the movement as a whole. Neither social activism nor the health and wealth gospel are ambiguous; what is ambiguous is the indecision that one or the other characterizes Pentecostals as a whole. More precisely, in the contexts of global Christianity, 'ambiguity is the coming together of the local and specific with the global and open-ended'.[111] Pentecostalism is closely tied to local socio-economic contexts and the particular conditions experienced by its members but 'is sufficiently adaptable to forge links with very different social formations'.[112] Much of this ambiguity is the result of organizational dynamics among Pentecostals that are typically in the hands of small groups, congregations, and pastoral leadership rather than denominations, regional, national, or international organizations.[113] Ambiguity is necessary for a global movement like Pentecostalism that exists not as a ready-made global system but is in the process of becoming a worldwide phenomenon 'by constant adjustment on the ground'.[114] These adjustments have shaped Pentecostalism as a utilitarian movement without forcing the pragmatic stance in any particular direction.

A third way to characterize the social consciousness among Pentecostals is to speak of Pentecostal social engagement as a multifarious phenomenon summarized with the motto, 'many tongues, many practices'.[115] This motto embraces the contradictions and ambiguity of the movement without attempting to force the phenomenology of Pentecostalism into a normative account of a single social practice. Instead, a multiplicity of socio-political forms and structures are already anticipated in the biblical account of Pentecost from which modern-day Pentecostalism derives its meaning and which forms the central motif of the Pentecostal worldview and spirituality. This multiplicity corresponds to a pluralism of responses from the Christian world to the struggle for social, economic, and political justice in general.[116] An intentional multiplicity of responses and practices are therefore seen as constitutive of the distinct Pentecostal contributions to the global Christian landscape.[117] This perspective does not interpret the idea of 'many tongues and many practices' as a temporary phenomenon but as a posture that may well represent the face(s) of global Christianity in the near future. Contradictions and ambiguity are part of Pentecostalism's determination 'to engage the public square in some senses on its own Christian terms rather than on the terms set by the 'world''.[118] Social engagement and the health and wealth gospel are both expressions of a multifarious Christian existence echoing the many tongues of the Spirit given on the day of Pentecost and characterizing the Pentecostal world today.

If these characterizations are correct, then the contradictory, ambiguous, and multifarious social consciousness and behaviour of modern-day Pentecostalism is not temporary but here to stay. Even when there is evidence that Pentecostal social ethics are solidifying under pressure of socialization, institutionalization, and seculari-zation, the resulting expressions cannot be seen as normative for the entire movement.[119] This pluralistic identity should not be understood as relativism, that is, an intentional lack of direction and decision-making on behalf of social justice. It is perhaps more adequately identified as a form of 'prophetic activism' that has come to include progressive and conservative means of Christian social engagement.[120] As prophetic, Pentecostal social activism takes place in the 'borderlands' of globalization, internationalization, urbani-zation, and industrialization.[121] In these places, the forms of social engagement are as varied as the challenges. Pentecostalism is still in the process of finding an ethical methodology that enables it to respond to the reality and crisis of pluralism characteristic of the twenty-first century world.[122] The worldwide economic down-turn and various dramatic socio-economic and political changes since the end of the twentieth century have contributed to a widening of these borderlands across the globe. The corresponding need to face the various social struggles in these transitional contexts anticipates the further spread of Pentecostalism in its diverse range from social activism to triumphalism.

CHAPTER SIX

Egalitarian practices and institutionalism

Hot debates, often to the boiling point, have erupted in many Pentecostal circles over issues of gender and race. The existence of such disagreements is particularly surprising in light of the fact that Pentecostalism is widely considered an egalitarian movement. Divisions over the representation and authority of Pentecostals across the lines of gender and race stand in sharp contrast to the emphasis on the prophethood of all believers. These tensions have permeated the movement and brought it to the brink of separation, often held together only by the joint affirmation that the Spirit of God has been poured out on all flesh and that the gifts of the Spirit are available to everyone without measure. On the one hand, the outpouring of the Spirit is seen as an act of liberation and reconciliation across the limits of age, gender, race, class, and ethnicity. On the other hand, some postpone these achievements as eschatological promises to the time of a new creation while holding on to established institutional patterns.

Reasons for the tensions between egalitarianism and institutionalism are complex, often depending on the heritage, social make-up and context, as well as history of particular Pentecostal groups. Divisions over gender and race stand out with particular force and contrast with the desires of Pentecostalism as a global charismatic and ecumenical movement. The present chapter presents this contrast and the underlying motivations with particular focus on the exorbitant tensions surrounding the authority of women in ministry and the divisions between black Pentecostalism and white congregations. The first part of this chapter introduces the egalitarian impulse of the Pentecostal movement, focusing on the ideals of the outpouring of the Holy Spirit, the priesthood of all believers, and the end of partiality in the body of Christ. The second part describes the contrasting divisions over race and gender dominant among Pentecostal groups worldwide. In the final part, the influence of institutionalism, the bias of Pentecostal scholarship, and a segregated doxology are highlighted as the key contributors to maintaining the tensions between egalitarianism and institutionalism among Pentecostals today.

The egalitarian impulse of Pentecostalism

Pentecostalism is a movement of the people. Stereotypes, sometimes based on dominant historiographies of the movement, tend to regard Pentecostalism as an isolated religious sect, the social religious movement of a disenfranchised and underprivileged minority occupied with peculiar religious concerns. In this portrait, the typical Pentecostal cannot be identified with the general image of society and is not concerned with the social struggle. A less biased approach, however, suggests rather the opposite, namely that Pentecostalism can indeed be identified as a movement of the masses.[1] Various models, including theories relating Pentecostalism to the phenomenon of deprivation, restorationism, revivalism, accommodation, modernism, and postmodernism, are utilized in the attempt to understand the existence and composition of the global movement.[2] The common denominator of these models is the attempt to explain what motivations exactly have made Pentecostalism one of the most vibrant contemporary religious movements. Among the most outstanding features emerging from this discussion is the universal appeal of Pentecostalism as an egalitarian model of the Christian life that disregards barriers of class, social status, race, ethnicity, gender, education, and age. In their place, Pentecostals emphasize the outpouring of the Holy Spirit on all flesh, the prophethood of all believers, and the equality of the body of Christ.

The universal outpouring of the Holy Spirit

Pentecostals unmistakably understand themselves as participants in the work of the Holy Spirit. More explicitly, Pentecostalism itself is typically regarded as a movement of the Spirit in the world. As such, Pentecostals seek to display in the movement the characteristics of the Spirit's presence and activity. These features are derived initially from a reading of the New Testament, particularly Luke-Acts, in light of the Spirit-oriented perspective surrounding the day of Pentecost:[3] The church is portrayed as a community anointed with the Spirit of Jesus, whose own ministry is interpreted in light of his anointing with the Spirit of God (see Acts 10.38) and in fulfilment of the prophets (Lk. 4.18–19; see Isa. 61.1–2). Characterized as a ministry to the poor, the captives, the blind, and the oppressed, Jesus is known for his fellowship (Lk. 5.30; 7.34; 15.1) with men, women, and children, the religious elite, sinners and tax collectors, the sick, demon-possessed, and disabled – social outcasts in various ways.[4] The Spirit-filled ministry of Jesus oversteps the boundaries of social structures and establishments and represents for Pentecostals a paradigm for a new egalitarian movement.

The day of Pentecost marks the beginning of the outpouring of the Holy Spirit. Acts 2.17–18 became the central passage for the interpretation of the work of the Spirit by most Pentecostals: 'In the last days it will be, God declares, that I will pour out my Spirit upon all flesh, and your sons and your daughters shall prophesy, and your young men shall see visions, and your old men shall dream dreams. Even upon my slaves, both men and women, in those days I will pour out my Spirit; and they shall prophesy.' In these words, Pentecostals find affirmation that the outpouring of the Spirit has initiated a new social order, a community of equals among the rich and the poor, masters and servants, men and women, old and young (see Gal. 3.28; Col. 3.11).[5] All are seen as baptized, filled, and empowered by the Spirit, often reversing established cultural, socio-economic, political, or ecclesiastical structures.

In addition to this reading of the Scriptures, Pentecostals interpret themselves as the fulfilment of the biblical promises of the day of Pentecost. This recognition is nowhere more evident than in the widely publicized events of the Azusa Street Mission and revival of 1906–9 that embraced, in the midst of the segregationist environment prevalent in North America at the time, persons from different races, genders, cultures, ethnicities, and nationalities.[6] Participation in the outpouring of the Spirit joined diverse people together in outbursts and celebrations of socially aberrant and typically unacceptable behaviours. The common association with Pentecostals ostracized them as a group quickly from the rest of society. The group itself, however, understands its existence as a result of the revelation that God shows no partiality; men and women, fathers and mothers, sons and daughters (see Acts 10.34), all are recipients of the gift of the Holy Spirit.

The outpouring of the Holy Spirit without partiality is interpreted as both gift and mandate. As a gift from God, Pentecostals are convinced that the modern-day Pentecost marks the beginning of the end time, an eschatological signpost for the imminent return of Christ, the judgment of the world, and the new creation.[7] The universal gift of the Spirit is the final invitation to a dying world to receive salvation, sanctification, and empowerment in the last days. For Pentecostals, the outpouring of the Spirit penetrates the last dominion of Satan, demonic strongholds throughout the world including governments, political structures, destructive public and social organizations, false religions, oppression, poverty, and persecution. No places, publics, or persons are excluded from the fulfilment of the promises of God heralded by the coming of the Holy Spirit.

As mandate, Pentecostals see themselves as harbingers of the outpouring of the Spirit to the ends of the earth. The baptism of the Spirit is seen as the source of divine power available to everyone for the sanctification, conversion, and salvation of the whole world.[8] In turn, the outpouring of the Spirit is the sign that this mandate has been received around the globe. This mandate to share the universal availability of the Holy Spirit with the world marks the seedbed of worldwide Pentecostalism. Since the Spirit has been poured out on all, the mandate is service to all – ministry to the children and youth, adults, and the elderly, men and women, the sick, the dying, the homeless, natives, immigrants, businesses, schools, hospitals, the unevangelized, and those who have heard the gospel but know nothing of the power of the Spirit.[9] The conviction of the outpouring of the Spirit on all flesh inspires, at least in expectation and enthusiasm, an environment of democratic, egalitarian ideals.

In its most dramatic form, the ideal of the outpouring of the Spirit on 'all flesh' is seen as bursting open the chains of social, economic, political, and religious segregation. Put negatively, the promise of the Spirit is given not exclusively to one society or nation; it is not limited to the political, economic, cultural, or religious elite, the church or the believer, the priest or the clergy, the educated, the adult, man or woman. Put positively, the outpouring of the Spirit makes possible the engagement of all creation and therefore its ultimate reconciliation with God.[10] Pentecostals understand themselves as a prophetic voice announcing the final transformation in the relationship of God and the world in which the whole of creation is subject to the presence and activity of God's Spirit. 'Pentecost' in this sense becomes a watchword for the transformation of creation, its conversion and empowerment to participate in the Spirit's redemption. At least theologically, the participation of creation in this redemptive process knows no boundaries.

The prophethood of all believers

The notion of the universal outpouring of the Holy Spirit has immediate connotations for the Pentecostal view of Christian vocation, ministry, and service. Since Pentecostals believe that the gifts of the Spirit are available to all, everyone who has received the Spirit is in principle equipped and empowered to participate in all aspects of the life of the church. The immediate consequence of this perspective has been formulated as the slogan, 'the church belongs to the people'.[11] Historically, this notion is akin to the Protestant emphasis on the priesthood of all believers, and Pentecostals have indeed consistently emphasized the mobilization of all people for the preaching of the gospel, mission, evangelization, the healing of the sick, prophecy, exorcism, and the exercise of other spiritual gifts. At the same time, priestly forms of ministry do not identify a central concern among Pentecostals as they did among the Protestant Reformers. The Pentecostal emphasis on the restoration of the apostolic age gives to the people all Christian vocations found in the New Testament: apostles, prophets, evangelists, pastors, teachers (Eph. 4.11), overseers, elders, and deacons (Phil. 1.1) – but the notion of the priesthood is reserved for Christ (Heb.

7.24) and serves primarily as a metaphor for the whole church (1 Pet. 2.5, 9).[12] It is therefore more accurate to identify the egalitarian impulse in Pentecostalism as an emphasis on the prophethood of all believers.

The prophethood of all believers emphasizes the charismatic functions of anyone who is subject to the anointing of the Holy Spirit regardless of social, economic, religious, or cultural status. Gender, age, race, ethnicity, or education are not indicative of the anointing of the Spirit and therefore do not imply a measure of authority, vocation, or position. The ideal of this egalitarian image of Christian ministry derives immediately from the recovery of Joel's ancient prophecy by the apostle Peter on the day of Pentecost (Acts 2.17–18). Modern-day Pentecostals interpret this passage not only as an indication of the restoration of prophecy but as an expansion of the gift of the Spirit and the prophetic anointing to all. The result is a dynamic image of the Christian life with focus on worship and participation in a fellowship of mutuality by all who believe and have received the Spirit.[13] This emphasis seeks to evade the polarity between priest and people, ordained and laity, church and world, office and spiritual gift, or any other similar distinction that locates the active exercise of the Christian vocation in the hands of a particular individual or group.

The emphasis on the participation of all believers in the life of the church has resulted in a lack of focus on developing an official doctrine of the church, and many Pentecostals reject traditional, hierarchical patterns in favour of congregational and independent forms of organization. The prophethood of all believers here functions in an original 'protestant' sense as a counter-cultural critique that exposes existing ecclesiastical structures as restricting the full participation of all believers in the body of Christ.[14] From a Pentecostal perspective, it is the gift of the Holy Spirit and not the office of the church that establishes spiritual authority. The universal outpouring of the Spirit, captured in the image of Spirit baptism, inspires a reinterpretation and reconstruction of the world, frequently offering a critical, biblical, political, theological, and ethical alternative to the established institutional patterns of the orthodox establishment that favour more restrictive forms of participation and authority.

Particularly in the Charismatic Movements in the established churches, democratic and egalitarian tendencies among Pentecostals depend on the idea of the spiritual anointing of all believers without thereby questioning the authority of the priestly ministry. One could say that the focus of Pentecostalism is not the individual – whether priest or prophet – but the community of faith. In this ecclesiological mindset, the Spirit poured out on all flesh leads not only to the charismatic endowment of all believers but ultimately to a charismatic church.[15] Nonetheless, the prophetic function of the underprivileged, particularly the ministry of women as well as those with no formal clerical training or those who previously held priestly functions in non-Christian religions, has posed severe challenges to the established institutions.[16] The challenges pertain not only to the integration of charismatic manifestations in all churches but to the role and extent of participation in the church's service and ministry by those who manifest such gifts regardless of the dictates of class, society, history, and culture. In other words, the realization of Pentecostal egalitarian ideals requires their tangible manifestation as practices of equality among all believers in the body of Christ.

Egalitarian practices in the body of Christ

The biblical foundations for the prophethood of all believers and the attributing of spiritual gifts to those ordinarily separated from the privilege of leadership in the church lead to egalitarian practices that have earned Pentecostals the reputation of being a counter-cultural and postcolonial movement. This perception stands out nowhere more forcefully than in the sensitive areas of race and gender, in which the Pentecostal image of the outpouring of the Spirit on men and women of all colour and age holds a unique position, sometimes interpreted as a resistance to domination that is itself a gift of the Holy Spirit.[17] These egalitarian practices find illustrations in various contexts of the global movement.

In the ethnic context of South Africa, for example, both black and white Pentecostals have repeatedly engaged in the fight against apartheid.[18] The Pentecostal outpouring of the Spirit, understood as a promise given to both the oppressed and their oppressors, has nurtured an attitude of resistance and hope concentrated in the idea of liberating the structures that hold both sides prisoners. In India, the Dalit Pentecostals have become synonymous with

the liberation of a caste of untouchables by a religious movement
that promises an egalitarian future for all Spirit-filled and baptized
Christians.[19] While the turn to Christianity for liberation is not
unusual, the institutional structures of the established churches
have often hindered the removal of social segregation. Pentecostals,
in turn, have invited the social outcasts into a fellowship of equals
where they are no longer untouchables but brothers and sisters.
Others see the black Pentecostal experience in Britain as a model
for the worldwide struggle against oppression and for the reconciliation of races.[20]

In the racially divided context of North America during the
twentieth century, early Afro-Pentecostalism emerged as a major
constituent of Black civil society.[21] More than 30 years before the
advent of the Civil Rights Movement, the impact of the Pentecostal
revival in America was described as washing away the 'color line'.[22]
The dialogue on racial reconciliation among classical Pentecostals
spans the twentieth century in diverse forms that find a high point
in the so-called 'Memphis miracle' of 1994. A candid discussion
of the racial divisions among classical Pentecostals at a meeting
in Memphis led the all-white Pentecostal Fellowship of North
America to be re-established as the racially inclusive Pentecostal/
Charismatic Churches of North America.[23] This decision of a
group of Pentecostals to share leadership with both African
American Pentecostals and women emerged from an environment
of repentance, the celebration of the Lord's Supper, and joint
participation in a spontaneous act of interracial foot-washing. The
most tangible result from this meeting is the 'Pentecostal Partners
Racial Reconciliation Manifesto', which reaffirms the egalitarian
impulse of the Pentecostal pioneers and repudiates all forms of
racism, culminating in a strategy for racial reconciliation for the
twenty-first century.[24] Seen as a step on the way toward a future of
full reconciliation, the miracle of Memphis has opened the doors
for a multicultural and trans-ethnic movement that transcends the
borders of culture, colour, and gender.

Concerns for gender equality among Pentecostals have made
similar headlines, often coupled with political movements. The
African Instituted Churches with a strong leadership of women,
especially among the Charismatic churches in West Africa,
have left an indelible mark on African Christianity including a
reshaping of traditional patriarchal institutions and concepts of

ordained male authority.[25] In the North American context, the influence of African egalitarian attitudes on black Pentecostal communities has contributed to shaping new opportunities for women in leadership.[26] The migration of Pentecostal communities from Africa, Asia, and Latin America has initiated similar transformational processes in Europe.[27] In Latin America, the Pentecostal revival has strengthened the public voice and authority of women.[28] Similar observations across the developing world have shown advantages given to women and young people among many Pentecostal groups.[29] In many countries, Pentecostalism has become a movement on behalf of women especially among the poor. Some describe the movement consequently as 'a modern egalitarian impulse'.[30] Others speak cautiously of Pentecostalism as exhibiting an 'egalitarian patriarchialism'.[31] Both characterizations imply significant revisions of established patterns of authority, yet without suggesting that Pentecostalism has fully succeeded as a mechanism of social transformation. Egalitarian ideals have significantly contributed to the image of the Pentecostal movement today. A neglect of this important dimension would fail to account for a central dynamic in the way Pentecostals engage the world. At the same time, the concrete realization of Pentecostal ideals has encountered significant challenges and resistance not only among Pentecostal groups worldwide.

Institutionalism in the Pentecostal movement

The egalitarian model of Pentecostalism stands in sharp contrast to the visible reality among many Pentecostal denominations and institutions. Pentecostal groups have found it difficult to put into practice the breadth of equality, impartiality, and democracy demanded by their ideals. Opportunities to become a pioneer for equal rights of race and gender during the twentieth century were squandered, and many of the accomplishments presented in the previous section were late achievements at the end of a slow gravitation toward equal opportunities. While the seed of egalitarian ideals remains at the heart of the Pentecostal ethos, and the fight against racism and patriarchalism is raging incessantly among

Pentecostals worldwide, the movement is torn between its idealistic intentions and the reality of complicity in racial segregation and gender discrimination.

Complicity in racial segregation

The origins of Pentecostalism worldwide are interracial, or to put it more mildly, distributed among different races. This environment provided frequent opportunities for bias, opposition, separation, and unjust persecution on both sides. In the racially discriminating environment of North America during the first half of the twentieth century, the colour-line that allegedly had been washed away among Pentecostals was quickly re-drawn when the revivals were in need of lasting organization.[32] Many Pentecostals, supported by the customs of American society, were strictly opposed to the egalitarian convictions supporting racial unity. Some rejected the joint forms of worship and interracial association that had come to characterize the Azusa Street revival and mission. Membership in the Ku Klux Klan and participation in the Pentecostal movement were not always seen as mutually exclusive.[33] Others began to associate certain theological convictions with racial identification, which not only led to a racial separation of doctrines among Pentecostals but institutionalized the racial divide.[34] This development has led to a predominantly African American membership in Wesleyan Pentecostalism and Oneness Pentecostalism and predominately white and Hispanic membership in Reformed Pentecostal groups.[35] Particularly in the American South, Pentecostals did little to broach the subject of race or to expose the spread of racism in its less subtle forms.[36] As a result, the heartland of classical Pentecostalism produced and sustained denominations split along racial lines. Even in the wake of the Civil Rights Movement of the 1960s and 1970s, black Pentecostals were almost non-present in the predominantly white Pentecostal denominations.[37] Communion is stronger between black and Hispanic Pentecostals, even across doctrinal convictions, than fellowship with or among white Pentecostals.[38] The Memphis manifesto advocating racial reconciliation has yet to be followed by concrete and continual measures that confront racial separation and tangible forms of racism across religious, social, economic, and political lines. The collective memory among

Pentecostals in North America is not yet strong enough to support the realization of a racially integrative Pentecostalism.

Latina/o and Hispanic Pentecostalism bears similar experiences of racial segregation. The biological and cultural intermixture representative of this branch of Pentecostalism has been commonly termed as *mestizaje* and helped give a voice to articulate the experiences of cultural, racial, and ethnic marginalization and oppression.[39] While the term *mestizaje* has been widely used to paint a homogenous image of the inclusion of different cultural and racial groups among Pentecostals, the implementation of this ideal has turned out to be quite ambiguous under the reality of heterogeneity that characterizes the Latina/o people.[40] Internal tensions and different types of racism, which often exclude indigenous and African peoples, have created a false image of homogeneity that favours particular national identities. The Latin American contexts that inspired the notion of *mestizaje* are ill-fit for the heterogeneous situation in the United States and elsewhere and have expanded among Pentecostals the dominant black/white rhetoric to include also the *mestizo*, indigenous, and African identities in addition to cross-over trends toward European and white features that promise affluence and power.

Similar concerns arise in the history of apartheid in South Africa that has posited many classical Pentecostal churches against the Charismatic Movement and neo-Pentecostal communities. Widely accepted studies paint the image of the charismatic churches as conservative, anxious, and neurotic communities that largely support the status quo of racial segregation.[41] Widespread discussion over the extent of such discrimination has led to divisive reactions among many Pentecostal streams in South Africa, not least between classical Pentecostal groups and African Indigenous Pentecostals.[42] In a similar manner as the Memphis manifesto, some charismatic associations publicized a joint confession in 1991 that acknowledged their neglect both to effectively oppose apartheid and to put into practice existing egalitarian ideals.[43] Despite their penetrating presence among the poor and socially dislocated, which were found among all population groups in the country during the twentieth century, Pentecostals struggled to define their own role in the process of recovery.[44] A false anthropology favouring racial discrimination, and a low ecclesiology suppressing the unity and equality of all races in the body of Christ, have failed to disallow for complicity with apartheid.[45] Changes in Pentecostal practices are due to the rise of Afrikaner nationalism, the anti-apartheid movement, and the general political changes in South Africa rather than the realization of their egalitarian ideals.

These images can be expanded in many places where sensitive racial relations characterize the composition of Pentecostalism and its location in existing cultural and socio-political contexts. Pentecostals struggle with the racial divide in leadership, government, doctrine, rituals, and worship. Pentecostal denominations, churches, and smaller fellowships continue to demarcate racial affiliation instead of racial reconciliation. As a result, Pentecostals have squandered the opportunity to become a tangible force in a global racial reconciliation.

The Pentecostal gender paradox

The demands of putting into practice the deep-seated egalitarian ideals of the Pentecostal movement have also affected the relationship of men and women, particularly in positions of public leadership and authority. The contrast between democratic impulses in principle and sexual discrimination in practice has prompted several observers to speak of a 'gender paradox' in the Pentecostal movement.[48]

> An unresolved tension remains between the *de jure* system of patriarchal authority in church and home and the *de facto* establishment of a way of life which decisively shifts the domestic and religious priorities in a direction that benefits women and children while morally restraining the traditional autonomy of the male and the selfish or irresponsible exercise of masculine power. The implicit deal seems to be that a substantive shift towards greater gender equality will be tolerated so long as women are not seen to be publicly exercising formal authority over men.[49]

Pentecostalism appears amidst the tensions characterizing it as a revolutionary egalitarian religion and at the same time a chauvinist conservative and fundamentalist movement. The gender paradox perpetuates the difficulties of reconciling the religious sense of the outpouring of the Holy Spirit on sons *and daughters* with the social, economic, and political changes that outpouring brings to their relationship with one another.

The gender paradox is particularly visible in Pentecostal communities where patriarchy is a deeply ingrained system in society and culture. Some of the most significant voices of gender discrimination come from Latin America, where the paradox stands out sharply between the disproportionately large numbers of women converting to a Pentecostalism that does not give them an institutional place of authority.[50] In Brazil, for example, the suppression of women in Pentecostal churches is closely connected with racial discrimination and identity. Women have been left out of positions of authority not only because they are women but also because they are black.[51] On the other hand, the image of women also contrasts starkly with traditional Latino patriarchal ideology and the image of male authority. Pentecostalism in Colombia shows the clear effects of this ideology in the relegation of women's roles to the private sphere of the household.[52] The process of integrating women in public religious life is slow and difficult. Women's leadership remains widely unofficial, and opportunities offered to women typically exclude prominent and highly visible positions. Pentecostals in Bolivia manifest the continuing difficulties in unmasking the implicit affirmation of traditional relations of domination between men and women and the perpetuation of gender inequality in their midst.[53] Here and elsewhere in Latin America, an egalitarian Pentecostalism is still very much in development.

The religious scene in North America has become a similar point of contention for the equality of women in Pentecostal leadership. The roots of antifeminism can be located in the notable influence of fundamentalism on the North American religious system.[54] While the typically negative connotation of fundamentalism has contributed to false stereotypes of Pentecostalism, classical Pentecostals did adopt many of the patriarchal and authoritarian dimensions and strict boundaries prevalent among fundamentalist Evangelicals in the United States.[55] Although women shared significantly in the success of the early Pentecostal revivals, their names and contributions were often covered or reduced to the sidelines.[56] Others have made traditional European forms of church hierarchy responsible for the institution and perpetuation of the marginalization and subordination of women.[57] Obtaining and retaining a position of authority for female Pentecostal preachers and pastors often entails additional work and the relinquishing of other rights.[58] Most Pentecostal denominations grant women a limited form of ordination; many continue to exclude women from the highest positions of ecclesiastical and episcopal authority.

Similar manifestations of the Pentecostal gender paradox can be found in Europe, Africa, Asia, and the Caribbean. In Sicily, for example, a stronghold of patriarchism in Western Europe, Pentecostal churches emulate the configuration of the Sicilian family, where men are the head of the family while women do most of the physical and emotional work.[59] African Pentecostalism exhibits forms of a gendered charisma, where women are accepted as 'founders, sisters, first ladies, and Jezebels' but excluded from leadership on the basis of supposedly different charismatic abilities.[60] In Korea, the adoption of Presbyterian forms of church government from the West confirmed the already existing patriarchal structures of society and has kept the Pentecostal leadership on an official level almost exclusively in the hands of men.[61] In Jamaica, a highly embodied form of faith confronted with a strict moral order continues to affirm the gender divide and the position of the male pastor.[62] These and other examples confirm that the gender paradox in Pentecostal churches is alive and well throughout the world. The conundrum of global Pentecostalism is that it has become a women's religion that has barred women from entrance to the male-dominated hierarchy.

It is important to acknowledge these tensions between democratic egalitarianism and divide of race and gender in contemporary Pentecostalism. Exclusively identifying one side has led to false stereotypes of the movement on a global scale that does no justice to its diverse contexts. The heart of these tensions is formed by the difficulties existing in putting into practice the egalitarian impulse in the sensitive environments of race and gender worldwide. Failure to reconcile intentions and practices of reconciliation has further contributed to critical questions of the movement's overall concern for issues of social justice.[63] The perplexity of this situation is best explained by shifting attention to the factors that contribute to the coexistence of egalitarian ideals and their practical counterparts in Pentecostal communities.

Pentecostal egalitarianism-in-the-making

The previous overview of the tensions existing among Pentecostals with regard to the equality of race and gender suggests that we cannot speak in general terms of Pentecostalism as an egalitarian movement. The existence of the racial divide and the gender paradox are undeniable features of much of the visible Pentecostal landscape, at least on the organizational and denominational level. On the other hand, Pentecostals cannot be described simply as racists and chauvinists. The egalitarian impulse, even if estimated carefully, forms a foundational component of the worldview and spirituality that informs modern-day Pentecostalism. The global and historical development of Pentecostalism suggests that it is a movement toward a democratic, egalitarian identity. It is therefore more accurate to speak of Pentecostalism as an egalitarian movement-in-development.[64] The tensions existing between the egalitarian heart and the divisive practices among Pentecostals cannot be forged easily into a homogeneous image. Chief among the factors contributing to the coexistence of egalitarianism and its contradictions is the high degree of institutionalism that accompanies the emergence of the Pentecostal movement. A neglect and bias in the scholarship and study of Pentecostalism and a segregated doxology further consolidate the institutional basis. How quickly Pentecostalism can become a fully egalitarian movement depends largely on the ability and willingness to meet the crucial demands posed by these challenges.

Institutionalism and Pentecostal hierarchy

A high demand for institutionalization and institution-building characterizes the modern-day Pentecostal movement since its inception. The unprecedented expansion of the movement across the world, the growth of membership, and the lack of organizational structures at the original revivals soon demanded a higher degree of organizational leadership. The initial institutionalization of classical Pentecostalism progressed in broad stages, including a selective focus on particular doctrines, a formulation of doctrinal structures to protect and formalize the selective perspective, and the ecclesial solidification of such structures.[65] The later integration of the Charismatic Movement in the mainline churches represented its own challenges when confronted with the traditional hierarchical structures that many took as restrictive to the emergence of charismatic manifestations.[66] Moreover, the organizational forms of recent neo-Pentecostal groups exhibit a high degree of transition and differentiation, often depending on the founding figures and frequently resembling traditional hierarchical structures and a strong focus on the demands of the local church.[67] Max Weber's dominant theory of the pressures of institutionalization and routinization has been successfully applied to Pentecostalism and suggests several dilemmas concentrated on the delimitation, power, and administrative order of the movement as a whole.[68] The unresolved tensions between egalitarian ideals and the reality of racial and gender discrimination among Pentecostals are a result of the difficulties of coping with the growing institutionalization of the movement, the demands of unfamiliar organizational structures, and the adoption of the socio-political norms that accompanied the establishment of such configurations.

The demands and effects of institutionalization among Pentecostals point to a dominance of sacerdotal and episcopal forms of ecclesiastical organization and administration. Put differently, a high degree of institutionalism defined by the authority of the socio-cultural group dominant during the early phase of Pentecostal history has led to a priestly form of Pentecostalism that is foreign to the original self-understanding of most Pentecostals as a prophetic movement.[69] This inherited ecclesial ideology affects Pentecostal practices in terms of both gender and race and has led to the preponderance of churches and denominations following sexually and racially exclusive patterns of fellowship, worship, doctrine, and government.

The original motivation of the prophetic as a counter-cultural and critical mechanism for a revolutionary Pentecostal movement has turned into a ghetto for the culturally suppressed groups of colour and gender.[70] Under the auspices of a prophetic ministry, all are equal: No hierarchical system applies to the prophetic realm. At the same time, the hierarchical view of the priesthood adopted by most Pentecostals today contains features of vocational and ontological selectivity.[71] All priests can be prophets, but not all prophets can be priests. This paradigm has been enforced with particular sharpness in the exclusion of women from influence on church polity and government. The result is a confrontation of spiritual egalitarianism with ecclesial pragmatism.[72] While the two are not necessarily antithetical, the core values and beliefs of individuals conflict with the practices developed to establish and support Pentecostal institutions. The office of the priest, dominated by a division of race and gender, can coexist with the prophethood of all believers, since the latter does not possess official status in the decision-making of the churches. The perpetuation of this artificial division is largely responsible for the endurance of the gender divide and racial separation at least among the leadership of Pentecostal denominations into the foreseeable future.

Biased Pentecostal scholarship

Pentecostal scholarship has at least two central dimensions: it consists of Pentecostalism as the object of study, on the one hand, and of Pentecostal scholars, on the other hand, who may or may not focus their scholarship on the study of Pentecostalism. Both sides are relatively recent developments originating with the second half of the twentieth century.[73] Pentecostalism as the subject and object of contemporary scholarship has been only marginally explored, often with highly visible bias. Stereotypes and prejudices abound in early assessments and dismissals of Pentecostalism across scientific and academic disciplines. Pentecostal scholars themselves spent much of the early decades of Pentecostal scholarship occupied with internal issues of doctrine and church government. On both sides, the concerns of gender and race were largely overlooked.

African and African American origins of classical Pentecostalism, for example, remain a neglected topic. Despite the influence of the black preacher William J. Seymour and other African American leaders on the origins and development of Pentecostalism in North America, few scholars have developed a comprehensive argument on the racial landscape of Pentecostals. The recovery of African American contributions was hindered for many decades by the dominance of two competing theories of Pentecostal beginnings that identified either white or black origins.[74] Theories on the influence of African slaves or a Black oral liturgy on the predominantly white camp-meeting revivals and the urbanization and subsequent growth of a racially diverse Pentecostalism have not been widely examined.[75] Interracial origins and the diversity of influences within different racial traditions are only recently becoming a topic of study, and the much larger questions of the relationship of particular racial theories of Pentecostal origins to the racial composition of global Pentecostalism are only in their infancy.[76] These deficiencies are compounded by an almost exclusive look at the male leadership in both the white and black Pentecostal communities.[77] The concerns of gender and race have not yet come to occupy a central place in the study of Pentecostalism. The absence of these concerns is a central factor in the persistence of the gender divide and racial segregation. Pentecostal scholarship is only beginning to break free from the influence of institutionalism toward a broader egalitarian profile.

Pentecostal scholarship in its beginnings has been overly dependent on institutional deficiencies in the broader academy. Social theories of Pentecostalism frequently treat the experience of white Pentecostals and men as representative of the entire movement, silencing the experiences of women and the different racial or ethnic voices.[78] The underrepresentation of women and different races and ethnicities in the academic world has contributed to a significant shortage of research related to the issues of gender and race in general. This deficiency has penetrated Pentecostal scholarship in its composition as a still largely male-dominated academy and in the isolation of racially divided theological concentrations and motivations. The results of this situation are particularly visible in the long neglect to identify the Pentecostal gender paradox, even among the populations that experienced substantial Pentecostal growth and those scholars most occupied with gender and family.[79] Pentecostalism also hardly fits in the global analysis of feminism and women's movements.[80] A healthy revision of these areas of scholarship and the recent shift in focus to both Pentecostalism and women is among the most important factors to help Pentecostals understand the tensions of gender in the movement. The growth of Black theology and the increasing significance of African American scholarship promise further egalitarian practices toward racial reconciliation. An increasing number of studies of the socio-theological dynamics in Pentecostal churches worldwide have begun to shed light on the role of gender and race in the everyday life of the movement. The political debates fought over women in positions of official authority and inter-racial leadership positions have begun to alert the wider public to the unresolved tensions in Pentecostalism. Above all, the rise of Pentecostal scholarship worldwide, both as the subject and object of study, has made visible the internal conflicts of the global movement and the importance of contextualizing our under-standing of an egalitarian Pentecostalism in different geographical, cultural, political, and economic settings as a contemporary devel-opment not yet concluded.

Segregated doxology

Pentecostalism has always been characterized as a kinaesthetic movement allowing for the physical expressions of the whole body. Speaking in tongues, prophesying, shouting, singing, dancing, jumping, clapping, swaying, and other physical expressions of worship have penetrated also into the established mainline churches and particularly into modern Evangelicalism.[81] Especially dominant is the penetration of African spirituality and worship across cultures.[82] At the same time, white forms of worship have remained largely isolated and stagnant. The differences are the visible result of institutionalization. At the same time, the doxological divide further perpetuates the divisions of gender and race.

The confrontation of black and white forms of worship in classical Pentecostalism is visible since the pioneering years of the movement. As the rural liturgy of the early camp meetings confronted the Pentecostal revivals in urban North America, external observers and Pentecostals alike joined in criticism of interracial forms of worship.[83] The rejection is apparent not only in the separation of black and white churches but in the isolation of black and white forms of worship that perpetuated a visible separation of a black and white Pentecostalism. As white American Pentecostals returned frequently to dominant Anglo-European forms of worship, African American Pentecostals utilized contem-porary media, technology, and culture to establish themselves as a dominant religious phenomenon. In response, many white congregations have adopted black styles of preaching, praying, and singing, while the black gospel worship of the African American community is hardly influenced by white Pentecostal doxology. It is more unusual to see white Pentecostals in a predominantly black congregation than it is to find black Pentecostals in a predominantly white church. This segregated doxology represents the most visible and potent means of reinforcing the institutional practices of a racially divisive Pentecostalism into the foreseeable future.

The confrontation of worship practices found in North American Pentecostalism has been experienced in a similar manner by the countries that received classical Pentecostal missionaries, particularly those with a history of racial segregation. As a country or region becomes conscious of their indigenous doxology, dominant cultural forms of worship frequently conflict with the racially and ethnically informed practices of missionaries or those now associated with a particular existing minority. Conflicts also arise between culturally dominant forms of Christianity as well as indigenous religious practices that differ from Pentecostal rituals.[84] In turn, the Pentecostal war against many indigenous religions has contributed to further segregation by identifying Pentecostal practices with the behaviour of a select socio-cultural group.[85] Race and ethnicity frequently distinguish different degrees of expressive forms of Pentecostal worship. Those who eventually find together under the roof of a Pentecostal congregation are frequently associated in worship by similarities of gender, race, and class. On the one hand, Pentecostals are divided over the question of how worship as Pentecostals relates to how Pentecostals worship in public.[86] On the other hand, a dominant problem is the mistaking of certain highly visible forms of Pentecostal worship as representative of the whole movement. Pentecostal forms of worship can be perceived as a potential of renewal and reconciliation.[87] However, the accepted patterns of many Pentecostal groups have uncritically enforced many existing tensions in contexts already divided over issues of race.

The doxological separation in terms of gender is often more subtle than the racial divide. While few churches separate female members from all leadership functions, women are typically highly visible and audible in Pentecostal worship, supported by the fact that most congregations consist of a majority of women. In contrast to many of the established traditions, Pentecostals have opened the directing and practising of worship in a variety of ways to women, who lead and engage in worship, prayer, singing,

preaching, witnessing, and many other activities that have little
equivalent in the mainline traditions. At the same time, patriarchal
forms of worship and liturgy also dominate many Pentecostal
forms of worship; patriarchal heritage and male imagery often
used in hymns and songs stand in contrast to the egalitarian ideals.
Although women are allowed to speak, shout, testify, sing, preach,
pray, and prophesy, their voices are not always heard; although
they can be seen, they are not always acknowledged or remembered.
Only recent scholarship has unearthed the significant presence of
women in the history of Pentecostalism and emphasized the loss of
their company from the overwhelming majority of records about
men.[88] In patriarchal cultures where women are rarely seen in the
public square, Pentecostals have not yet resisted the patterns that
allow women as participants but not as leaders in worship.[89] The
prophetic anointing evident among women is allowed to direct
the worship as long as it does not stand in contrast to its priestly
leadership. The divide that separates the two is not always clearly
visible in the separation of pulpit and altar from platform and pew.

Pentecostal doxology encourages a high level of participation; it
is the backbone of egalitarian practices. For most Pentecostals, the
reconciliation of gender and race is ultimately realized in worship.
Consequently, Pentecostals have created a church culture in which
such practices are the foundation and goal of the Christian life. A
realistic view of the Pentecostal movement shows that Pentecostal
spirituality and worldview afford to the practices of worship the
ideals of freedom and liberty to a degree that holds unsurpassed
opportunities for the reconciliation of gender and race. At the same
time, worship is the chief catalyst in the realization of egalitarian
ideals primarily on the grassroots level. The tensions existing
among Pentecostals have hindered this realization throughout
much of the history of the movement. An intellectual basis for the
realization of egalitarian practices has also not yet been established.
These and other less visible elements support incompatible institutional practices that are primarily responsible for maintaining
a conflicting global reality among many Pentecostals communities. Nonetheless, while these insights do not justify bigotry,
injustice, and racism, a closer look at the Pentecostal movement
indicates a tendency toward the reconciliation of gender and race.
The perplexing situation that characterizes Pentecostalism today
justifies its designation as an egalitarian movement in-the-making.

CHAPTER SEVEN

Scholarship and anti-intellectualism

This concluding chapter addresses the intellectual dimension of Pentecostalism: Pentecostal attitudes toward education, pedagogy, and academia, the development of Pentecostal scholarship, and the stereotypes and tensions inherent in the expanding field of Pentecostal studies. Since the late twentieth century, Pentecostalism has garnered increasing attention with the rise of Pentecostal scholarship, the Charismatic Movement among North American universities, the establishment of Pentecostal academic societies and institutions of higher education, and the penetration of different fields of intellectual inquiry by Pentecostal scholars. At the same time, the beginnings of modern-day Pentecostalism also signal a persistent stance of anti-intellectualism, a rejection of higher education and learning, and criticism of the academic world.

Both the alleged anti-intellectualism as well as the growing Pentecostal scholarship have shaped the social face and perception of the movement. On the one hand, Pentecostals are seen as outsiders with no apparent theological tradition, no underlying intellectual system, and no interest in developing and formulating an intellectual structure that compares or contrasts with existing traditions. On the other hand, Pentecostal scholarship seems poised to become a central player in the theological academy. Pentecostals have begun to rescript the movement in its intellectual dimensions beyond the theological disciplines and have entered the humanities and sciences explicitly as Pentecostals. While a persistent anti-intellectualism has neglected to create mechanisms that help in the traditioning of the Pentecostal ethos to subsequent generations, Pentecostal scholarship is forming an emerging tradition that includes the origins of the movement while moving far beyond them. This chapter confronts this contrast of scholarship and anti-intellectualism by outlining first the anti-intellectual ethos and its motivations among classical Pentecostals. The second part of the chapter introduces the still largely uncharted territory of Pentecostal scholarship, its development and current state of affairs. In the concluding part, the tensions of anti-intellectualism and Pentecostal scholarship are brought into dialogue in a conversation about the future of Pentecostal studies. This conversation suggests that Pentecostals are shaping the movement into a holistic tradition that is likely to play a central role in the telling of the intellectual history of the twenty-first century.

Anti-intellectualism in classical Pentecostalism

Pentecostal pioneers hardly appear on the lists of the intellectual elite of their time. We search in vain for an organized Pentecostal scholarship during the first half of the twentieth century. For most of the century, there is no visible attempt to formulate a Pentecostal pedagogy. Most of the first generation of Pentecostals in North America only received a basic education and did not or could not engage in the challenges of continued academic instruction.[1] Apart from Bible schools, there were few attempts to build Pentecostal institutions of higher education, and the limited number of Pentecostal scholars typically received their training at non-Pentecostal schools and universities. Some Pentecostals who pursued scholarly careers felt forced to leave their denominations.[2] Others were reluctant to engage in academic education and professional scholarship altogether or voiced suspicion of the scholastic tendencies in the history of Christianity.[3] From the perspective of post-Enlightenment scientific and academic history, classical Pentecostals (along with the Holiness and Fundamentalist traditions) have been dismissed as a profoundly anti-intellectual movement.[4] In turn, Pentecostals worldwide have not succeeded in correcting this interpretation.[5] On the contrary, the rise of world

Pentecostalism has confirmed the stereotype that Pentecostals in many places possess a 'strong anti-theological, anti-academic prejudice'.[6] This section presents the motivations behind this alleged anti-intellectualism in order to provide a more exact definition of this attitude and identification of the Pentecostal position.

Motivations for anti-intellectualism

The first generations of classical Pentecostals lacked the motivation to engage in intellectual activities and organizations. This is to say that historical sources of early Pentecostals show a passive attitude toward education and scholarship rather than active resistance. Simply put, Pentecostal pioneers were not professional scholars, even though they clearly engaged in the intellectual dimensions of faith. However, these intellectual activities were carried out on an informal level, dependent on the education of a person and the limited resources available. Pentecostal pioneers are therefore more aptly described as 'amateurs' compelled by faith and experience rather than trained writers who obeyed literary rules and scholarly conventions.[7] Pentecostals did not possess a particular educational model. They did not reject the idea of traditioning their beliefs, values, and practices. However, the idea of developing a genuine Pentecostal 'catechesis' was not a concern among the early generations; it was deemed neither necessary nor helpful. Instead, the pursuit of scholarship was often considered a hindrance to the determination shared by Pentecostals that the gospel of salvation was to be proclaimed to a world facing the coming of the kingdom of God.

The determination and urgency felt by Pentecostals in the task of evangelization and mission formed the most immediate context for the amateur status of early Pentecostal scholarship. Many Pentecostals departed almost immediately to other parts of the country or to the mission field abroad in order to preach the gospel, typically without preparation and training.[8] The missionary spirit of these Pentecostals relied heavily on their 'faith' and the experience of the baptism in the Spirit manifested in the speaking with tongues. The latter was frequently interpreted as the gift of foreign languages, which would help Pentecostals to preach the message of salvation to other nations without the need for biblical, theological,

and academic training. Pentecostal publications proclaimed enthusiastically that God had 'given languages to the unlearned'[9] and
equipped the 'simple, unlearned members of the body of Christ'.[10]
This missionary zeal was fuelled by divine revelation rather than
'deep tiresome thinking' that wasted precious time by 'searching'
and 'counting' and 'special study' instead of obtaining the 'deeper,
spiritual experiences' made available through the Holy Spirit.[11] The
critical voices did not dismiss learning and education entirely but
voiced a lack of patience at the prospect of forsaking or postponing
the spread of the gospel as the result of the formal educational
process.[12]

This impatience was closely wedded to the eschatological
mindset among classical Pentecostals and its influence on missionary
practices. Despite the fact that many Pentecostals found themselves
unable to speak the foreign languages they had anticipated, only a
minority returned to their homeland.[13] They simply did not possess
the luxury of time to engage in the formal study of languages,
or for that matter, in theological education. The prospect of
lengthy formal study conflicted with the eschatological urgency of
Pentecostals who had little time to enter into schools and universities at the prospect of Christ's imminent return.[14] Moreover,
Pentecostals not only were convinced about Christ's return but
also believed that the kingdom of God would not arrive until
the gospel had been proclaimed to all nations.[15] The Pentecostal
mission was therefore the evangelization of the world in the power
of the Spirit, words, signs, and wonders that hastened the day of
Christ's coming.[16] Consequently, the missionaries received only
minimal training, often bypassing long-term college or seminary
degree programmes.[17] Even when Bible institutes became more
prominent in the 1920s and 1930s, many Pentecostals went into
the mission field without credentials and formal studies.[18] They did
not reject the intellect or those dedicated to the life of the mind but
questioned the purpose of engaging in such study at this crucial
point in salvation history. The eschatological urgency of the times
demanded immediate engagement with those who had not yet
heard the gospel.

Consequently, Pentecostals saw their anti-intellectual attitude
as a rather pragmatic and appropriate form of the Christian life
during the last days of the world. Emphasis was placed on worship,
witness, and mission rather than preparation, training, and study.[19]

Insisting on the prophethood of all believers, Pentecostals found affirmation in the signs and wonders accompanying their efforts that formal education and long-term training were, at best, not necessary or, at worst, delaying the work of each Christian on behalf of God's kingdom. Under the experience of the baptism with the Holy Spirit, Pentecostals felt sufficiently equipped to do the work of God. This work focused on oral worship and witness rather than written scholarship, research, and study.[20] Schools, if necessary, were designed as 'shortcuts' into the work of evangelization and mission.[21] Pentecostal vocabulary (in sermons, pamphlets, testimonies, hymns, spirituals and other venues) emphasized the immediacy of 'service' in which all believers could and should participate. Others simply lacked the finances, time, and dedication necessary to enrol in colleges and seminaries for an extended period. Continuing education and dedication to the life of the mind were simply not practical aspects of Pentecostal worldview and spirituality.

These indirect forms of resistance to long-term intellectual pursuits were often supplanted by the more direct and negative perception that an intellectualization of the Christian faith was resisting or suppressing the work of the Holy Spirit. The life of the Spirit and the demands of an intellectual career were seen as opposites that do not readily mix.[22] Pentecostals perceive themselves in discontinuity with the history of the church whose institutionalization and intellectualization has displaced the power of the Spirit.[23] For Pentecostals, the Spirit has been driven out of the church and is replaced with a reliance on the intellectual abilities of human beings evidenced in speculative thinking, creeds, doctrines, theories, and criticisms that challenge the gospel and paralyse the faithful.[24] The resulting divisions and schisms continue to form the seedbed for Pentecostal resistance to formal theological education.[25] The latter is typically seen as liberal (in contrast to a biblical conservatism), unbiblical (rejecting especially methods of higher criticism), formal (suppressing the liberty of the Holy Spirit), and out-of-touch with reality (particularly the demands on the mission field). When combined with pragmatic, eschatological, and evangelistic convictions, these criticisms present the most potent challenges to Christian and Pentecostal scholarship.

The nature of Pentecostal anti-intellectualism

Anti-intellectualism was not untypical for nineteenth-century America.[26] However, the nature of Pentecostal anti-intellectualism does not readily fit the historical paradigms and cannot be judged as fundamentally opposed to the life of the mind.[27] Motivated by an evangelistic and eschatological pragmatism that centres on the work of the Holy Spirit, the history of classical Pentecostals exhibits a reluctance to engage in existing forms and institutions of education without thereby rejecting the intellect entirely. Even with the waning of eschatological urgency among contemporary Pentecostals as well as the establishment of Pentecostal schools and the rise of Pentecostal scholarship since the twentieth century, a form of anti-intellectualism persists across the movement primarily as scepticism towards culturally and socially dominant models of Christian pedagogy.

This scepticism toward the intellectual world exists even among Pentecostal scholars, particularly when academic scholarship is associated with an overdependence on the intellect at the cost of involving the entire person in the life of faith. Some scholars have argued that the dominant pedagogical model that connects Christian faith and scholarship advocates a restrictive view of Christian learning and seems ill-fit for Pentecostal concerns.[28] Others suggested, from the opposite perspective, that Pentecostals themselves possess a genuine pedagogy emerging from the Pentecostal worldview and spirituality, which are not easily integrated in the dominant liberal arts curriculum and the research university.[29] Again others have painted this contrast on the bigger canvas of the shift from modernity to postmodernity and portray Pentecostal beliefs and practices as conflicting with the intellectualism and rationalism of the modern world and as more equipped to speak to the postmodern realm.[30] The resulting image is either a rather uneasy relationship of scholarship and Pentecostalism or an opportunity for Pentecostals to enrich the contemporary philosophy of education. On the one hand, Pentecostals are struggling to emancipate themselves from the dominant but ill-fitting educational paradigms; on the other hand, the Pentecostal commitment to signs and wonders could help reform the current world of academic scholarship.[31] The challenges exist for both Pentecostals and the scholarly world: the former must find ways to speak intelligibly to the established traditions, disciplines, and institutions; the latter must learn to take seriously Pentecostal education, scholarship, and praxis.[32] The inherent distinctions between both worlds can be summarized with a few outstanding characteristics.

First, on a foundational level, Pentecostal scholarship arises from the affections rather than intellectual ability. The emphasis on love, passion, desire, feeling, or emotion rejects the sole rule of the intellect while attempting to integrate the right affections (orthopathy) with the right thinking (orthodoxy) and the right practices (orthopraxy).[33] For Pentecostals, orthopathy consists of 'abiding dispositions which dispose the person toward God and the neighbor in ways appropriate to their source and goal in God'.[34] The principle of orthopathy is not intellectual knowledge but the identification, solidarity, and transformation of the human condition in light of the kingdom of God.[35] Pentecostal 'thinking', if that term is appropriate, happens at the affective, unconscious, predeliberative level aimed at witness and worship before it enters the cognitive, deliberate world of understanding.[36] The persistent form of anti-intellectualism does not deny the significance of the intellect, but it rejects its dominance for the full pursuit of knowledge.

Second, and arising from the pursuit of affective knowledge, Pentecostal scholarship is dominated by the imagination rather than reason.[37] Put differently, Pentecostal pedagogy functions on an epistemological level that is aesthetic rather than noetic.[38] This aesthetic is marked by a vision of the world that centres on the manifestation of the Holy Spirit in the world and the interpretation of that world in light of the biblical witness and the community of faith.[39] This Pentecostal hermeneutic 'engages the human being and the world factually, corporeally, relationally, communally, morally, and spiritually'.[40] The imagination stands in contrast to the dominance of reason and order; it is more improvisational, more playful than the productivity, performance, and instrumentality demanded by the established institutions, disciplines, languages, and methodologies of the modern academy.[41] Implicit in the Pentecostal imagination is a sacramentality that both sees reality and looks beyond reality as the necessary presuppositions for engaging this world.[42] Although Pentecostal scholars are deeply committed to a realism that participates in human struggle and suffering, they rarely critique the intellectual world for withdrawal to an ivory-tower mentality.[43] Instead, their critique is directed more explicitly at the pessimism and failure of modern scholarship to speak to the hope and transformation of the world. The Pentecostal 'imagining of the world otherwise'[44] places less trust in purely cognitive knowledge than in participatory 'action-reflection in the Spirit'.[45] Pentecostal anti-intellectualism does not reject the rational pursuit of meaning, but it questions the dominance of reason alone as a proper and sufficient instrument for the discernment of truth.

Third, Pentecostal scholarship operates on the level of oral rather than written discourse. Put differently, Pentecostal scholars operate at the limits of speech and are more comfortable with testimony, stories, songs, preaching, and praise than with the definitions, concepts, theses, systems, philosophies, and methodologies that dominate the world of writing, publishing, and scholarly conversation.[46] The emphasis on orality denotes not a simple preference of oral over written discourse but signals an inherent inability for the Pentecostal imagination to function in the dominant mode of the intellectual world. Pentecostal tongues resist the function and categorization of language(s) and operate in a realm outside of the reality that provides and affirms their meaning.[47] This resistance shapes a rather messy, noisy, and untidy pedagogy when compared to the clean and orderly models of liberal arts and scientific knowledge.[48] Glossolalia are the flagship of the Pentecostal resistance to the dominance of human language and the discourse of meaning. Where the intellect fails to grasp their meaning and purpose, the Pentecostal relies on the affections and the imagination to allow the utterances to stand. Pentecostal anti-intellectualism does not reject human language, but it questions the ability of the human word to capture the world in its manifold dimensions.

The portrayal of Pentecostalism as anti-intellectual is appropriate if such a characterization captures the evangelistic, missionary, pragmatic, and pneumatological emphasis of Pentecostals and places them in contrast to the dominant models of scholarship and learning. Pentecostals cannot be stereotyped as rejecting education, academia, and the intellectual dimensions of life. However, the uneasiness, scepticism, and mostly passive resistance to purely cognitive, rational, and scientific modes of knowing can also not simply be diminished. Less important than placing Pentecostalism among current pedagogical models is the identification of the ethos that forms the heart of Pentecostal 'knowing' in terms of a dynamic, experiential, and relational knowledge.[49] The emphasis on the affections, imagination, and the limits of speech explains not only the anti-intellectual attitude among Pentecostals but also shapes the unprecedented rise of Pentecostal scholarship.

The rise of Pentecostal scholarship

The intellectual history of modern-day Pentecostalism has not yet been written. The first part of this chapter described the beginnings of Pentecostal scholarship in terms of an amateur-status of most Pentecostals at the start of the twentieth century. Professional scholarly publications by Pentecostals did not appear until the 1960s, when the Charismatic Movement swept through many North American universities and began to stir up questions about the relationship of the Spirit-filled life and academic scholarship. Nonetheless, Pentecostals had been active in educational and pedagogical efforts from the early decades of the twentieth century. Largely ignored by mainstream scholarship, Pentecostalism was typically neglected as a subject matter and ridiculed as a dialogue partner. This situation changed dramatically when the 1970s saw an unprecedented increase of Pentecostal scholars, the emergence of Pentecostal studies in the theological academy, the formation of academic societies among Pentecostals, and the establishment of Pentecostal institutions of higher education. In light of the preceding characterization of Pentecostal anti-intellectualism, this section traces the history of the rise of the Pentecostal academy. This portrait is followed by an assessment of the character of Pentecostal scholarship.

The emergence of the Pentecostal academy

The history of Pentecostal scholarship can be divided into five periods of development, each focusing on the formation of a particular vocation: (1) Pentecostal missionaries, (2) Pentecostal historians, (3) Pentecostal biblical scholarship, (4) Pentecostal theologians, and (5) Pentecostal scientists. The first period spans beyond the first half of the twentieth century, the beginnings of historical and biblical scholarship among Pentecostals can be located in the 1970s, theological scholarship arose prominently with the end of the twentieth century, and the entrance of Pentecostals into the human and natural sciences marks the most recent phase of Pentecostal involvement in the academic world.

The origins of Pentecostal scholarship at the beginning of the twentieth century are synonymous with the training of Pentecostal missionaries. Missionary training schools and Bible institutes became dominant in North America during the 1920s and '30s as many Pentecostals leaving the country to evangelize the world found themselves in need of instruction and training.[50] A. B. Simpson's model of the Missionary Training Institute led to the first Bible institute in North America and was enthusiastically embraced by Pentecostals.[51] Pentecostal groups and denominations established so-called Bible Schools, Bible Institutes, Bible Training Schools, Bible Colleges, Bible and Missionary Institutes, and Missionary Training Schools, particularly in urban areas, across the country.[52] Popular institutions, such as Aimee Semple McPherson's Lighthouse of International Foursquare Evangelism (LIFE), trained thousands of missionaries and led the way in raising the standard of education among Pentecostal men and women.[53] The first generations of classical Pentecostals are also the first generations to struggle with the integration of Pentecostal spirituality, pragmatism, and anti-intellectualism in the educational and academic landscape of the twentieth century.

The second phase of Pentecostal scholarship began in the late 1960s with the work of Walter J. Hollenweger.[54] Emerging as probably the foremost authority on worldwide Pentecostalism, Hollenweger published his extensive research while many Pentecostal scholars completed graduate programmes in environments that neglected or obstructed the interaction of critical scholarship and Pentecostal faith and praxis.[55] With his work emerged a wave of Pentecostal historians wishing to preserve the early history of the Pentecostal movement. The remarkable spread of the Charismatic Movement, in particular, encouraged Pentecostals to rediscover their own roots and to confront historiographical models that failed to account for the rise and persistence of modern-day Pentecostalism. These scholars laid the groundwork for Pentecostal archives across the world that today offer countless resources, newspaper articles, pamphlets, letters, sermons, and testimonies narrating the intellectual history among Pentecostals.[56] As a result, Pentecostal historians helped not only to distribute the Pentecostal perspective of the movement's history but also to reformulate dominant historical accounts and thus to reshape the historical disciplines.[57] Descriptive historical studies and social scientific research shifted scholarly attention gradually to the Pentecostal movement worldwide and softened the hard anti-intellectual base of classical Pentecostalism.

A third wave of Pentecostal scholarship surfaced in the 1970s among biblical scholars. These scholars investigated both the biblical sources most relevant to the Pentecostal self-description, particularly Luke-Acts, and the dominant interpretations of such texts. Questions concerning cessationism, dispensationalism, Spirit baptism, and hermeneutics led Pentecostals to discussions genuine to Pentecostal concerns.[58] On the one hand, conservative Evangelical exegesis with the establishment of the historical-critical method as its flagship severely challenged Pentecostal hermeneutics.[59] On the other hand, Pentecostal biblical scholars began to engage in these and other discourses emerging in the circles of the Society for Biblical Literature and challenged the viability of such discourse for the reflection of their own pneumatological focus and charismatic experiences in the biblical texts.[60] This conversation produced a substantial amount of literature on distinctive Pentecostal concerns, including Spirit baptism and speaking in tongues, that helped shape a distinctive Pentecostal hermeneutic in response to both liberalism and fundamentalism.[61] Pentecostal biblical and historical scholarship engaged the wider academy and eventually laid the groundwork for the Society for Pentecostal Studies in North America, the first independent academic society among Pentecostals.[62] Other academic societies followed in Europe (1979), Latin America (1992), Africa (1998), and Asia (1998). These societies contributed significantly to the next wave of an emerging theological scholarship among Pentecostals.

The fourth wave of Pentecostal scholarship began during the 1990s with the emergence of constructive theological research. Beginning with an emphasis on the distinctives of the Pentecostal faith, sometimes cast in the language of apologetics, this generation of scholars has entered the broad range of theological disciplines.[63] Theological scholarship among Pentecostals has developed

a theology of the Spirit-filled life that attempts to integrate the
various distinctive emphases of Pentecostals, such as speaking in
tongues or spiritual gifts, in the broader theological and ecumenical
discussions.[64] In a subsequent development, a new generation of
Pentecostal theologians has begun to reconsider existing doctrines
in a more systematic fashion that include soteriology, ecclesiology,
pneumatology, the doctrine of God, the doctrine of creation,
dialogue with religions, and a theology of culture.[65] These scholars
have begun to suggest explicit ways in which Pentecostal theology
contributes to the theological agenda of the twenty-first century.[66]
The new discussions have led to deliberations on the nature of
Pentecostal theology, in general, and have begun to shape a new
generation of Pentecostal scholarship that goes beyond the traditional historical, biblical, and internal theological conversations.

The fifth and most current wave of Pentecostal scholarship
consists of an expansion into the human and natural sciences.
This generation of scholars coincides with the formulation of a
new rationale for the vitality and future of Pentecostal scholarship
able to overcome the juxtaposing of spirituality and science and
to encourage Pentecostals to enter scientific careers explicitly as
Pentecostals.[67] Pentecostal scholarship has moved into questions of
scientific knowledge and methodology, physics, biology, chemistry,
psychology, medicine, anthropology, sociology, and technology.[68]
In turn, interdisciplinary perspectives, particularly in the social
sciences, humanities, and theology, have engaged Pentecostals in
the broader scholarly conversations.[69] For some, the coming of age
of Pentecostal scholarship necessitates that Pentecostals ultimately
engage in all scientific disciplines; for others, the increasing exposure
of the scientific world to the phenomenon of Pentecostalism has
only just initiated that journey. Both perspectives anticipate significant changes in the nature of Pentecostal scholarship during the
twenty-first century.

The nature of Pentecostal scholarship

Pentecostal scholarship refers to the coexistence as well as the
interpenetration of Pentecostal and scholarly commitments. This
distinction between scholarship *and* Pentecostalism, on the one
hand, and scholarship *as* a Pentecostal, on the other hand, can

be seen across the Pentecostal scholarly world. The number of scholars, academicians, and scientists who are Pentecostal is virtually unknown but promises to be much larger than the number of scholars who deliberately carry out their scholarship as Pentecostals. Many Pentecostal scholars and scientists are hesitant to voice their Pentecostal persuasions in environments that look sceptically at the involvement of religion and science. Others question how scientific instruments and empirical data can benefit from a Pentecostal faith and praxis.[70] At the same time, the global emergence of Pentecostal seminaries, colleges, universities, and centres of higher education promises a shift in public perception, liberal-arts education, and professional and scientific programmes.[71] General assessments of Pentecostal scholarship do not yet exist. Nonetheless, a few elements stand out as defining the character of Pentecostal scholarship during the first century of the Pentecostal movement.

First and foremost, Pentecostal scholarship is experiential. This foundational dimension refers to the central importance of an encounter with the Holy Spirit for the Christian life. Some scholars have therefore described the whole of Pentecostal theology as a theology of encounter.[72] All Pentecostal scholarship can be understood as an attempt 'to articulate this normative encounter with God'[73] in the diverse forms, methods, and vocabulary of the scholarly and scientific communities. The Pentecostal experiences are at the core defined theologically. In disciplines not directly associated with theological inquiry, the experience of the Spirit-filled life often carries over in terms of the Pentecostal worldview and spirituality in general, which are more visible in the motivation for the Pentecostal scholar to pursue a particular vocation than in the measurable forms of pedagogy, research, and writing. On a more visible level, the experience of the Holy Spirit places Pentecostal scholarship at the crossroads of the scientific and theological worlds.[74] The outpouring of the Holy Spirit, when understood in the whole context of creation, directs Pentecostal scholars to pursue a spirit-oriented scholarship in the experimental and empirical worlds of science.[75] While this pneumatological pursuit may not always yield explicit references to the Holy Spirit, it is nonetheless radically informed by the anticipation that the Holy Spirit can be discovered in all of life and thereby directs all of life toward God.

Second, Pentecostal scholarship operates on the principle of play rather than performance. This playful orientation stands in contrast to the performance-oriented and utilitarian categories of traditional scholarship under the tyranny of rationalism, seriousness, and work.[76] Thus, Pentecostal thinking sometimes stands critically over against established scholarly norms and operates on the level of 'pure means' or 'pure self-presentation'.[77] Pentecostal scholarship presents itself as a restlessness caused both by the encounter with God's Spirit in the present and the anticipation of the kingdom of God in which the fullness of life in the Spirit is yet to be fully realized. The playfulness of Pentecostal scholarship in the midst of this restlessness can be seen as the pursuit of 'a way of being that is radically open to divine surprises, always at work resisting obstacles to human flourishing, and committed to creating, broadening, and deepening new possibilities of life'.[78] Put positively, the playfulness of Pentecostal scholarship is the radical consequence of a deliberate dependence on and openness to the divine freedom. Put negatively, playful scholarship does not reject critical reflection, logic, and order but refuses to submit to their exclusive claim of dominance. Instead, the playful dynamic of Pentecostal scholarship embraces the logic of intellectual rigour in the broadest sense as an ethical commitment to conscientization. At the beginning of the twenty-first century, Pentecostal scholarship is still in the process of raising its self-consciousness as a means to engage in the struggle against the structures that hinder human flourishing and direct the human being to God.[79] At the same time, while avoiding becoming submerged in the dominant models of scholarship, Pentecostals are themselves establishing a new consciousness based on the pneumatological focus inherent in their worldview and spirituality.

Third, Pentecostal scholarship is in an important sense always embodied scholarship. For most Pentecostals, this emphasis reflects a going-beyond the mere intellectual pursuit of knowledge to include holistic modes of learning and being. On the one hand, embodied scholarship strives towards interdisciplinary and multidisciplinary inquiry; on the other hand, it reconsiders existing ways of understanding the world, human nature, and the human encounter with God.[80] This interdependence refers both to the influence of embodiment on Pentecostal scholarship and the product of such scholarly efforts. In the simplest terms, embodiment refers to an expressiveness that connects the personal experience with the community, social structure, and human concerns.[81] In the written discourse of modern scholarship, this expressiveness is seen in the evangelistic, inspirational, expository, sermonic, and thematic emphases of many Pentecostal publications that include testimony, exhortation, prayer, praise, and other elements not typical for scholarly conventions.[82] In the more radical sense, embodiment seeks the (often dramatic) expressions of the charismatic life: the prophetic, spontaneous, and unadorned desire to let the Holy Spirit speak through the work of the scholar. While such work seldom receives scholarly recognition from the wider academy, it represents the important desire of Pentecostal scholarship to shed the role of the objective observer for the sake of passionate participation.[83]

Finally, Pentecostal scholarship is based on a comprehensive hermeneutic that in the broadest sense can be characterized as analogical. Pentecostal scholars have more typically spoken of the analogical imagination as a 'this-is-that' hermeneutic.[84] Foundational to this hermeneutic is the interpretation of the present in terms of the past, the Christian life in terms of the biblical texts, and the Pentecostal experience in terms of the story of Pentecost. The principle of analogy defines and correlates the Pentecostal interpretation of Scripture and of the contemporary world.[85] Pentecostal scholarship engages reality, not unlike the apostle Peter, by rejecting dominant perceptions and offering alternative interpretations. The biblical records (Acts 2.15–16) show a two-fold dynamic in Peter's sermon on the day of Pentecost: he rejects the dominant perception of the crowd ('these are not drunk') and offers an alternative interpretation ('this is what was spoken through the prophet Joel').[86] Similarly, Pentecostal scholarship operates on the basis of a hermeneutic that acknowledges the tension between 'this' reality of the human life and 'that' reality of God by suggesting that this relationship can only be expressed as analogy. Such correlation is essential to the theologian as much as to the scientist; both interpret the world in their respective disciplines as a witness to God – even if such analogy fails when the experience of God cannot be correlated to any existing event. The principle of analogy has driven Pentecostals from a primary occupation with internal debates during the early years to an expansion of their scholarship. This expansion also includes the critical evaluation and correction of existing analogies and interpretative models. The integration of the experiential, playful,

embodied, and analogical dimensions of understanding and participating in the world promises to take Pentecostal scholars not
only to various disciplines but to the forefront of the renewal and
revitalization of the academic world.

The future of Pentecostal studies

Pentecostalism shows itself as neither a complete intellectual or
anti-intellectual movement. Although both elements are present
among Pentecostals worldwide, the sole emphasis on either characterization would misrepresent the state of affairs. Moreover, the
perplexing nature of Pentecostalism escapes us if we neglect to
account for the existing tension between anti-intellectualism and
Pentecostal scholarship. The coexistence of both attitudes is representative of the struggle to come to terms with the scope and depth
of the Pentecostal ethos. While this coexistence cannot be easily
reconciled, the dimensions of anti-intellectualism as described in
this chapter shed important light on the future of Pentecostal scholarship. The final section of this chapter presents this prospect with
regard to three intersecting dimensions of the contemporary world
of Pentecostal studies: the groundwork of Pentecostal pedagogy,
Pentecostal scholarship as counter-culture, and the emergence of
Renewal scholarship as a distinct identity of Pentecostal studies.

The groundwork of Pentecostal pedagogy

The study of Pentecostalism shows a struggle among Pentecostals
to find and express a pedagogical model concomitant with the
Pentecostal worldview and spirituality and to integrate such a
model in the dominant Western methodologies that pervade the
academic world. Much of this struggle takes place not in the
academy but in the churches, schools, and homes of Pentecostals.
The battle for a Pentecostal pedagogy is fought not only among
those involved in and seeking higher education but more significantly in the testimonies, conversations, debates, sermons, and
arguments of congregations, which often span the whole breadth
of educational upbringing.

The formation of Pentecostal pedagogy takes place to a large extent in the 'ordinary' world of 'everyday' life, the 'contextual', 'non-academic' and 'lived' world of the 'ground level'.[87] At this level of folk religion, assembled beliefs, values, experiences, and practices connecting individuals and communities, the primary task among Pentecostals remains first of all to accurately observe, interpret, and portray their intellectual history and position. The shaping of a common pedagogy among Pentecostals worldwide emerges largely at the junction of individual efforts relating to congregational life and denominational history and tradition.[88] The groundwork consists above all in a more explicit advocacy among Pentecostal congregations for reason, logic, and education, for theology, the defence of the faith, philosophy, and science.[89] Postgraduate Pentecostal scholarship remains the exception rather than the norm. On the ground, the development of a Pentecostal pedagogy depends on the basic formation of Pentecostal congregations, including the increase of literacy, the institution of continuing education, the diversification of the church curriculum, the building of educational structures and libraries, and the marrying of faith and understanding in the whole of the Christian life.[90]

All of these efforts are in principle a form of conscientization as part of the attempt to build a Pentecostal catechesis on the ground. The most visible struggle of this catechesis remains the integration and transformation of Pentecostal 'amateurism' vis-à-vis the accepted norms of the professional academic world.[91] This transformation emphasizes 'the oral nature of a Pentecostal hermeneutic and the dynamics of Pentecostal liturgy ... a dynamic and active role of the Holy Spirit and ... the full participation of all members of the community of faith'.[92] The result of this unfolding catechesis on the ground is unlikely to be the full intellectualization of Pentecostal faith and praxis but rather the traditioning of a holistic spirituality.[93] In light of the intellectual history of Pentecostalism, catechesis among Pentecostals will exceed mere cognitive transformation toward reflective action.[94] The goal of this groundwork is no more (and no less) than the faithful and critical awareness of and response to God's revelation in the world in all circumstances of life. A scholarly community among Pentecostals will continue to emerge only gradually on this catechetical basis.

Pentecostal scholarship as counter-culture

A conscious and critical Pentecostal catechesis is increasingly visible
in both the gradual integration of Pentecostal scholarship in the
academic world and the continuing resistance to such integration
by Pentecostal scholars. It is inevitable that Pentecostals will
eventually teach and research at the elite universities of the world,
although much of that integration still depends on the cultural
significance of Pentecostalism in particular contexts and the consequent interest of institutions in Pentecostal scholarship. While most
academic institutions are no longer hostile to Pentecostals, many
universities and colleges, not only those affiliated with a particular
religious tradition, invite few Pentecostals to participate in the
broader academic conversations. Similarly, Pentecostal scholars
resist invitations to associate themselves fully with existing institutions that question or contradict the Pentecostal worldview and
spirituality. Pentecostal scholarship retains its counter-cultural
stance in its concerns not only for the content of study but also
for the formation of the scholar, the methods and instruments of
scholarship, and the relevance of the results. The anti-intellectual
dimension of Pentecostal scholarship finds its most potent contemporary expression in this counter-culture.

In popular perception, the speaking with tongues based upon
the broad image of Spirit baptism remains the most significant
counter-cultural practice of Pentecostals.[95] Pentecostal scholarship
as tongue speech may solicit the image of interrupting 'proper'
academic norms and behaviours. Such a perception is not entirely
incorrect. However, Pentecostal scholarship has re-described the
critical function of tongues as a call for an 'affective and embodied
epistemology', 'holistic spirituality', and 'non-reductionistic
worldview'.[96] Where popular Pentecostal language speaks of 'letting
go and letting God', Pentecostal scholarship acknowledges 'the
pretentiousness of the critical scientific mind'.[97] This *via negativa*,
perhaps even deconstructive nature of Pentecostal studies, is the
irrevocable element of Pentecostal spirituality despite its silencing
to often no more than a hidden protest in academic conversations
and publications.[98] The tension between social activism and sectarianism evident among Pentecostals is also reflected in the discrepancy
between those scholars who have become comfortable and those
who remain homeless in the contemporary academic world.[99]

The counter-culture of Pentecostal scholarship speaks to the 'homelessness' of Pentecostal studies. The objectification of knowledge, depersonalization of education, individualization of critical thinking, separation of the subject and object of knowing, anonymity of the academic community, and separation of the academy from church and world are just a few of the reasons held responsible for this dilemma.[100] Underlying the homelessness of Pentecostal scholarship is the fundamental theological commitment of Pentecostals, even in the humanities and social and natural sciences, that sees education itself as a transformative practice in light of the encounter with the Holy Spirit.[101] Where Pentecostals have started to make themselves at home, this critical function of Pentecostal scholarship has become less visible. Explicitly critical Pentecostal scholarship, on the other hand, maintains the personal, pedagogical, and epistemological priority of dependence on the Holy Spirit in all realms of engaging and changing the world.[102] This dependence has carried Pentecostal scholarship out of the realm of internal Pentecostal concerns to diverse multidisciplinary conversations.

From Pentecostal studies to Renewal scholarship

Pentecostal studies has transitioned during the twentieth century from preoccupation with internal concerns, including wide-ranging debates about Spirit baptism, glossolalia, sanctification, Pentecostal distinctives, or church government, to dialogue with constituencies and topics far beyond the original reach. While Pentecostals have not abandoned internal affairs, these discussions have been integrated in and expanded to multidisciplinary and ecumenical conversations. Pentecostal scholarship today can be described as a Spirit-oriented pursuit of the religious, social, political, economic, and scientific dimensions of life and engages with these dimensions on spiritual, experiential, and intellectual grounds. This pursuit has expanded the horizon of Pentecostal scholarship from a church-dominated audience to a dialogue partner with diverse publics in the church, academy, and society. The significant expansion and transition of Pentecostal scholarship has become known in some circles by the term 'Renewal studies'.

Renewal Studies shows both an indebtedness to Pentecostalism
and a drive beyond any narrowly constructed Pentecostal scholarship, in other words, a tendency towards the renewal of
Pentecostalism itself. The underlying motif for Renewal studies is
not Pentecostalism but Pentecost, or more precisely, the renewing
work of the Holy Spirit.[103] The pneumatological motif, exemplified
at Pentecost and in the modern-day Pentecostal movement, refers
to the experiential and theological start with the Spirit that
proceeds to engagement and dialogue with other perspectives and
disciplines and represents a procedure whereby that interaction is
opened up to what the Spirit is saying and where the interpretation
of the Spirit's direction is leading. Thus Renewal studies functions
as an important corrective to Pentecostal scholarship, as a tool
for its assessment as well as an invitation to enter into theoretical,
practical, and theological interaction with other fields.[104] In this
sense, renewal is that counter-critical and prophetic element
within a pneumatological framework that allows the Pentecostal
consciousness to expand in ongoing critical conversation. The
renewal focus is perhaps adequately described as a 'Pentecostal
pneumatology of quest'.[105]

The quest for renewal emerges for Pentecostals from 'a distinctive
modality of Spirit-filled lifelong teaching and learning that has been
the legacy of Pentecostal and Charismatic institutions of higher
education in the twentieth century'.[106] This modality is based on
the existence of many voices, many gifts, many tongues, and many
practices among Pentecostals that seek to engage the world in 'a
polyphonic perspectivalism'.[107] Comfortable with this pluralism of
the late modern world, renewal is for Pentecostals 'a methodology
for inquiry rather than just a subject of teaching and research'.[108]
The focus is not limited to the study of Pentecostalism but open to
a non-sectarian emphasis on the renewing work of the Holy Spirit
in all phenomena of life. This focus is inherently motivated by an
underlying 'Renewal theology'.[109] Yet the centrality of the person
and work of the Holy Spirit that upholds and penetrates this kind
of theology expands the theological emphasis immediately to other
fields of inquiry and thereby challenges the established structures,
tasks, and procedures of modern-day scholarship. Renewal, in this
progressive sense, because of its critical and anti-intellectual under-
tones, is taking Pentecostal scholarship to the frontiers of religion,
science, technology, politics, economics, and other fields.[110] The

result is not only the continuing transformation of Pentecostal studies but the prospect of renewal of contemporary Christian pedagogy and scholarship in the twenty-first century.

EPILOGUE

A conclusion to this brief portrait of the perplexing reality of Pentecostalism would be out of place; it might give the impression that the development of Pentecostalism has in some sense been determined when rather the opposite is true. Pentecostalism has just started. At the beginning of the twenty-first century, we can at best speak of the adolescent years of Pentecostalism, a movement characterized by a perplexing variety of tensions often only in their infancy. Not only historically but also in its worldwide varieties, languages, tongues, beliefs, practices, and experiences, Pentecostalism exhibits different, often contrasting, elements that compete to define the core persuasions of the movement. There are difficulties not only with understanding the depth of these tensions, but also significant disagreements on whether and how these disagreements can be reconciled in order to speak of a single form of Pentecostalism. In light of the various tensions presented in this volume, the labelling of Pentecostalism as a 'movement' remains the most suitable form of its identification.

Pentecostalism has been termed a movement from the early years of the twentieth century, often with reference to what was anticipated as a mere temporary existence. Outsiders to the movement gave Pentecostalism a relatively short lifespan, seeing it as an insignificant repetition of ecstatic religion that is not unusual for Christian history. Insiders typically highlighted the eschatological significance of the movement and viewed Pentecostalism as the final phase before the imminent consummation of the kingdom of God. Both perspectives have been disappointed by the longevity of the movement. Both sides are confounded by the changes and transitions that continue to shape modern-day Pentecostalism.

The reasons for the perplexity of the Pentecostal movement lie in its transitional character. While the designation of Pentecostalism as a 'movement' is often applied to Pentecostalism in its relation to others, the reference to the transitional character of that movement emphasizes that Pentecostalism is itself in movement and thereby continues to be transformed. The term 'Renewal' perhaps best identifies the nature and goal of that transition as a transformation by the Spirit of God. The heart of this identification of Pentecostalism as a Renewal movement is the insight that Pentecostalism by its very nature cannot be static but remains subject to its inherent renewal impetus. As a transitional phenomenon, Pentecostalism at this time can only be captured by embracing the tensions within the movement as identifiers of that transition. Any subjugation of one extreme under another only leads to a biased stereotyping that is perhaps more palatable but does not capture the movement in its fullness.

The designation of Pentecostalism as a Renewal movement avoids any romanticized or triumphalist notion of that definition. If Pentecostalism is a movement, then the direction of that movement is not always altogether clear. The movement travels, so to speak, in different directions, and yet, it is precisely this unbalanced transition that keeps Pentecostalism in movement. Rather than becoming a disjointed phenomenon, Pentecostalism has expanded to include many multifarious elements among its constituencies. The extremes of the Pentecostal movement belong at this point in their development to the nature of Pentecostalism worldwide. The movement as a whole, if such a designation is justified, shows little concern for the existence of such inconsistencies. On the contrary, the unqualified identification of such developments as 'tensions', 'extremes', and 'inconsistencies' betrays a critical perspective foreign to the character of a movement that is comfortable with the playful variations of its perplexing existence.

The extremes of pluralism, charismatic excessiveness, denominationalism, sectarianism, triumphalism, institutionalism, and anti-intellectualism are confronted by the local roots, holistic spirituality, ecumenical ethos, orthodoxy, social engagement, egalitarian practices, and scholarship of the movement. The resulting tensions are not absorbed or cancelled out but held in opposition. In other words, for a movement in transition, as Pentecostalism is best described today, the critical tensions that remain mark the energy of that transition. If measured in this way, Pentecostalism is a movement with a constant tendency to go beyond itself.

A dominant perception maintains that Pentecostalism is primarily, or exclusively, a religious movement. However, the extremes held in opposition by the contemporary movement suggest that the dynamics of Pentecostals worldwide far exceed the religious realm. The perplexities of Pentecostalism identified in the previous chapters represent the struggle of a worldwide movement to identify its place and position in the global Christian landscape. While the tensions identified in this study are among the most visible elements of global Pentecostalism today, some less visible aspects were mentioned only marginally or could not be addressed. Among the tensions that add to the perplexing nature of the Pentecostal movement, but that are only in their early phase of development, is the Pentecostal emphasis on salvation through Christ alone in contrast to the emerging Pentecostal dialogue with other religions or the prominence of supernaturalism in contrast to the developing dialogue with the natural sciences. More specifically theological aspects that also exhibit a perplexing range of contrasting positions include the apolitical or anti-political stance in contrast to an emerging Pentecostal political theology, debates about the theology of creation, and the discussion of the very nature of theology as it is or should be done by Pentecostals. Finally, there are a number of internal tensions that could be added to the picture, including debates about the initial (physical) evidence of Spirit baptism or the nature of sanctification. Adding these tensions to the portrait of modern-day Pentecostalism would only solidify the assessment that Pentecostalism is a movement in transition. Significant for the future of the Pentecostal movement is the extent to which these tensions within Pentecostalism are seen as exemplary of a religious movement and representative of the global state of the Christian world.

The perplexing tensions of Pentecostalism are symptomatic not only for the changing face of the Pentecostal movement but for the dramatic transitions of global Christianity. In this sense, Pentecostalism is merely a representative of the dynamics of the late modern Christian social, cultural, and religious milieu. However, these developments also far exceed the realm of religion and expand ultimately into all dimensions of life. Pentecostalism has become a movement beyond the concerns of religion. Modern-day Pentecostalism is occupied with all questions of human flourishing, understanding, and transformation and engages the religious, social, cultural, political, economic, scientific, and spiritual dimensions of human existence. This characterization may explain much of the bewildering character of the movement and suggests that the immediate future of Pentecostalism will show an even greater variety of perplexities. At the least, those curious to understand Pentecostalism are forced to look beyond the realm of religion. At the end of this brief guide, we arrive at yet one more perplexing insight: To understand Pentecostalism, one has to look beyond Pentecostalism.

NOTES

Chapter One

1   Todd M. Johnson and Brian J. Grim (eds), *World Religion Database: International Religious Demographic Statistics and Sources* (Leiden: Brill, 2008), http://www.worldreligiondatabase. org, accessed April 22, 2012.

2   Pew Forum on Religion and Public Life (ed.), *Spirit and Power: A 10-Country Survey of Pentecostals* (Washington, DC: Pew Research Center, 2006), http://pewforum.org/Christian/Evangelical-Protestant-Churches/Spirit-and-Power.aspx, accessed April 22, 2012.

3   World Christian Database, available at http://www. worldchristiandatabase.org/wcd/, accessed April 22, 2012.

4   Center for the Study of Global Christianity (ed.), 'Christianity 2010: A View from the New Atlas of Global Christianity', *IBMR* 34, no. 1 (2010), pp. 29–36 (36).

5   Patrick Johnstone and Jason Mandryk, *Operation World: 21st Century Edition. Updated and Revised Edition* (Carlisle, UK: Paternoster Press, 2001), p. 3.

6   See Cecil M. Robeck Jr., 'Global and Local', *Christian Century*, 7 March 2006, p. 34.

7   Cf. Hugh Osgood, 'Pentecostalism: Global Trends and Local Adjustments', *JEPTA* 28, no. 1 (2008), pp. 62–75.

8   See Allan Anderson, *An Introduction to Pentecostalism* (Cambridge: Cambridge University Press, 2004), pp. 19–183; Walter J. Hollenweger, *The Pentecostals: The Charismatic Movement in the Churches* (Minneapolis: Augsburg, 1972), pp. 21–6.

9   See Donald E. Miller and Tetsunao Yamamori, *Global Pentecostalism: The New Face of Christian Social Engagement* (Berkeley, CA: The University of Berkeley Press, 2007), pp. 5–7.

10 Hollenweger, *The Pentecostals*, p. 29.

11 See Charles W. Conn, *Like a Mighty Army: The History of the Church of God* (Cleveland, TN: Pathway, 1996), pp. 3–16.

12 Vinson Synan, *The Holiness-Pentecostal Movement in the United States* (Grand Rapids: Eerdmans, 1971), pp. 100–2.

13 Cecil M. Robeck, Jr., *The Azusa Street Mission and Revival: The Birth of the Global Pentecostal Movement* (Nashville: Thomas Nelson, 2006), pp. 87–8.

14 Wolfgang Vondey, *Beyond Pentecostalism: The Crisis of Global Christianity and the Renewal of the Theological Agenda* (PM 3; Grand Rapids: Eerdmans, 2010), pp. 119–29.

15 Eifon Evans, *The Welsh Revival of 1904* (Bridgend, UK: Evangelical Press of Wales, 1969), pp. 190–6.

16 Michael Bergunder, *The South Indian Pentecostal Movement in the Twentieth Century* (Grand Rapids: Eerdmans, 2008), pp. 23–6.

17 Young-hoon Lee, *The Holy Spirit Movement in Korea: Its Historical and Theological Development* (Oxford: Regnum, 2009), pp. 25–33.

18 Ogbu Kalu, *African Pentecostalism: An Introduction* (Oxford: Oxford University Press, 2008), pp. 3–83.

19 *Ibid.*, pp. 41–64.

20 Allan H. Anderson, *African Reformation: African Initiated Christianity in the 20th Century* (Asmara, Eritrea: Africa World Press, 2001), pp. 69–190.

21 Cf. Manuel J. Gaxiola-Gaxiola, 'Latin American Pentecostalism: A Mosaic within a Mosaic', *Pneuma* 13, no. 2 (1991), pp. 107–29; Jean-Pierre Bastian, *Le protestantisme en Amérique Latine: Une approche sociohistorique* (Histoire et société 27; Geneva: Labor et Fides, 1994), pp. 257–70; Mike Berg and Paul Pretiz, *Spontaneous Combustion: Grass-Roots Christianity, Latin American Style* (Pasadena, CA: William Carey Library, 1996).

22 Leonardo Boff, *Ecclesiogenesis: The Base Communities Reinvent the Church,* trans. Robert R. Barr (Maryknoll, NY: Orbis, 1986), pp. 1–9.

23 *Ibid.*, p. 23.

24 Karl-Wilhelm Westmeier, *Protestant Pentecostalism in Latin America: A Study in the Dynamics of Mission* (Madison: Associated University Presses, 1999).

25 Daniel H. Bays, 'Christian Revival in China, 1900–1937', *Modern*

Christian Revivals, (eds) Edith Blumhofer and Randall Balmer (Urbana: University of Illinois Press, 1993), pp. 163–75.

26 Paul Tsuchido Shew, 'History of the Early Pentecostal Movement in Japan: The Roots and Development of the Pre-war Pentecostal Movement in Japan (1907–1945)', unpublished doctoral dissertation (Fuller Theological Seminary, 2003).

27 See the essays in Allan Anderson and Edmond Tang (eds), *Asian and Pentecostal: The Charismatic Face of Christianity in Asia* (Oxford: Regnum, 2005), pp. 177–571.

28 David Martin, *Pentecostalism: The World Their Parish* (Oxford: Blackwell, 2002), p. 67.

29 Cf. Isgard S. Peter, *Der Unsichtbaren Religion auf der Spur: Eine soziologische Studie zur Pfingstbewegung in Deutschland* (Saarbrücken: Verlag Dr. Müller, 2007), pp. 25–59.

30 Hollenweger, *The Pentecostals*, pp. 206–17.

31 Valdis Teraudkalns, 'Pentecostalism in the Baltics: Historical Retrospection', *JEPTA* 21 (2001), pp. 91–108.

32 See Kevin Ranaghan and Dorothy Ranaghan, *Catholic Pentecostals* (New York: Paulist, 1969), pp. 6–106.

33 Miller and Yamamori, *Global Pentecostalism*, pp. 25–8.

34 *NIDPCM*, p. xx.

35 See Wolfgang Vondey, 'The Denomination in Classical and Global Pentecostal Ecclesiology: A Historical and Theological Contribution', in *Denomination: Assessing an Ecclesiological Category*, (eds) Paul M. Collins and Barry Ensign-George (EI 1; London: Continuum, 2011), pp. 100–16.

36 Robeck, *The Azusa Street Mission and Revival*, pp. 214–34.

37 Synan, *The Holiness-Pentecostal Movement*, pp. 33–54.

38 Russel E. Richery, 'Revivalism: In Search of a Definition', *WeslTJ* 28, no. 1 and 2 (1993), pp. 165–75.

39 Robert Mapes Anderson, *Vision of the Disinherited: The Making of American Pentecostalism* (New York: Oxford University Press, 1979), p. 152; Grant Wacker, *Heaven Below: Early Pentecostals and American Culture* (Cambridge: Harvard University Press, 2001), p. 216.

40 Gary B. McGee, *Miracles, Missions, and American Pentecostalism* (Maryknoll, NY: Orbis, 2010), pp. 3–98.

41 Allan Anderson, *Spreading Fires: The Missionary Nature of Early Pentecostalism* (Maryknoll, NY: Orbis, 2007).

42 David D. Daniels, '"Everybody Bids You Welcome": A Multicultural Approach to North American Pentecostalism', in *The Globalization of Pentecostalism: A Religion Made to Travel*, (eds) Murray W. Dempster, Byron D. Klaus, Douglas Petersen (Oxford: Regnum, 1999), pp. 222–58.

43 Vondey, *Beyond Pentecostalism*, pp. 119–29.

44 Daniel E. Albrecht, *Rites in the Spirit: A Ritual Approach to Pentecostal/Charismatic Spirituality* (*JPTSupp* 17; Sheffield: Sheffield Academic Press, 1999).

45 See Vondey, *Beyond Pentecostalism*, pp. 150–8.

46 Susan A. Maurer, *The Spirit of Enthusiasm: A History of the Catholic Charismatic Renewal, 1967–2000* (Lanham, MD: University Press of America, 2010), pp. 36–54.

47 Richard M. Riss, *A Survey of 20th-Century Revival Movements in North America* (Peabody: Hendrickson, 1988), pp. 148–52.

48 See David Wilkerson, *The Cross and the Switchblade* (New York: Random House, 1963).

49 Amos Yong, 'Pentecostalism and the Theological Academy', *TTod* 64, no. 2 (2007), pp. 244–50.

50 See Kilian McDonnell, *Presence, Power, Praise: Documents on the Charismatic Renewal* (3 vols; Collegeville: Liturgical Press, 1980).

51 See Wolfgang Vondey, *Pentecostalism and Christian Unity: Ecumenical Documents and Critical Assessments* (Eugene, OR: Pickwick, 2010).

52 André Droogers, 'Globalisation and Pentecostal Success', in *Between Babel and Pentecost: Transnational Pentecostalism in Africa and Latin America*, (eds) André Corten and Ruth Marshall-Fratani (Bloomington: Indiana University Press, 2001), pp. 41–61.

53 William K. Kay, *Pentecostalism: A Very Short Introduction* (Oxford: Oxford University Press, 2011), pp. 89–105.

54 Miller and Yamamori, *Global Pentecostalism*, pp. 91–4, 135–6.

55 Sturla J. Stålsett (ed.), *Spirits of Globalization: The Growth of Pentecostalism and Experiential Spiritualities in a Global Age* (London: SCM, 2006).

56 See Dempster, Klaus, and Petersen, *The Globalization of Pentecostalism*.

57 See Roland Robertson, *Globalization: Social Theory and Global Culture* (London: Sage, 1992), pp. 49–60.

58   Cf. Birgit Meyer, 'Pentecostalism and Globalization', in *Studying Global Pentecostalism: Theories and Methods*, (eds) Allan Anderson et al. (Berkeley, CA: University of California Press, 2010), pp. 113–30.

59   See Wolfgang Vondey, 'Christian Amnesia: Who in the World Are Pentecostals?' *AJPS* 4, no. 1 (2001), pp. 21–39.

60   Karla Poewe (ed.), *Charismatic Christianity as a Global Culture* (Columbia, SC: University of South Carolina Press, 1994), p. 17.

61   See Jean-Daniel Plüss, 'Globalization of Pentecostalism or Globalization of Individualism? A European Perspective', in Dempster, Klaus, and Petersen, *The Globalization of Pentecostalism*, pp. 170–82.

62   Ivan M. Satyavrata, 'Contextual Perspectives on Pentecostalism as a Global Culture: A South Asian View', *ibid.*, pp. 203–21.

63   Cf. Brian Howell, 'Practical Belief and the Localization of Christianity: Pentecostal and Denominational Christianity in Global Perspective', *Rel* 33 (2003), pp. 233–48.

64   Roland Robertson, 'Glocalization: Time-Space and Homogeneity-Heterogeneity', in *Global Modernities*, (eds) Mike Featherstone, Scott Lash, and Roland Robertson (London: Sage, 1995).

65   Robertson, *Glocalization*, pp. 25–8.

66   See Robertson, *Globalization*, pp. 50–7.

67   Meyer, 'Pentecostalism and Globalization', pp. 113–30 (114–16).

68   Ogbu U. Kalu, 'Changing Tides: Some Currents in World Christianity at the Opening of the Twenty-First Century', in *Interpreting Contemporary Christianity: Global Processes and Local Identities*, (eds) Ogbu U. Kalu and Alaine M. Low (Grand Rapids: Eerdmans, 2008), pp. 3–23; Ruth Marshall-Fratani, 'Mediating the Global and Local in Nigerian Pentecostalism', in Corten and Marshall-Fratani, *Between Babel and Pentecost*, pp. 80–105.

69   See the essays on Pentecostal mobility in *PentecoStudies* 9, no. 2 (2010), pp. 145–250; Corten and Marshall-Fratani, *Between Babel and Pentecost*, pp. 124–308; Kalu and Low, *Interpreting Contemporary Christianity*, pp. 207–316.

70   Michael Bergunder, 'Pfigstbewegung, Globalisierung und Migration', in *Migration und Identität: Pfingstlich-charismatische Migrationsgemeinden in Deutschland* (Frankfurt: Otto Lembeck, 2006), pp. 155–69.

71   Cf. David Martin, *Tongues of Fire: The Explosion of Protestantism in Latin America* (Oxford: Blackwell, 1993), p. 122.

72   Margaret Poloma, 'A Reconfiguration of Pentecost', in *'Toronto' in Perspective: Papers on the New Charismatic Wave of the Mid 1990s*, (ed.) David Hilborn (Carlisle, UK: ACUTE, 2001), pp. 123–5.

73   See Robertson, *Globalization*, pp. 164–81.

74   See Veli-Matti Kärkkäinen (ed.), *The Spirit in the World: Emerging Pentecostal Theologies in Global Contexts* (Grand Rapids: Eerdmans, 2009), xiii–xx.

Chapter Two

1   See Martin William Mittelstadt, *Reading Luke–Acts in the Pentecostal Tradition* (Cleveland, TN: CPT Press, 2010).

2   See Donald Dayton, *The Theological Roots of Pentecostalism* (Peabody: Hendrickson, 1998), pp. 19–22.

3   See Frank D. Macchia, *Baptized in the Spirit: A Global Pentecostal Theology* (Grand Rapids: Zondervan, 2006).

4   Roger Stronstad, *The Charismatic Theology of St. Luke* (Grand Rapids: Baker, 1984), pp. 75–82.

5   See Robert P. Menzies, *Empowered for Mission: The Spirit in Luke–Acts*, (*JPTSupp* 2; Sheffield: Sheffield Academic Press, 1995).

6   See J. D. G. Dunn, *Baptism in the Holy Spirit: A Re-examination of the New Testament Teaching on the Gift of the Spirit in Relation to Pentecostalism Today* (London: SCM, 1970).

7   See Wolfgang Vondey, *Beyond Pentecostalism: The Crisis of Global Christianity and the Renewal of the Theological Agenda* (PM 3; Grand Rapids: Eerdmans, 2010), pp. 16–46.

8   See Amos Yong, 'The Spirit Hovers over the World: Toward a Typology of "Spirit" in the Religion and Science Dialogue', *Digest* 4, no. 12 (2004), n. p.

9   Grant Wacker, *Heaven Below: Early Pentecostals and American Culture* (Cambridge: Harvard University Press, 2001), pp. 87–98.

10   See Emmanuel Kingsley Larbi, 'The Nature of Continuity and Discontinuity of the Ghanaian Pentecostal Concept of Salvation in African Worldview', *AJPS* 5, no. 1 (2002), pp. 87–106.

11   Macchia, *Baptized in the Spirit*, p. 281.

12   See Stephen E. Parker, *Led by the Spirit: Toward a Practical Theology of Pentecostal Discernment and Decision Making* (*JPTSupp* 7; Sheffield: Sheffield Academic Press, 1996).

13 Steven Jack Land, *Pentecostal Spirituality: A Passion for the Kingdom* (*JPTSupp* 1; Sheffield: Sheffield Academic Press, 1993), pp. 136–61.

14 For this distinction see Ralph Del Colle, 'The Holy Spirit: Presence, Power, Person', *TS* 62, no. 2 (2001), pp. 322–40.

15 See Margaret M. Poloma, *Main Street Mystics: The Toronto Blessing and Reviving Pentecostalism* (Walnut Creek, CA: AltaMira, 2003).

16 See Veli-Matti Kärkkäinen (ed.), *The Spirit in the World: Emerging Pentecostal Theologies in Global Contexts* (Grand Rapids: Eerdmans, 2009).

17 Cf. Keith Warrington, *Pentecostal Theology: A Theology of Encounter* (London: T & T Clark, 2008), pp. 206–45.

18 See Jon Ruthven, *On the Cessation of the Charismata: The Protestant Polemic on Postbiblical Miracles* (*JPTSupp* 3; Sheffield: Sheffield Academic Press, 1993).

19 See S. M. Horton, *What the Bible Says about the Holy Spirit* (Springfield, MO: Gospel Publishing House, 1976), p. 208.

20 Land, *Pentecostal Spirituality*, pp. 119–21.

21 See David K. Bernard, *Spiritual Gifts* (Hazelwood: Word Aflame, 1997); Max Turner, *The Holy Spirit and Spiritual Gifts* (Peabody: Hendrickson, 1996); Arnold Bittlinger, *Gifts and Ministries*, trans. Clara K. Dyck (Grand Rapids: Eerdmans, 1973).

22 Amos Yong, *The Spirit Poured Out on All Flesh: Pentecostalism and the Possibility of Global Theology* (Grand Rapids: Baker Academic, 2005), pp. 294–6.

23 See Francis A. Sullivan, *Charisms and Charismatic Renewal: A Biblical and Theological Study* (Ann Arbor: Servant Books, 1982); Donald Bridge and David Phypers, *Spiritual Gifts and the Church* (Downers Grove: InterVarsity, 1973).

24 See Robert G. Gromacki, *The Modern Tongues Movement* (Philadelphia: Presbyterian and Reformed Publishing Company, 1972).

25 See Clarke Garrett, *Spirit-Possession and Popular Religion: From the Camisards to the Shakers* (Baltimore: John Hopkins University Press, 1987).

26 See Horace S. Ward, 'The Anti-Pentecostal Argument', in *Aspects of Pentecostal-Charismatic Origins*, (ed.) Vinson Synan (Plainfield, NJ: Logos International, 1975), pp. 99–122.

27 Ward, 'The Anti-Pentecostal Argument', pp. 99–122.

28 Vinson Synan, *The Holiness-Pentecostal Movement in the United States* (Grand Rapids: Eerdmans, 1971), pp. 141–5.

29 Richard Quebedeaux, *The New Charismatics: The Origins, Development and Significance of Neo-Pentecostalism* (New York: Doubleday, 1976).

30 O. Talmadge Spence, *Charismatism: Awakening of Apostasy?* (Greenville, NC: Bob Jones University Press, 1978), p. vii.

31 See Hank Hanegraaff, *Counterfeit Revival: Looking for God in All the Wrong Places* (Dallas: Word Publishing, 1997).

32 John F. MacArthur, Jr., *Charismatic Chaos* (Grand Rapids: Zondervan, 1992).

33 *Ibid.*, p. 130.

34 Hakon J. Stolee, *Speaking in Tongues* (Minneapolis: Augsburg, rev. edn, 1963), pp. 75–93.

35 Poloma, *Main Street Mystics*, pp. 59–85.

36 David W. Cloud, *The Laughing Revival: From Azusa to Pensacola* (Oak Harbor, WA: Way of Life Literature, 1998), pp. 91–119.

37 See the essays in David Hilborn, *'Toronto' in Perspective: Papers on the New Charismatic Movement of the 1990s* (Exeter, UK: Paternoster, 2001), pp. 3–127.

38 Hugh F. Pyle, *The Truth about Tongues and the Charismatic Movement* (Murfreesboro, TN: Word of the Lord, 1989), pp. 11–25.

39 Cf. Peter Mullen, *Strange Gifts? A Guide to the Charismatic Movement* (Oxford: Basil Blackwell, 1984), pp. 97–106.

40 Robert Mapes Anderson, *Vision of the Disinherited: The Making of American Pentecostalism* (New York: Oxford University Press, 1979), pp. 156–7.

41 *Ibid.*, p. 157.

42 See Vinson Synan, 'The Role of Tongues as Initial Evidence', in *Spirit and Renewal: Essays in Honor of J. Rodman Williams*, (ed.) Mark W. Wilson, (*JPTSupp* 5; Sheffield: Sheffield Academic Press, 1994), pp. 67–82.

43 *Ibid.*, pp. 75–8.

44 Gerard Roelofs, 'Charismatic Christian Thought: Experience, Metonymy, and Routinization', in *Charismatic Christianity as a Global Culture*, (ed.) Karla Poewe (Columbia, SC: University of South Carolina Press, 1994), pp. 217–33.

45 See Kilian McDonnell, *Presence, Power, Praise: Documents on the Charismatic Renewal* (3 vols; Collegeville: Liturgical Press, 1980).

46 James C. Logan, 'Controversial Aspects of the Movement', in *The Charismatic Movement*, (ed.) Michael P. Hamilton (Grand Rapids: Eerdmans, 1975), pp. 33–46.

47 Cf. Allan H. Anderson, 'Stretching the Definitions? Pneumatology and "Syncretism" in African Pentecostalism', *JPT* 10, no. 1 (2001), pp. 98–119.

48 Ogbu Kalu, *African Pentecostalism: An Introduction* (Oxford: Oxford University Press, 2008), pp. 171–3.

49 Julie C. Ma, 'Santuala: A Case of Pentecostal Syncretism', *AJPS* 3, no. 1 (2000), pp. 61–82.

50 Doongsoo Kim, 'The Healing of *Han* in Korean Pentecostalism', *JPT* 15 (1999), pp. 123–39.

51 Mark R. Mullins, 'Japanese Pentecostalism and the World of the Dead: A Study of Cultural Adaptation in Iesu no Mitama Kyōkai', *Japanese Journal of Religious Studies* 17, no. 4 (1990), pp. 353–74.

52 See Vondey, *Beyond Pentecostalism*, pp. 171–201.

53 See Stefan Huber and Odilo W. Huber, 'Psychology of Religion', in *Studying Global Pentecostalism: Theories and Methods*, (eds) Allan Anderson et al. (Berkeley: University of California Press, 2010), pp. 133–55; Steven A. Gritzmacher, Brian Bolton, and Richard H. Dana, 'Psychological Characteristics of Pentecostals: A Literature Review and Psychodynamic Synthesis', *Journal of Psychology and Theology* 16 (1988), pp. 233–45.

54 Huber and Huber, 'Psychology of Religion', pp. 133–55 (135).

55 See William K. Kay, 'The Mind, Behavior and Glossolalia – A Psychological Perspective', in *Speaking in Tongues: Multi-Disciplinary Perspectives*, (ed.) Mark J. Cartledge (Milton Keynes: Paternoster, 2006), pp. 174–205.

56 Cf. Gritzmacher, Bolton, and Dana, 'Psychological Characteristics', pp. 233–45 (234).

57 See Kilian McDonnell, *Charismatic Renewal and the Churches* (New York: Seabury, 1976), pp. 79–109.

58 Huber and Huber, 'Psychology of Religion', pp. 133–55 (136–40).

59 *Ibid.*, 135; Gritzmacher, Bolton, and Dana, 'Psychological Characteristics', pp. 233–45 (235).

60 Cf. Huber and Huber, 'Psychology of Religion', pp. 133–55 (140–51).

61   *Ibid.*, p. 141.

62   Cf. Yong, *The Spirit Poured Out on All Flesh*, p. 28; Vondey, *Beyond Pentecostalism*, pp. 16–46.

63   Cf. James K. A. Smith, *Thinking in Tongues: Pentecostal Contributions to Christian Philosophy* (PM 1; Grand Rapids: Eerdmans, 2010), pp. 22–31.

64   Amos Yong, *Spirit-Word-Community: Theological Hermeneutics in Trinitarian Perspective* (Eugene, OR: Wipf and Stock, 2002), pp. 123–49.

65   *Ibid.*, p. 134.

66   Cf. Leon-Joseph Suenens, *Renewal and the Powers of Darkness* (Malines Document 4; Ann Arbor: Servant Books, 1983), pp. 57–9; Amos Yong, 'The Demonic in Pentecostal/Charismatic Christianity and in the Religious Consciousness of Asia', in *Asian and Pentecostal: The Charismatic Face of Christianity in Asia*, (eds) Allan Anderson and Edmond Tang (Oxford: Regnum Books International, 2005), pp. 93–128.

67   See Opal L. Reddin (ed.), *Power Encounter: A Pentecostal Perspective* (Springfield, MO: Central Bible College Press, rev. edn, 1999) and C. Peter Wagner, *Confronting the Powers* (Ventura, CA: Regal Books, 1996).

68   Cf. Land, *Pentecostal Spirituality*, pp. 119–21.

69   See Amos Yong, 'Spiritual Discernment: A Biblical-Theological Reconsideration', in *The Spirit and Spirituality: Essays in Honor of Russel P. Spittler,* (eds) Wonsuk Ma and Robert P. Menzies (*JPTSupp* 24; London: T. & T. Clark, 2004), pp. 83–107.

70   *Ibid.*, p. 102.

71   Cf. Parker, *Led by the Spirit*, pp. 20–38.

72   *Ibid.*, p. 37.

73   Yong, *Spirit-Word-Community*, p. 197.

74   Cf. *ibid.*, pp. 164–75.

75   Albrecht, *Rites in the Spirit*, pp. 196–208.

76   Vondey, *Beyond Pentecostalism*, pp. 109–40.

Chapter Three

1   See Wolfgang Vondey (ed.), *Pentecostalism and Christian Unity: Ecumenical Documents and Critical Assessments* (Eugene, OR: Pickwick, 2010).

2   Cf. Wolfgang Vondey, 'Pentecostalism and Ecumenism', in Cecil M. Robeck, Jr., and Amos Yong (eds), *The Cambridge Companion to Pentecostalism* (Cambridge: Cambridge University Press, 2012).

3   See Walter J. Hollenweger, *Pentecostalism: Origins and Development Worldwide* (Peabody, MA: Hendrickson, 1997), pp. 334–400.

4   Donald W. Dayton, *Theological Roots of Pentecostalism* (Peabody, MA: Hendrickson, 1987), pp. 23–8.

5   Charles W. Conn, *Like a Mighty Army: A History of the Church of God, Definitive Edition* (Cleveland, TN: Pathway, 1996), pp. 12–14.

6   William J. Seymour, 'The Apostolic Faith Movement', *AF* 1, no. 1 (1906), p. 2.

7   Frank Bartleman, *Azusa Street* (South Plainfield, NJ: Bridge Publishing, 1925, repr. 1980), p. 68.

8   Thomas B. Barratt, *In the Days of the Latter Rain* (London: Simpkin, Marshall, Hamilton, Kent & Co. Ltd., 1909), p. 145. Emphasis original.

9   See Cornelis van der Laan, *Sectarian against His Will: Gerrit Roelof Polman and the Birth of Pentecostalism in the Netherlands* (SiE 11; London: Scarecrow, 1991), p. 268.

10 *Ibid.*, pp. 105–30; Hollenweger, *Pentecostalism*, pp. 334–49.

11 Cf. Douglas Jacobsen, 'The Ambivalent Ecumenical Impulse in Early Pentecostal Theology in North America', in Vondey, *Pentecostalism and Christian Unity*, pp. 3–19.

12 Cecil M. Robeck, Jr., 'The Challenge Pentecostalism Poses to the Quest for Ecclesial Unity', in *Kirche in ökumenischer Perspektive: Kardinal Walter Kasper zum 70. Geburtstag*, (eds) Peter Walter, Klaus Krämer, and George Augustin (Freiburg: Herder, 2003), pp. 306–20.

13 Richard Shaull and Waldo Cesar, *Pentecostalism and the Future of the Christian Churches: Promises, Limitations, Challenges* (Grand Rapids: Eerdmans, 2000).

14 Carmelo E. Álvarez, 'Joining the World Council of Churches:

The Ecumenical Story of Pentecostalism in Chile', in Vondey, *Pentecostalism and Christian Unity*, pp. 35–43.

15 See Christian Churches Together in the USA at http://www.christianchurchestogether.org, accessed April 22, 2012.

16 Paul van der Laan, 'Guidelines for Ecumenical Dialogue with Pentecostals: Lessons from the Netherlands', in Vondey, *Pentecostalism and Christian Unity*, pp. 46–65; Jerry L. Sandidge, *Roman Catholic/Pentecostal Dialogue (1977–82): A Study in Developing Ecumenism*, vol. 1 (Frankfurt: Peter Lang, 1986), pp. 352–59.

17 Frank Macchia, 'From Azusa to Memphis: Evaluating the Racial Reconciliation Dialogue among Pentecostals', *Pneuma* 17, no. 2 (1995), pp. 203–18.

18 Allan H. Anderson and Walter J. Hollenweger (eds), *Pentecostals after a Century: Global Perspectives on a Movement in Transition* (*JPTSupp* 13; Sheffield: Sheffield Academic Press, 1999), pp. 33–107.

19 Allan H. Anderson, 'The Struggle for Unity in Pentecostal Mission Churches', *Journal of Theology for Southern Africa* 82 (1993), pp. 67–77.

20 Cf. Wolfgang Vondey, 'Presuppositions for Pentecostal Engagement in Ecumenical Dialogue', *JMER* 30, no. 4 (2001), pp. 344–58.

21 See Vondey, *Pentecostalism and Christian Unity*, pp. 101–98; Sandidge, *Roman Catholic/Pentecostal Dialogue*, I:60–279.

22 Cecil M. Robeck, Jr., 'Lessons from the International Roman Catholic-Pentecostal Dialogue', in Vondey, *Pentecostalism and Christian Unity*, pp. 82–98.

23 Hollenweger, *Pentecostalism*, pp. 377–84.

24 Huibert van Beek, *A Handbook of Churches and Councils: Profiles of Ecumenical Relationships* (Geneva: World Council of Churches, 2006).

25 See Vondey, *Pentecostalism and Christian Unity*, pp. 199–227.

26 Institute for Ecumenical Research (ed.), *Lutherans and Pentecostals in Dialogue* (Strasbourg: Institute for Ecumenical Research, 2010), pp. 7–21.

27 Huibert van Beek (ed.), *Revisioning Christian Unity: The Global Christian Forum* (SGC; Oxford: Regnum, 2009).

28 See Center for the Study of Global Christianity (ed.), 'Christianity

2010: A View from the New Atlas of Global Christianity', *IBMR* 34, no. 1 (2010), pp. 29–36.

29 See Todd M. Johnson and Brian J. Grim (eds), *World Religion Database: International Religious Demographic Statistics and Sources* (Leiden: Brill, 2008).

30 World Christian Database, available at http://www. worldchristiandatabase.org/wcd/, accessed April 22, 2012.

31 Jacobsen, 'The Ambivalent Ecumenical Impulse', pp. 3–19.

32 Cf. Wolfgang Vondey, 'Appeal for a Pentecostal Council for Ecumenical Dialogue,' *Mid-Stream* 40, no. 3 (2001), pp. 45–56.

33 Cf. Robeck, 'Lessons from the International Catholic-Pentecostal Dialogue', pp. 82–98.

34 Grant Wacker, 'Playing for Keeps: The Primitivist Impulse in Early Pentecostalism', in *The American Quest for the Primitive Church*, (ed.) Richard T. Hughes (Urbana: University of Illinois Press, 1988), pp. 196–219.

35 D. William Faupel, *The Everlasting Gospel: The Significance of Eschatology in the Development of Pentecostal Thought* (*JPTSupp* 10; Sheffield: Sheffield Academic Press, 1996), pp. 44–76.

36 Veli-Matti Kärkkäinen, '"Anonymous Ecumenists?" Pentecostals and the Struggle for Christian Identity', *JES* 37, no. 1 (2000), pp. 13–27.

37 Robert Mapes Anderson, *Vision of the Disinherited: The Making of American Pentecostalism* (New York: Oxford University Press, 1979), pp. 192–4.

38 Cecil M. Robeck Jr., 'The Assemblies of God and Ecumenical Cooperation 1920–1965,' in *Pentecostalism in Context: Essays in Honor of William W. Menzies*, (eds) Wonsuk Ma and Robert P. Menzies (*JPTSupp* 11; Sheffield: Sheffield Academic Press, 1997), pp. 107–50.

39 Cf. Vondey, 'The Denomination in Classical and Global Pentecostal Ecclesiology: A Historical and Theological Contribution', in *Denomination: Assessing an Ecclesiological Category*, (eds) Paul M. Collins and Barry Ensign-George (*EI* 11; London: Continuum, 2011), pp. 100–16.

40 See Vondey, *Beyond Pentecostalism*, pp. 146–50.

41 Cf. Allan Anderson, *Spreading Fires: The Missionary Nature of Early Pentecostalism* (London: SCM Press, 2007).

42 Cf. Vondey, *Beyond Pentecostalism*, p. 155.

43 Faupel, *The Everlasting Gospel*, pp. 187–227.

44 Cf. Vinson Synan, *The Holiness-Pentecostal Movement in the United States* (Grand Rapids: Eerdmans, 1971), pp. 77–93.

45 Vondey, *Beyond Pentecostalism*, pp. 155–7.

46 Cf. Anderson, *Vision of the Disinherited*, pp. 192–4.

47 *Ibid.*, p. 194.

48 Cf. Kärkkäinen, 'Anonymous Ecumenists', pp. 15–18.

49 Vondey, *Beyond Pentecostalism*, pp. 1–15.

50 Cf. Veli-Matti Kärkkäinen, *An Introduction to Ecclesiology: Ecumenical, Historical and Global Perspectives* (Downers Grove: InterVarsity, 2002), pp. 68–78.

51 Vondey, 'Presuppositions for Pentecostal Engagement', pp. 344–58.

52 Cf. Frank D. Macchia, 'The Nature and Purpose of the Church: A Pentecostal Reflection on Unity and *Koinonia*', in Vondey, *Pentecostalism and Christian Unity*, pp. 243–55.

53 See 'Perspectives on *Koinonia*. Final Report of the Dialogue between the Roman Catholic Church and Some Classical Pentecostal Churches and Leaders, 1985–1989', in Vondey, *Pentecostalism and Christian Unity*, pp. 133–58.

54 Macchia, 'The Nature and Purpose of the Church', pp. 243–55.

55 'Perspectives on *Koinonia*', pp. 150–3.

56 Wolfgang Vondey, 'Pentecostal Perspectives on *The Nature and Mission of the Church*: Challenges and Opportunities for Ecumenical Transformation', in *Receiving 'The Nature and Mission of the Church': Ecclesial Reality and Ecumenical Horizons for the Twenty-First Century*, (eds) Paul M. Collins and Michael A. Fahey (*EI* 1; London: Continuum, 2008), pp. 55–68.

57 Kärkkäinen, 'An Exercise on the Frontiers of Ecumenism: Almost Thirty Years of Roman Catholic-Pentecostal Dialogue', *JMER* 29, no. 2 (2000), pp. 156–71.

58 See Melvin Hodges, *A Theology of the Church and Its Mission: A Pentecostal Perspective* (Springfield, MO: Gospel Publishing House, 1977).

59 Heribert Mühlen, 'Kirche in Bewegung – keine neue Bewegung in der Kirche', *Erneuerung in Kirche und Gesellschaft* 2 (1977), pp. 22–5.

60 Cf. Miroslav Volf, *After Our Likeness: The Church as the Image of the Trinity* (Grand Rapids: Eerdmans, 1998).

61   *Ibid.*, pp. 228–33.

62   See Daniel E. Albrecht, *Rites in the Spirit: A Ritual Approach
      to Pentecostal/Charismatic Spirituality* (*JPTSupp* 17; Sheffield:
      Sheffield Academic Press, 1999).

63   Bobby C. Alexander, 'Pentecostal Ritual Reconsidered:
      Anti-Structural Dimensions of Possession', *JRitS* 3, no. 1 (1989),
      pp. 109–28.

64   Cf. Amos Yong, *The Spirit Poured Out on All Flesh: Pentecostalism
      and the Possibility of Global Theology* (Grand Rapids: Baker
      Academic, 2005), pp. 121–66.

65   Cf. Vondey, 'The Denomination in Classical and Global Pentecostal
      Ecclesiology', pp. 100–16.

66   See Heribert Mühlen, *Una Mystica Persona: Die Kirche als das
      Mysterium der heilsgeschichtlichen Identität des Heiligen Geistes
      in Christus und den Christen; Eine Person in vielen Personen*
      (Paderborn: Schöningh, 1967), pp. 74–172.

Chapter Four

1   See 'Oneness-Trinitarian Pentecostal Final Report, 2002–2007',
     Pneuma 30, no. 2 (2008), pp. 203–24 (nos. 9 and 10).

2   Cf. Wolfgang Vondey, *Beyond Pentecostalism: The Crisis of Global
     Christianity and the Renewal of the Theological Agenda* (PM 3;
     Grand Rapids: Eerdmans, 2010), pp. 78–108.

3   See Dale M. Coulter, 'The Development of Ecclesiology in the
     Church of God (Cleveland): A Forgotten Contribution?' *Pneuma*
     29, no. 1 (2007): pp. 64–7.

4   See Martin William Mittelstadt, *Reading Luke-Acts in the
     Pentecostal Tradition* (Cleveland, TN: CPT Press, 2010), pp. 18–43.

5   See Shane Clifton, 'The Spirit and Doctrinal Development: A
     Functional Analysis of the Traditional Pentecostal Doctrine of the
     Baptism in the Holy Spirit', *Pneuma* 29, no. 1 (2007), pp. 5–23.

6   Cf. Joseph Randall Guthrie, 'Pentecostal Hymnody: Historical,
     Theological, and Musical Influences', unpublished D. MA.
     Dissertation (Southwestern Baptist Theological Seminary, 1992),
     pp. 29–88.

7   See Steven Jack Land, *Pentecostal Spirituality: A Passion for the
     Kingdom* (*JPTSupp* 1; Sheffield: Sheffield Academic Press, 1993),
     pp. 32–47.

8   Cf. Simon Chan, 'The Church and the Development of Doctrine',
    JPT 13, no. 1 (2004), pp. 57–77.

9   See Christopher A. Stephenson, 'The Rule of Spirituality and
    the Rule of Doctrine: A Necessary Relationship in Theological
    Method', *JPT* 15, no. 1 (2006), pp. 83–105.

10 See Jean-Daniel Plüss, *Therapeutic and Prophetic Narratives in
    Worship: A Hermeneutic Study of Testimony and Visions* (Bern:
    Peter Lang, 1988).

11 Cf. Amos Yong, *The Spirit Poured Out on All Flesh: Pentecostalism
    and the Possibility of Global Theology* (Grand Rapids: Baker
    Academic, 2005), pp. 91–8.

12 Cf. Donald W. Dayton, *Theological Roots of Pentecostalism*
    (Peabody, MA: Hendrickson, 1987), pp. 19–23.

13 See Yong, *The Spirit Poured Out on All Flesh*, p. 28.

14 'Jesus Saves', *Evangel Songs* (Springfield, MO: Gospel Publishing
    House, 1931), p. 68.

15 Henry Date (ed.), *Pentecostal Hymns* (Chicago: Hope Publishing,
    1894), p. 111.

16 S. L. Flowers and C. B. Widmeyer, *Songs of the Pentecostal Flame*
    (Boulder, CO: Flowers Publishing, 1910), p. 46.

17 Land, *Pentecostal Spirituality*, pp. 59–60.

18 *Ibid.*, p. 32.

19 See Ralph Del Colle, 'Spirit-Christology: Dogmatic Foundations
    for Pentecostal-Charismatic Spirituality', *JPT* 3 (1993),
    pp. 91–112.

20 See Richard Shaull and Waldo Cesar, *Pentecostalism and the Future
    of the Christian Churches: Promises, Limitation, Challenges* (Grand
    Rapids: Eerdmans, 2000), pp. 184–92.

21 'Breathe upon Us', *Evangel Songs*, p. 92.

22 Cf. Del Colle, 'Spirit-Christology', pp. 91–112.

23 'Send the Fire', *Evangel Songs*, p. 41.

24 Frank D. Macchia, *Baptized in the Spirit: A Global Pentecostal
    Theology* (Grand Rapids: Zondervan, 2006), p. 89.

25 *Ibid.*, pp. 113–29.

26 Talmadge L. French, *Our God Is One: The Story of the Oneness
    Pentecostals* (Indianapolis: Voice and Vision, 1999), pp. 227–34,
    253–83.

27 *Ibid.*, pp. 127–58.

28   See Gregory Boyd, *Oneness Pentecostals and the Trinity* (Grand Rapids: Baker, 1992).

29   Cf. William B. Chalfant, *Ancient Champions of Oneness* (Hazelwood, MO: Word Aflame, 1981), pp. 137–48.

30   David K. Bernard, *Oneness and Trinity, A.D. 100-300: The Doctrine of God in Ancient Christian Writings* (Hazelwood, MO: Word Aflame, 1991), pp. 165–74.

31   David K. Bernard, *The Trinitarian Controversy in the Fourth Century* (Hazelwood, MO: Word Aflame, 1993), pp. 9–23.

32   David K. Bernard, 'The Future of Oneness Pentecostalism', in *The Future of Pentecostalism in the United States*, (eds) Eric Patterson and Edmund Rybarczyk (Lanham: Lexington Books, 2007), pp. 123–36, at 123.

33   Bernard, *Oneness and Trinity*, pp. 121–8.

34   See William B. Chalfant, 'The Fall of the Ancient Apostolic Church', in *Symposium on Oneness Pentecostalism, 1988 and 1990* (Hazelwood, MO: Word Aflame, 1990), pp. 351–85.

35   See David K. Bernard, *The Oneness View of Jesus Christ* (Hazelwood, MO: Word Aflame, 1994).

36   David A. Reed, *'In Jesus' Name': The History and Beliefs of Oneness Pentecostals* (JPTSupp 31; Blandford Forum, UK: Deo Publishing, 2008), pp. 227–306.

37   Daniel L. Butler, *Oneness Pentecostalism: A History of the Jesus Name Movement* (Bellflower, CA: International Pentecostal Church, 2004), pp. 89–90.

38   Cf. Vondey, *Beyond Pentecostalism*, pp. 88–98.

39   Bernard, *The Oneness View of Jesus Christ*, p. 16.

40   'Oneness-Trinitarian Pentecostal Final Report', no. 42.

41   *Ibid.*, no. 37.

42   Gordon Magee, *Is Jesus in the Godhead or Is the Godhead in Jesus?* (Hazelwood, MO: Word Aflame, 1988), p. 25.

43   'Oneness-Trinitarian Pentecostal Final Report', no. 39.

44   David K. Bernard, *Understanding the Articles of Faith: An Examination of United Pentecostal Beliefs* (Hazelwood, MO: Word Aflame, 1992), p. 27.

45   'Oneness-Trinitarian Pentecostal Final Report', no. 40.

46   See Bernard, *The Oneness of God*, pp. 128–9.

47   See *ibid.*, pp. 182–3.

48 *Ibid.*, p. 184.

49 *Ibid.*, p. 185.

50 *Ibid.*, p. 196.

51 French, *Our God Is One*, p. 206.

52 See the responses to the report in *Pneuma* 30, no. 2 (2008), pp. 225–69.

53 See Keith Warrington, *Pentecostal Theology: A Theology of Encounter* (London: T&T Clark, 2008), pp. 17–27; Miller and Yamamori, *Global Pentecostalism*, pp. 129–59.

54 Cf. Vondey, *Beyond Pentecostalism*, pp. 98–103.

55 Cf. Warrington, *Pentecostal Theology*, pp. 20–7.

56 See Yong, *The Spirit Poured Out on All Flesh*, pp. 83–91.

57 'Oneness-Trinitarian Pentecostal Final Report', pp. 206–7.

58 Reed, *'In Jesus' Name'*, p. 352.

59 See Ralph Del Colle, 'Oneness and Trinity: A Preliminary Proposal for Dialogue with Oneness Pentecostalism', *JPT* 10 (1997), pp. 85–110.

60 Reed, *'In Jesus' Name'*, pp. 9–68.

61 See Jeff Astley, *Ordinary Theology: Looking, Listening and Learning in Theology* (Surrey, UK: Ashgate, 2002).

62 See Mark J. Cartledge, *Testimony in the Spirit: Rescripting Ordinary Pentecostal Theology* (Surrey, UK: Ashgate, 2010), pp. 15–18.

63 Arlene M. Sanchez-Walsh, 'Christology from Latino/a Perspective: Pentecostalism', in *Jesus in the Hispanic Community: Images of Christ from Theology to Popular Religion*, (eds) Harold J. Recinos and Hugo Magallanes (Louisville, KY: Westminster John Knox, 2009), pp. 92–104.

64 *Ibid.*, pp. 94–102.

65 Sammy Alfaro, *Divino Compañero: Toward a Hispanic Pentecostal Christology* (Eugene, OR: Pickwick, 2010), pp. 94–114.

66 See Clifton R. Clarke, *African Christology: Jesus in Post-Missionary African Christianity* (Eugene, OR: Pickwick, 2011).

67 *Ibid.*, pp. 172–3.

68 Cf. Ogbu Kalu, *African Pentecostalism: An Introduction* (Oxford: Oxford University Press, 2008), pp. 249–69.

69 Clarke, *African Christology*, pp. 130–68.

70 See Thomas A. Smail, *The Forgotten Father* (Grand Rapids: Eerdmans, 1980).

71 See Del Colle, 'Spirit-Christology', pp. 91–112.

72 Amos Yong, *Spirit-Word-Community: Theological Hermeneutics in Trinitarian Perspective* (Eugene, OR: Wipf and Stock, 2002), pp. 119–217.

73 *Ibid.*, p. 316.

74 *Ibid.*, p. 254.

75 See Veli-Matti Kärkkäinen (ed.), *The Spirit in the World: Emerging Pentecostal Theologies in Global Contexts* (Grand Rapids: Eerdmans, 2009).

76 See Michael Welker (ed.), *The Work of the Spirit: Pneumatology and Pentecostalism* (Grand Rapids: Eerdmans, 2006).

77 See James K. A. Smith and Amos Yong (eds), *Science and the Spirit: A Pentecostal Engagement with the Sciences* (Bloomington: Indiana University Press, 2010); Amos Yong (ed.), *The Spirit Renews the Face of the Earth: Pentecostal Forays in Science and Theology of Creation* (Eugene, OR: Pickwick, 2009).

78 Cf. Telford Work, 'The Science Division: Pneumatological Relations and Christian Disunity in Theology-Science Dialogue', *Zygon* 43, no. 4 (2008), pp. 897–908.

79 Amos Yong, 'Reading Scripture and Nature: Pentecostal Hermeneutics and Their Implications for the Contemporary Evangelical Theology and Science Conversation', *JASA* 63, no. 1 (2011), pp. 3–15.

80 Cf. Yong, *The Spirit Poured Out on All Flesh*, pp. 292–302.

81 Chan, 'The Church and the Development of Doctrine', pp. 57–77.

Chapter Five

1 See Robert Mapes Anderson, *Vision of the Disinherited: The Making of American Pentecostalism* (Oxford: Oxford University Press, 1979).

2 Cf. David Martin, *Pentecostalism: The World Their Parish* (Oxford: Blackwell, 2002), pp. 1–27.

3 See Cecil Bradfield, *Neo-Pentecostalism: A Sociological Assessment* (Lanham, MD: University Press of America, 1979), pp. 1–17.

4 David Martin, *Tongues of Fire: The Explosion of Protestantism in Latin America* (Oxford, UK: Blackwell, 1990), pp. 163–268.

5   Cf. Donald E. Miller and Tetsunao Yamamori, *Global Pentecostalism: The New Face of Christian Social Engagement* (Berkeley, CA: The University of Berkeley Press, 2007), pp. 31–4.

6   Todd M. Johnson and Brian J. Grim (eds), *World Religion Database: International Religious Demographic Statistics and Sources* (Leiden: Brill, 2008), available at http://www.worldreligiondatabase.org, accessed April 22, 2012.

7   United Nations Development Program (ed.), *Human Development Report 2010: The Real Wealth of Nations. Pathways to Human Development* (New York: UNDP, 2010), pp. 161–3.

8   See Robert D. Woodberry, 'Pentecostalism and Economic Development', in *Markets, Morals and Religion*, (ed.) Jonathan B. Imber (New Brunswick, NJ: Transaction, 2008), pp. 157–77.

9   World Christian Database, available at http://www.worldchristiandatabase.org/wcd/, accessed April 22, 2012.

10   *Ibid.*

11   This is the focus of Miller and Yamamori, *Global Pentecostalism.*

12   Anderson, *Vision of the Disinherited*, pp. 223–40.

13   *Ibid.*, p. 152.

14   Cf. Virginia H. Hine, 'The Deprivation and Disorganization Theories of Social Movements', in *Religious Movements in Contemporary America*, (eds) Irving I. Zaretsky and Mark P. Leone (Princeton: Princeton University Press, 1974), pp. 646–61.

15   Veli-Matti Kärkkäinen, 'Are Pentecostals Oblivious to Social Justice? Theological and Ecumenical Perspectives', *MIR* 24, no. 4 (2001), pp. 417–31.

16   See John Loftland and Rodney Stark, 'Becoming a World-Saver: A Theory of Religious Conversion', *ASR* 30, no. 6 (1965), pp. 862–74.

17   Luther P. Gerlach and Virginia H. Hine, *People, Power, Change: Movements of Social Transformation* (Indianapolis: Bobbs-Merrill, 1970), pp. xxii–xxiii.

18   Martin, *Tongues of Fire*, pp. 271–95.

19   Miller and Yamamori, *Global Pentecostalism*, pp. 41–3.

20   Helen S. Dyer, *Pandita Ramabai: The Story of Her Life* (New York: Fleming H. Revell, 1900).

21   Clementia Butler, *Pandita Ramabai Sarasvati: Pioneer in the Movement for the Education of the Child-Widow of India* (New York: Fleming H. Revell, 1922).

22 Cf. Allan Anderson, *Spreading Fires: The Missionary Nature of Early Pentecostalism* (London: SCM Press, 2007), pp. 75–102.

23 Rebecca Samuel Shah and Timothy Samuel Shah, 'How Evangelicanism—Including Pentecostalism—Helps the Poor: The Role of Spiritual Capital', in *The Hidden Form of Capital: Spiritual Influences in Societal Progress*, (eds) Peter L. Berger and Gordon Redding (London: Anthem Press, 2010), pp. 61–90.

24 Cf. David Martin, *Pentecostalism: The World Their Parish*, pp. 132–52.

25 Ogbu Kalu, *African Pentecostalism: An Introduction* (Oxford: Oxford University Press, 2008), pp. 211–12.

26 See Sandy Johnston, *Under the Radar: Pentecostalism in South Africa and Its Potential Social and Economic Role* (Johannesburg: Centre for Development and Enterprise, 2008).

27 Lawrence Schlemmer, *Dormant Capital: Pentecostalism in South Africa and Its Potential Social and Economic Role* (Johannesburg: Centre for Development and Enterprise, 2008).

28 Roger Southall and Stephen P. Rule, *Faith on the Move: Pentecostalism and Its Potential Contribution to Development* (Johannesburg: Centre for Development and Enterprise, 2008).

29 Kalu, *African Pentecostalism*, pp. 213–17.

30 John Burdick, 'Struggling against the Devil: Pentecostalism and Social Movements in Urban Brazil', in *Rethinking Protestantism in Latin America*, (eds) Virginia Garrard-Burnett and David Stoll (Philadelphia: Temple University Press, 1993), pp. 20–44.

31 R. Andrew Chesnut, *Born Again in Brazil: The Pentecostal Boom and the Pathogens of Poverty* (New Brunswick, NJ: Rutgers University Press, 1997), pp. 104–7; Cecilia Loreto Mariz, *Coping with Poverty: Pentecostals and Christian Base Communities in Brazil* (Philadelphia: Temple University Press, 1994), pp. 95–100.

32 Mariz, *Coping with Poverty*, pp. 101–51.

33 Rowan Ireland, *Kingdoms Come: Religion and Politics in Brazil* (Pittsburgh: University of Pittsburgh Press, 1991), pp. 93–108.

34 See Frans H. Kamsteeg, *Prophetic Pentecostalism in Chile: A Case Study on Religion and Development Policy* (Lanham, MD: Scarecrow Press, 1998), pp. 169–227.

35 *Ibid.*, pp. 229–48.

36 See Frans Kamsteeg, 'Pentecostalism and Political Awakening

in Pinochet's Chile and Beyond', in *Latin American Religion in Motion*, (ed.) Christian Smith and Joshua Prokopy (New York: Routledge, 1999), pp. 187–204.

37 Kamsteeg, *Prophetic Pentecostalism*, pp. 182–5.

38 Cf. Amos Yong, *In the Days of Caesar: Pentecostalism and Political Theology* (Grand Rapids: Eerdmans, 2010), pp. 3–38.

39 See Martin, *Tongues of Fire*, pp. 237–45; Cornelia Butler Flora, *Pentecostalism in Columbia: Baptism by Fire and Spirit* (Cranberry, NJ: Associated University Presses, 1976), pp. 204–29.

40 Cf. Omar M. McRoberts, *Streets of Glory: Church and Community in a Black Urban Neighborhood* (Chicago: The University of Chicago Press, 2003), pp. 100–21.

41 Miller and Yamamori, *Global Pentecostalism*, pp. 99–128.

42 See Gordon D. Fee, *The Disease of the Health and Wealth Gospel* (Beverly, MA: Frontline, 1985).

43 Cf. Milmon F. Harrison, *Righteous Riches: The Word Faith Movement in Contemporary African American Religion* (Oxford: Oxford University Press, 2005), pp. 3–19, 134–58.

44 Harrison, *Righteous Riches*, pp. 134–7.

45 *Ibid.*, pp. 138–40.

46 Stephanie Y. Mitchem, *Name It and Claim It? Prosperity Preaching in the Black Church* (Cleveland: Pilgrim, 2007), pp. 104–17.

47 Ogbu U. Kalu, 'Black Joseph: Early African American Charismatic and Pentecostal Linkages and Their Impact on Africa', in *Afro-Pentecostalism: Black Pentecostal and Charismatic Christianity in History and Culture*, (eds) Amos Yong and Estrelda Alexander (New York: New York University Press, 2011), pp. 209–32 (228).

48 See Asonzeh F.-K. Ukah, '"Those Who Trade with God Never Lose": The Economics of Pentecostal Activism in Nigeria', in *Christianity and Social Change in Africa: Essays in Honor of J. D. Y. Peel, (ed.) Toyin Falola* (Durham, NC: Carolina Academic Press, 2005), pp. 253–74.

49 Cf. David Maxwell, *African Gifts of the Spirit: Pentecostalism and the Rise of a Zimbabwean Transnational Religious Movement* (Oxford: James Currey, 2006), pp. 217–18.

50 Rijk van Dijk, 'The Pentecostal Gift: Ghanaian Charismatic Churches and the Moral Influence of the Global Economy', in *Modernity on a Shoestring: Dimensions of Globalization,*

Consumption and Development in Africa and Beyond, (eds) Richard Fardon, Wim van Binsbergen, Rijk van Dijk (Leiden: EIDOS, 1999), pp. 71–89.

51 Cf. Tabona Shoko, 'Healing in Hear the Word Ministries Pentecostal Church Zimbabwe', in *Global Pentecostalism: Encounters with Other Religious Traditions,* (ed.) David Westerlund (London: I. B. Tauris, 2009), pp. 43–55.

52 Jean-Pierre Olivier de Sardan, 'African Corruption in the Context of Globalization', in Fardon, Binsbergen, van Dijk, *Modernity on a Shoestring,* pp. 247–68.

53 Katharine L. Wiegele, *Investing in Miracles: El Shaddai and the Transformation of Popular Catholicism in the Philippines* (Honolulu: University of Hawaii Press, 2005).

54 *Ibid.,* pp. 80–104.

55 *Ibid.,* pp. 142–69.

56 Sung-Gun Kim, 'Pentecostalism, Shamanism and Capitalism within Contemporary Korean Society', in *Spirits of Globalization: The Growth of Pentecostalism and Experiential Spiritualities in a Global Age,* (ed.) Sturla J. Stålsett (London: SCM, 2006), pp. 23–38.

57 Yong-gi Hong, "Encounter with Modernity: The McDonaldization and the Charismatization of Korean Mega-churches', *IRM* 92, no. 365 (2003), pp. 239–55.

58 Cf. George Ritzer, *The McDonaldization of Society* (Thousand Oaks, CA: Pine Forge Press, 1996; rev. (ed.)).

59 See the dedicated issue, 'Prosperity Theology and the Theology of Suffering', *ERT* 20, no. 1 (1996), pp. 3–94.

60 Bong Rin Ro, 'South Korea: Bankrupting the Prosperity Gospel', *CT* 42, no. 13 (1998), pp. 58–61.

61 Cf. David Lehmann, *Struggle for the Spirit: Religious Transformation and Popular Culture in Brazil and Latin America* (Cambridge, MA: Blackwell, 1996), pp. 205–7.

62 See Ari Pedro Oro and Pablo Séman, 'Brazilian Pentecostalism Crosses National Borders', in *Between Babel and Pentecost: Transnational Pentecostalism in Africa and Latin America,* (eds) André Corten and Ruth Marshall-Fratani (Bloomington: Indiana University Press, 2001), pp. 181–95.

63 Richard Shaull and Waldo Cesar, *Pentecostalism and the Future of the Christian Churches: Promises, Limitations, Challenges* (Grand Rapids: Eerdmans, 2000), pp. 28–31.

64 Yong, *In the Days of Caesar*, pp. 17–18.

65 Berge Furre, 'Crossing Boundaries: The "Universal Church" and the Spirit of Globalization', in Stålsett, *Spirits of Globalization*, pp. 39–51.

66 *Ibid.*, p. 46.

67 See Manuel Silva, 'A Brazilian Church Comes to New York', *Pneuma* 13, no. 2 (1991), pp. 161–5.

68 D. R. McDonnell, *A Different Gospel: A Historical and Biblical Analysis of the Modern Faith Movement* (Peabody, MA: Hendrickson, 1995), pp. 3–14.

69 Robert M. Bowman Jr., *The Word-Faith Controversy: Understanding the Health and Wealth Gospel* (Grand Rapids: Baker, 2001), pp. 57–84.

70 See E. W. Kenyon, *The Father and His Family: The Story of Man's Redemption* (Lynnwood, WA: Kenyon's Gospel Publishing Society, 1937).

71 E. W. Kenyon, *Identification: A Romance in Redemption* (Lynnwood, WA: Kenyon's Gospel Publishing Society, 1941).

72 Cf. Douglas Jacobsen, *Thinking in the Spirit: Theologies of the Early Pentecostal Movement* (Bloomington, IN: Indiana University Press, 2003), pp. 348–52.

73 E. W. Kenyon, *The Wonderful Name of Jesus*, 20th (ed.) (Lynnwood, WA: Kenyon's Gospel Publishing Society, 1964).

74 *Ibid.*, pp. 69–70.

75 Andrew Perriman (ed.), *Faith, Health and Prosperity: A Report on 'Word of Faith' and 'Positive Confession' Theologies by ACUTE* (Carlisle, UK: Paternoster, 2003), p. 34.

76 *Ibid.*, pp. 35–41.

77 Cf. Bruce Barron, *The Health and Wealth Gospel* (Downers Grove, IL: InterVarsity, 1987), pp. 108–11.

78 Harrison, *Righteous Riches*, pp. 10–11.

79 See Candy Gunther Brown (ed.), *Global Pentecostal and Charismatic Healing* (Oxford: Oxford University Press, 2011).

80 See Kimberly Ervin Alexander, *Pentecostal Healing: Models in Theology and Practice* (*JPTSupp* 29; Blandford Forum, UK: Deo, 2006).

81 Miller and Yamamori, *Global Pentecostalism*, pp. 149–54.

82 Cf. J. N. Horn, *From Rags to Riches: An Analysis of the Faith*

Movement and Its Relation to the Classical Pentecostal Movement (Pretoria: University of South Africa, 1989), pp. 85–112.

83   See Mitchem, Name It and Claim It?, pp. 37–103.

84   Perriman, Faith, Health and Prosperity, pp. 209–35.

85   Yong, In the Days of Caesar, pp. 265–8.

86   Horn, From Rags to Riches, pp. 1–68.

87   Anderson, Vision of the Disinherited, pp. 209–10.

88   Anderson, Spreading Fires, pp. 31–5.

89   Cf. D. William Faupel, The Everlasting Gospel: The Significance of Eschatology in the Development of Pentecostal Thought (JPTSupp 10; Sheffield: Sheffield Academic Press, 1996), pp. 307–9.

90   See Horn, From Rags to Riches, pp. 69–84.

91   David D. Daniels III, '"Doing All the Good We Can": The Personal Witness of African American Holiness and Pentecostal Churches in the Post-Civil Rights Era', in New Day Begun: African American Churches and Civic Culture in Post-civil Rights America, (ed.) R. Drew Smith (Durham, NC: Duke University Press, 2003), pp. 164–82.

92   David D. Daniels III, 'Navigating the Territory: Early Afro-Pentecostalism as a Movement within Black Civil Society', in Yong and Alexander, Afro-Pentecostalism, pp. 43–62.

93   Cf. Cheryl J. Sanders, Saints in Exile: The Holiness-Pentecostal Experience in African American Religion and Culture (New York: Oxford University Press, 1996).

94   Harrison, Righteous Riches, pp. 131–46.

95   See Cheryl J. Sanders, Empowerment Ethics for a Liberated People: A Path to African American Social Transformation (Minneapolis: Fortress, 1995).

96   Omar M. McRoberts, 'Understanding the "New" Black Pentecostal Activism: Lessons from Ecumenical Urban Ministries in Boston', SOR 60, no. 1 (1999), pp. 47–70.

97   McRoberts, Streets of Glory, pp. 100–21.

98   See Eldin Villafañe, The Liberating Spirit: Towards an Hispanic American Pentecostal Social Ethic (Grand Rapids: Eerdmans, 1993), pp. 1–132.

99   See E. L. Wilson and Jesse Miranda, 'Hispanic Pentecostalism', in NIDPCM, pp. 715–23.

100   Cf. Sidney Verba, Key Lehman Schlozman, Henry E. Brady (eds),

Voice and Equality: Civic Volunteerism in American Politics (Cambridge, MA: Harvard University Press, 1995).

101 See Gastón Espinosa, Virgilio Elizondo, Jesse Miranda, *Hispanic Churches in American Public Life: Summary of Findings* (Notre Dame, IN: Institute for Latino Studies at the University of Notre Dame, 2003).

102 Gastón Espinosa, 'Latino Clergy and Churches in Faith-Based Political and Social Action in the United States', in *Latino Religions and Civic Activism in the United States*, (eds) Gastón Espinosa, Virgilio Elizondo, Jesse Miranda (Oxford: Oxford University Press, 2005), pp. 279–306.

103 *Ibid.*, pp. 289–93.

104 Cf. Daniel Ramírez, 'Public Lives in American Hispanic Churches: Expanding the Paradigm', in Espinosa, Elizondo, Miranda, *Latino Religions*, pp. 177–95.

105 Espinosa, 'Latino Clergy and Churches', pp. 279–306.

106 See Paul Alexander, *Peace to War: Shifting Allegiances in the Assemblies of God* (Telford, PA: Cascadia, 2009); Charles W. Conn, *Like a Mighty Army: A History of the Church of God 1886-1995* (Cleveland, TN: Pathway Press, 1990), pp. 71–193.

107 Marion Dearman, 'Christ and Conformity: A Study of Pentecostal Values', *JSSR* 13, no. 4 (1974), pp. 437–53.

108 *Ibid.*, p. 454.

109 See John Jefferson Davis, *Evangelical Ethics: Issues Facing the Churches Today* (Phillipsburg, NJ: Presbyterian & Reformed Publishing Co., 3rd edn, 2004).

110 Martin, *Pentecostalism*, pp. 169–76.

111 *Ibid.*, p. 169.

112 *Ibid.*, 169.

113 See Miller and Yamamori, *Global Pentecostalism*, pp. 184–210.

114 Martin, *Pentecostalism*, p. 170.

115 Yong, *In the Days of Caesar*, pp. 109–11.

116 *Ibid.*, p. 110.

117 *Ibid.*, pp. 121–358.

118 *Ibid.*, p. 360.

119 Cf. Vondey, *Beyond Pentecostalism*, pp. 182–91.

120 See Helene Slessarev-Jamir, *Prophetic Activism: Progressive*

Religious Justice Movements in Contemporary America (New York: New York University Press, 2011).

121 *Ibid.*, pp. 22–6.

122 Cf. Nimi Wariboko, *The Pentecostal Principle: Ethical Methodology in New Spirit* (PM 5; Grand Rapids: Eerdmans, 2011).

Chapter Six

1 Cf. Albert G. Miller, 'Pentecostalism as a Social Movement: Beyond the Theory of Deprivation', *JPT* 9 (1996), pp. 97–114; Christian Lalive d'Epinay, *Haven of the Masses: A Study of the Pentecostal Movement in Chile* (London: Lutterworth, 1969).

2 See Stephen Hunt, 'Sociology of Religion', in *Studying Global Pentecostalism: Theories and Methods*, (eds) Allan Anderson et al. (Berkeley, CA: University of California Press, 2010), pp. 179–201.

3 Cf. Amos Yong, *The Spirit Poured Out on All Flesh: Pentecostalism and the Possibility of Global Theology* (Grand Rapids: Baker Academic, 2005), pp. 88–9.

4 See Wolfgang Vondey, *People of Bread: Rediscovering Ecclesiology* (New York: Paulist Press, 2008), pp. 141–94.

5 Matthias Wenk, *Community-Forming Power: The Socio-ethical Role of the Spirit in Luke-Acts* (JPTSupp 19; Sheffield: Sheffield Academic Press, 2000).

6 Cecil M. Robeck, Jr., *The Azusa Street Mission and Revival: The Birth of the Global Pentecostal Movement* (Nashville: Thomas Nelson, 2006), pp. 4–15.

7 Cf. D. William Faupel, *The Everlasting Gospel: The Significance of Eschatology in the Development of Pentecostal Thought* (JPTSupp 10; Sheffield: Sheffield Academic Press, 1996), pp. 187–227.

8 Gary B. McGee, *Miracles, Missions, and American Pentecostalism* (Maryknoll, NY: Orbis, 2010), pp. 101–18.

9 See Donald E. Miller and Tetsunao Yamamori, *Global Pentecostalism: The New Face of Christian Social Engagement* (Berkeley, CA: The University of Berkeley Press, 2007), pp. 39–128.

10 Yong, *The Spirit Poured Out on All Flesh*, pp. 292–301.

11 Cf. Miller and Yamamori, *Global Pentecostalism*, pp. 184–210.

12 Cf. Roger Stronstad, 'The Prophethood of All Believers: A Study in

Luke's Charismatic Theology', in *Pentecostalism in Context: Essays in Honor of William W. Menzies*, (eds) Wonsuk Ma and Robert P. Menzies (*JPTSupp* 11; Sheffield: Sheffield Academic Press, 1997), pp. 60–77.

13   See part 2 of, 'We Are the Church: New Congregationalism', in *Pentecostal Movements as an Ecumenical Challenge*, (eds) Jürgen Moltmann and Karl-Josef Kuschel (*Concilium* 3; London: SCM Press, 1996), pp. 17–44.

14   See Frank Macchia, 'Tongues as a Sign: Towards a Sacramental Understanding of Pentecostal Experience', *Pneuma* 15, no. 1 (1993), pp. 61–76.

15   Cf. Arnold Bittlinger (ed.), *The Church is Charismatic: The World Council of Churches and the Charismatic Renewal* (Geneva: World Council of Churches, 1981).

16   See Charles H. Barfoot and Gerald T. Sheppard, 'Prophetic vs. Priestly Religion: The Changing Role of Women Clergy in Classical Pentecostal Churches', *RevRR* 22, no. 1 (1980), pp. 2–17.

17   Harold Wells, 'Resistance to Domination as a Charism of the Holy Spirit', in *Spirits of Globalization: The Growth of Pentecostalism and Experiential Spiritualities in a Global Age*, (ed.) Sturla J. Stålsett (London, SCM, 2006), pp. 172–82.

18   See Allan H. Anderson and Gerald J. Pillay, 'The Segregated Spirit: The Pentecostals', in *Christianity in South Africa: A Political, Social, and Cultural History*, (eds) Richard Elphick and Rodney Davenport (Berkeley: University of California Press, 1997), pp. 227–41.

19   See T. S. Samuel Kutty, *The Place and Contribution of Dalits in Select Pentecostal Churches in Central Kerala from 1922 to 1972* (Delhi: ISPCK, 2000).

20   Roswith I. H. Gerloff, *A Plea for British Black Theologies: The Black Church Movement in Britain in Its Transatlantic Cultural and Theological Interaction with Special Reference to the Pentecostal (Oneness-) and Sabbatarian Movements*, vol. 1 (Frankfurt: Peter Lang, 1992), pp. 255–70.

21   David D. Daniels III, 'Navigating the Territory: Early Afro-Pentecostalism as Movement within Black Civil Society', in *Afro-Pentecostalism: Black Pentecostal and Charismatic Christianity in History and Culture*, (eds) Amos Yong and Estrelda Alexander (New York: New York University Press, 2011), pp. 43–62.

22 Frank Bartleman, *Azusa Street: The Roots of Modern-Day Pentecostalism* (Plainfield, NJ: Logos International, 1925; repr. 1980), p. 54.

23 See Frank Macchia, 'From Azusa to Memphis: Evaluating the Racial Reconciliation Dialogue among Pentecostals', *Pneuma* 17, no. 2 (1995), pp. 203–18.

24 *Ibid.*, pp. 215–18.

25 Andrea Hollingsworth and Melissa D. Browning, 'Your Daughters Shall Prophesy (As Long as They Submit): Pentecostalism and Gender in Global Perspective', in *A Liberating Spirit: Pentecostals and Social Action in North America*, (eds) Michael Wilkinson and Steven M. Studebaker (Eugene, OR: Pickwick, 2010), pp.161–84.

26 Cheryl Townsend Gilkes, 'The Role of Women in the Sanctified Church', *JRT* 43 (1986), pp. 24–41.

27 See Michael Bergunder and Jörg Haustein (eds), *Migration und Identität: Pfingstlich-charismatische Migrationsgemeinden in Deutschland* (Frankfurt: Otto Lembeck, 2006).

28 See Elizabeth E. Brusco, *The Reformation of Machismo: Evangelical Conversion and Gender in Columbia* (Austin: University of Texas Press, 1995).

29 Cf. Bernice Martin, 'The Pentecostal Gender Paradox: A Cautionary Tale for the Sociology of Religion', in *The Blackwell Companion to Sociology of Religion*, (ed.) Richard K. Fenn (Oxford: Blackwell, 2001), pp. 52–66.

30 *Ibid.*, p. 54.

31 Yong, *The Spirit Poured Out on All Flesh*, p. 41.

32 Cf. Iain MacRobert, *The Black Roots and White Racism of Early Pentecostalism in the USA* (New York: St. Martin's Press, 1988), pp. 60–76.

33 See Cecil M. Robeck, Jr., 'The Past: Historical Roots of Racial Unity and Division in American Pentecostalism', *CPCR* 14, http://www.pctii.org/cyberj/cyberj14/robeck.html, accessed April 22, 2012.

34 MacRobert, *The Black Roots*, pp. 63–7.

35 Cf. David D. Daniels, '"Everybody Bids You Welcome": A Multicultural Approach to North American Pentecostalism', in *The Globalization of Pentecostalism: A Religion Made to Travel*, (eds) Murray W. Dempster, Byron D. Klaus, Douglas Petersen (Oxford: Regnum, 1999), pp. 222–52.

36 Randall J. Stephens, *The Fire Spreads: Holiness and Pentecostalism in the American South* (Cambridge: Harvard University Press, 2008), pp. 209–14.

37 See Estrelda Y. Alexander, *Black Fire: One Hundred Years of African American Pentecostalism* (Downers Grove, IL: InterVarsity, 2011), pp. 249–92.

38 David D. Daniels, 'Dialogue among Black and Hispanic Pentecostal Scholars: A Report and Some Personal Observations', *Pneuma* 17, no. 2 (1995), pp. 219–28.

39 Samuel Solivan, *The Spirit, Pathos and Liberation: Toward an Hispanic Pentecostal Theology* (*JPTSupp* 14; Sheffield: Sheffield Academic Press, 1998), pp. 15–46.

40 See Nestor L. Medina, *Mestizaje: Remapping Race, Culture, and Faith in Latina/o Catholicism* (Maryknoll, NY: Orbis, 2009).

41 Cf. Manuel A. Vásquez, 'Rethinking Mestizaje', in *Rethinking Latino(a) Religion and Identity*, (eds) Miguel A. de la Torre and Gastón Espinosa (Cleveland, OH: Pilgrim Press, 2006), pp. 129–60.

42 E. S. Morran and L. Schlemmer, *Faith for the Fearful? An Investigation into the New Churches in the Greater Durban Area* (Durban: Center for Applied Social Sciences, 1984), pp. 170–9.

43 Cf. Karla Poewe-Hexham and Irving Hexham, 'Charismatic Churches and Apartheid in South Africa', in *All Together in One Place: Theological Papers from the Brighton Conference on World Evangelization*, (eds) Harold D. Hunter and Peter D. Hocken (*JPTSupp* 9; Sheffield: Sheffield Academic Press, 1993), pp. 73–83.

44 See Wynand J. de Kock, 'A Response to Karla Poewe-Hexham and Irving Hexham', in Hunter and Hocken, *All Together in One Place*, pp. 91–5.

45 See Peter Watt and Willem Saayman, 'South African Pentecostalism in Context: Symptoms of a Crisis', *Missionalia* 31, no. 2 (2003), pp. 318–33.

46 *Ibid.*, pp. 324–31.

47 Cf. Nico Horn, 'From Human Rights to Human Wrongs: The Dramatic Turn-About of the South African Pentecostal Movement', in *Christianity and Human Rights*, (ed.) Frederick M. Shepherd (Lanham, MD: Lexington Books, 2009), pp. 213–27.

48 See Martin, 'The Pentecostal Gender Paradox', pp. 52–66.

49 Martin, 'The Pentecostal Gender Paradox', p. 54.

50 Elizabeth Brusco, 'Gender and Power', in Anderson et al., *Studying Global Pentecostalism*, pp. 74–92.

51   Cf. John Burdick, *Blessed Anastacia: Women, Race, and Popular Christianity in Brazil* (New York: Routledge, 1998), pp. 119–48.

52   Brusco, *The Reformation of Machismo*, pp. 92–113.

53   Lesley Gill, '"Like a Veil to Cover Them": Women and the Pentecostal Movement in La Paz', *AE* 17, no. 4 (1990), pp. 708–21.

54   Cf. Margaret Lamberts Bendroth, *Fundamentalism and Gender, 1875 to the Present* (New Haven, CT: Yale University Press, 1993).

55   See Nancy Tatom Ammerman, *Bible Believers: Fundamentalists in the Modern World* (New Brunswick, NY: Rutgers University Press, 1987).

56   See R. Marie Griffith, 'Female Suffering and Religious Devotion in American Pentecostalism', in *Women and Twentieth-Century Protestantism*, (eds) Margaret Lambert Bendroth and Virginia Lieson Brereton (Urbana, IL: University of Illinois Press, 2002), pp. 184–208.

57   Cheryl Townsend Gilkes, *If It Wasn't for the Women: Black Women's Experience and Womanist Culture in Church and Community* (Maryknoll, NY: Orbis, 2000), pp. 92–117.

58   See Elaine J. Lawless, *Handmaidens of the Lord: Pentecostal Women Preachers and Traditional Religion* (Philadelphia: University of Pennsylvania Press, 1988).

59   Salvatore Cucchiari, 'Between Shame and Sanctification: Patriarchy and Its Transformation in Sicilian Pentecostalism', *AE* 17, no. 4 (1990), pp. 687–707.

60   Cf. Ogbu Kalu, *African Pentecostalism: An Introduction* (Oxford: Oxford University Press, 2008), pp. 147–65.

61   See Yoo, Boo-Woong, *Korean Pentecostalism: Its History and Theology* (Frankfurt: Peter Lang, 1987), pp. 98–102.

62   Diane J. Austin-Broos, *Jamaica Genesis: Religion and the Politics of Moral Orders* (Chicago: The University of Chicago Press, 1997), pp. 117–57.

63   Veli-Matti Kärkkäinen, 'Are Pentecostals Oblivious to Social Justice? Theological and Ecumenical Perspectives', *Missionalia* 29, no. 3 (2001), pp. 387–404.

64   Cf. Scott Billingsley, *It's a New Day: Race and Gender in the Modern Charismatic Movement* (Tuscaloosa, AL: University of Alabama Press, 2008).

65   Cf. Wolfgang Vondey, *Beyond Pentecostalism: The Crisis of Global*

Christianity and the Renewal of the Theological Agenda (PM 3; Grand Rapids: Eerdmans, 2010), p. 182.

66   Kilian McDonnell, *Charismatic Renewal and the Churches* (New York: Seabury, 1976), pp. 41–78.

67   Veli-Matti Kärkkäinen, *An Introduction to Ecclesiology: Ecumenical, Historical and Global Perspectives* (Downers Grove: InterVarsity, 2002), pp. 68–78.

68   Margaret M. Poloma, 'The Symbolic Dilemma and the Future of Pentecostalism: Mysticism, Ritual, and Revival', in *The Future of Pentecostalim in the United States*, (eds) Eric Patterson and Edmund J. Rybarczyk (Lanham, MD: Lexington Books, 2007), pp. 105–21.

69   Cheryl Bridges Johns, 'Pentecostal Spirituality and the Conscientization of Women', in Hunter and Hocken, *All Together in One Place*, pp. 153–65.

70   Cheryl Bridges Johns, 'Spirited Vestments: Or, Why the Anointing Is Not Enough', in *Philip's Daughters: Women in Pentecostal-Charismatic Leadership*, (eds) Estrelda Alexander and Amos Yong (Eugene, OR: Pickwick, 2009), pp. 170–84.

71   Kimberly Ervin Alexander and R. Hollis Gause, *Women in Leadership: A Pentecostal Perspective* (Cleveland, TN: Center for Pentecostal Leadership and Care, 2006).

72   Cf. Frederick L. Ware, 'Spiritual Egalitarianism, Ecclesial Pragmatism, and the Status of Women in Ordained Ministry', in Alexander and Yong, *Philip's Daughters*, pp. 215–33.

73   Amos Yong, 'Pentecostalism and the Theological Academy', *TTod* 64, no. 2 (2007), pp. 244–50.

74   See Allan Anderson, 'The Dubious Legacy of Charles Parham: Racism and Cultural Insensitivities among Pentecostals', *Pneuma* 27, no. 1 (2005), pp. 51–64.

75   Cf. Vondey, *Beyond Pentecostalism*, pp. 119–29.

76   Cf. Dale T. Irvin, 'Meeting Beyond These Stories: Black Pentecostalism, Black Theology, and the Global Context', in Yong and Alexander, *Afro-Pentecostalism*, pp. 233–47.

77   Cf. Alexander, *Black Fire*, pp. 293–341.

78   Nancy L. Eiesland, 'A Strange Road Home: Adult Female Converts to Classical Pentecostalism', in *Mixed Blessings: Gender and Religious Fundamentalism Cross Culturally*, (eds) Judy Brink and Joan Mencher (New York: Routledge, 1997), pp. 91–115.

79   Cf. Martin, 'A Pentecostal Gender Paradox', pp. 53, 58.

80   See Anne Motley Hallum, 'Taking Stock and Building Bridges: Feminism, Women's Movements, and Pentecostalism in Latin America', *Latin American Research Review* 38, no. 1 (2003), pp. 169–86.

81   Daniel E. Albrecht, *Rites in the Spirit: A Ritual Approach to Pentecostal/Charismatic Spirituality* (*JPTSupp* 17; Sheffield: Sheffield Academic Press, 1999), appendix.

82   Samuel Cruz, *Masked Africanisms: Puerto Rican Pentecostalism* (Dubuque, IA: Kendall/Hunt Publishing Company, 2005); Leonard E Barrett, 'African Roots in Jamaican Indigenous Religion', *JRT* 35, no. 1 (1978), pp. 7–26.

83   Cf. Vondey, *Beyond Pentecostalism*, pp. 125–9.

84   Cf. David Martin, *Pentecostalism: The World Their Parish* (Oxford: Blackwell, 2002), pp. 138–44.

85   André Droogers, 'Identity, Religious Pluralism, and Ritual in Brazil: Umbanda and Pentecostalism', in *Pluralism and Identity: Studies in Ritual Behaviour*, (ed.) Jan Platvoet and K. van der Toorn (Leiden: Brill, 1995), pp. 91–113.

86   Walter J. Hollenweger, *Pentecostalism: Origins and Development Worldwide* (Peabody, MA: Hendrickson, 1997), pp. 269–87.

87   Ronald Schouten, '"Rituals of Renewal": The Toronto Blessings as a Ritual Change of Contemporary Christianity', *JRitS* 17, no. 2 (2003), pp. 25–34.

88   See Estrelda Y. Alexander, *Limited Liberty: The Legacy of Four Pentecostal Women Pioneers* (Cleveland, OH: Pilgrim Press, 2008); eadem, *The Women of Azusa Street* (Cleveland, OH: Pilgrim Press, 2005).

89   Cf. Julie C. Ma, 'Changing Images: Women in Asian Pentecostalism', in Alexander and Yong, *Philip's Daughters*, pp. 203–14.

Chapter Seven

1   Cf. Douglas Jacobsen, *Thinking in the Spirit: Theologies of the Early Pentecostal Movement* (Bloomington, IN: Indiana University Press, 2003), pp. 5–8.

2   Cf. Paul. W. Lewis, 'Why Have Scholars Left Classical Pentecostal Denominations?', *AJPS* 11, no. 1–2 (2008), pp. 69–86.

3   Cf. Wolfgang Vondey, *Beyond Pentecostalism: The Crisis of Global Christianity and the Renewal of the Theological Agenda* (PM 1; Grand Rapids: Eerdmans, 2010), pp. 88–98.

4   See Mark A. Noll, *The Scandal of the Evangelical Mind* (Grand Rapids: Eerdmans, 1994), pp. 109–48.

5   Cf. Cheryl Bridges Johns, 'Partners in Scandal: Wesleyan and Pentecostal Scholarship', in *Pneuma* 21, no. 2 (1999), pp. 183–97.

6   Juan Sepúlveda, 'The Challenge for Theological Education from a Pentecostal Standpoint', *MF* 87 (1999), pp. 29–30.

7   Jacobsen, *Thinking in the Spirit*, p. 8.

8   Allan Anderson, *Spreading Fires: The Missionary Nature of Early Pentecostalism* (Maryknoll, NY: Orbis, 2007), pp. 46–72.

9   *AF* 1, no. 1 (September 1906), p. 1.

10   *AF* 1, no. 3 (November 1906), p. 1.

11   A. J. Tomlinson, *The Last Great Conflict* (Cleveland, TN: Walter E. Rogers, 1913), pp. 69, 74.

12   Cf. Grant Wacker, *Heaven Below: Early Pentecostals and American Culture* (Cambridge: Harvard University Press, 2001), p. 31.

13   Anderson, *Spreading Fires*, p. 58.

14   Cf. Wacker, *Heaven Below*, p. 31.

15   D. William Faupel, *The Everlasting Gospel: The Significance of Eschatology in the Development of Pentecostal Thought* (*JPTSupp* 10; Sheffield: Sheffield Academic Press, 1996), pp. 20–7.

16   See William K. Kay and Anne E. Dyer (eds), *Pentecostal and Charismatic Studies: A Reader* (London: SCM Press, 2004), pp. 25–46.

17   Gary B. McGee, *Miracles, Missions, and American Pentecostalism* (Maryknoll, NY: Orbis, 2010), pp. 153–6.

18   *Ibid.*

19   Steven J. Land, *Pentecostal Spirituality: A Passion for the Kingdom* (*JPTSupp* 1; Sheffield: Sheffield Academic Press, 1993), p. 19.

20   Cf. Vondey, *Beyond Pentecostalism*, pp. 30–3 and 61–6.

21   McGee, *Miracles, Missions, and American Pentecostalism*, p. 154.

22   See Lynne Price, 'Scholarship and Evangelism: Oil and Water?' in *Pentecostals after a Century: Global Perspectives on a Movement in Transition*, (eds) Allan H. Anderson and Walter J. Hollenweger (*JPTSupp* 13; Sheffield: Sheffield Academic Press, 1999), pp. 197–208.

23   See Richard G. Spurling, *The Lost Link* (Turtletown, TN: R. G. Spurling, 1920).

24   Del Tarr, 'Transcendence, Immanence, and the Emerging Pentecostal Academy', in *Pentecostalism in Context: Essays in Honor of William W. Menzies*, (eds) Wonsuk Ma and Robert P. Menzies (*JPTSupp* 11; Sheffield: Sheffield Academic Press, 1997), pp. 195–222.

25   Sepúlveda, 'The Challenge for Theological Education', p. 29.

26   See Richard Hofstadter, *Anti-Intellectualism in American Life* (New York: Knopf, 1963).

27   Rick M. Nañez, *Full Gospel, Fractured Minds? A Call to Use God's Gift of the Intellect* (Grand Rapids: Zondervan, 2005), pp. 116–22.

28   See Douglas Jacobsen and Rhonda Hustedt Jacobsen, 'Pentecostalism and the Academy', *Pneuma* 27, no. 1 (2005), pp. 106–9.

29   See Cheryl Bridges Johns, 'Athens, Berlin, and Azusa: A Pentecostal Reflection on Scholarship and Christian Faith', *Pneuma* 27, no. 1 (2005), pp. 136–47.

30   See Gordon Anderson, 'Pentecost, Scholarship, and Learning in a Postmodern World', *Pneuma* 27, no. 1 (2005), pp. 115–23.

31   Cf. David D. Daniels III, '"Wonder and Scholarship": Reflecting on Jacobsen and Jacobsen's Scholarship and Christian Faith: Enlarging the Conversation', *Pneuma* 27, no. 1 (2005), pp. 110–14.

32   Cf. Amos Yong, 'Academic Glossolalia? Pentecostal Scholarship, Multi-Disciplinarity, and the Science-Religion Conversation', *JPT* 14, no. 1 (2005), pp. 61–80.

33   Cf. Land, *Pentecostal Spirituality*, pp. 122–81.

34   *Ibid.*, p. 136.

35   Samuel Solivan, *The Spirit, Pathos and Liberation: Toward an Hispanic Pentecostal Theology* (*JPTSupp* 14; Sheffield: Sheffield Academic Press, 1998), pp. 80–6.

36   Cf. James K. A. Smith, *Thinking in Tongues: Pentecostal Contributions to Christian Philosophy* (PM 1; Grand Rapids: Eerdmans, 2010), pp. 71–80.

37   Cf. Vondey, *Beyond Pentecostalism*, pp. 16–46.

38   Smith, *Thinking in Tongues*, p. 81.

39   See Amos Yong, *Spirit-Word-Community: Theological Hermeneutics in Trinitarian Perspective* (Eugene, OR: Wipf and Stock, 2003), pp. 119–217.

40   Vondey, *Beyond Pentecostalism*, p. 40.

41   *Ibid.*, pp. 40–6.

42   Cf. Wolfgang Vondey and Chris W. Green, 'Between This and That: Reality and Sacramentality in the Pentecostal Worldview', *JPT*, 19, no. 2 (2010), pp. 243–64.

43   Cf. Douglas Jacobsen and Rhonda Hustedt Jacobsen, 'A Response to the *Pneuma* Essays on Faith and Scholarship', *Pneuma* 27, no. 1 (2005), pp. 157–60.

44   Smith, *Thinking in Tongues*, p. 80.

45   Land, *Pentecostal Spirituality*, p. 119.

46   Walter J. Hollenweger, *Pentecostalism: Origins and Developments Worldwide* (Grand Rapids: Baker Academic Press, 1997; 2005), pp. 194–7.

47   Cf. Smith, *Thinking in Tongues*, pp. 146–50.

48   Cf. Johns, 'Athens, Berlin, and Azusa', pp. 136–47.

49   Cheryl Bridges Johns, *Pentecostal Formation: A Pedagogy among the Oppressed* (*JPTSupp* 3; Sheffield: Sheffield Academic Press, 1993).

50   Cf. McGee, *Miracles, Missions, and American Pentecostalism*, pp. 154–5.

51   See Charles W. Nienkirchen, *A. B. Simpson and the Pentecostal Movement* (Peabody, MA: Hendrickson, 1992), pp. 43–6.

52   Cf. McGee, *Miracles, Missions, and American Pentecostalism*, pp. 156–7.

53   Cf. Matthew Avery Sutton, *Aimee Semple McPherson and the Resurrection of Christian America* (Cambridge, MA: Harvard University Press, 2007), pp. 204–10.

54   The English equivalent is Walter J. Hollenweger, *The Pentecostals: The Charismatic Movement in the Churches* (Minneapolis: Augsburg Publishing House, 1972).

55   Cf. Rick D. Moore, Steven J. Land, John Christopher Thomas, 'Editorial', *JPT* 1 (1992), pp. 3–5.

56   Cf. Amos Yong, 'Pentecostalism and the Theological Academy', *TTod* 64, no. 2 (2007), pp. 244–50.

57   See part two of Augustus Cerillo Jr. and Grant Wacker, 'Bibliography and Historiography of Pentecostalism in the United States', in NIDPCM, pp. 390–405.

58   Cf. Martin William Mittelstadt, *Reading Luke-Acts in the Pentecostal Tradition* (Cleveland, TN: CPT Press, 2010), pp. 64–80.

59   Cf. Yong, 'Pentecostalism and the Theological Academy', pp. 244–50.

60   *Ibid.*, p. 247.

61   See Kenneth J. Archer, *A Pentecostal Hermeneutic: Spirit, Scripture and Community* (Cleveland, TN: CPT Press, 2009), pp. 172–211.

62   See Vinson Synan, 'Fifteen Years of the Society for Pentecostal Studies', unpublished paper (Society for Pentecostal Studies, November 14–16, 1985), pp. 1–9.

63   Cf. Moore, Land, Thomas, 'Editorial,' pp. 3–5.

64   Cf. Yong, 'Pentecostalism and the Theological Academy', pp. 244–50 (248).

65   See Amos Yong, *The Spirit Poured Out on All Flesh: Pentecostalism and the Possibility of Global Theology* (Grand Rapids: Baker Academic, 2005).

66   Cf. Vondey, *Beyond Pentecostalism*, pp. 1–15.

67   See Yong, 'Academic Glossolalia', pp. 61–80.

68   See James K. A. Smith and Amos Yong (eds), *Science and the Spirit: A Pentecostal Engagement with the Sciences* (Bloomington, IN: Indiana University Press, 2010).

69   See Allan Anderson et al. (eds), *Studying Global Pentecostalism: Theories and Methods* (Berkeley: University of California Press, 2010).

70   Cf. James K. A. Smith and Amos Yong, 'Introduction: Science and the Spirit—Questions and Possibilities in the Pentecostal Engagement with Science', in Smith and Yong, *Science and the Spirit*, pp. 1–11.

71   See Jeff Hittenberger, 'The Future of Pentecostal Higher Education: The Ring, the Shire, or the Redemption of Middle Earth?' in *The Future of Pentecostalism in the United States*, (eds) Eric Patterson and Edmund Rybarczyk (Lanham, MD: Lexington Books, 2007), pp. 83–103.

72   See Keith Warrington, *Pentecostal Theology: A Theology of Encounter* (New York: Continuum, 2008).

73   Yong, 'Pentecostalism and the Theological Academy', p. 244–50.

74   Cf. Telford Work, 'What Have the Galapagos to Do with Jerusalem? Scientific Knowledge in Theological Context', in Smith and Yong, *Science and the Spirit*, pp. 15–33.

75   Cf. Wolfgang Vondey, 'Does God Have a Place in the Physical

Universe? Physics and the Quest for the Holy Spirit', Smith and Yong, *Science and the Spirit*, pp. 75–91.

76   Cf. Vondey, *Beyond Pentecostalism*, pp. 171–201.

77   Nimi Wariboko, *The Pentecostal Principle: Ethical Methodology in New Spirit* (PM 5; Grand Rapids: Eerdmans, 2011), pp. 165–71.

78   *Ibid.*, p. 207.

79   Cf. Johns, *Pentecostal Formation*, pp. 62–110.

80   Cf. Yong, 'Pentecostalism and the Theological Academy', pp. 244–50.

81   See Daniel E. Albrecht, *Rites in the Spirit: A Ritual Approach to Pentecostal/Charismatic Spirituality* (JPTSupp 17; Sheffield: Sheffield Academic Press, 1999), pp. 196–217.

82   See *ibid.*, pp. 255–6.

83   Cf. Yong, 'Pentecostalism and the Theological Academy', pp. 244–50 (249).

84   Cf. Mark Stibbe, 'This Is That: Some Thoughts Concerning Charismatic Hermeneutics', *Anvil* 13, no. 3 (1998), pp. 181–93.

85   See Kevin L. Spawn, 'The Principle of Analogy and Biblical Interpretation in the Renewal Tradition', in *Spirit and Scripture: Examining a Pneumatic Hermeneutic*, (eds) Kevin L. Spawn and Archie T. Wright (New York: Continuum, 2011), pp. 46–72.

86   Cf. Vondey and Green, 'Between This and That', pp. 243–64.

87   See Mark J. Cartledge, *Testimony in the Spirit: Rescripting Ordinary Pentecostal Theology* (Surrey, UK: Ashgate, 2010), pp. 15–16.

88   *Ibid.*, pp. 16–18.

89   Nañez, *Full Gospel, Fractured Minds*, pp. 135–95.

90   *Ibid.*, pp. 230–5.

91   Cf. Wonsuk Ma, 'Preparing for the Next Generation Pentecostal Thinkers in Asia', *AJPS* 9, no. 2 (2006), pp. 181–2.

92   Johns, *Pentecostal Formation*, p. 121.

93   Simon Chan, *Pentecostal Theology and the Christian Spiritual Tradition* (JPTSupp 21; Sheffield: Sheffield Academic Press, 2000), p. 31.

94   Johns, *Pentecostal Formation*, p. 139.

95   Cf. Frank Macchia, 'Sighs too Deep for Words: Toward a Theology of Glossolalia', *JPT* 1 (1992), pp. 47–73.

96 Cf. Yong, 'Academic Glossolalia', pp. 61–80 (64).

97 Johns, 'Partners in Scandal', pp. 183–97 (191).

98 *Ibid.*, p. 194.

99 See Butler, 'Pentecostal Traditions We Should Pass on', pp. 343–53.

100 Cf. Cheryl Bridges Johns, 'The Meaning of Pentecost for Theological Education', *MF* 87 (1999), pp. 42–7.

101 *Ibid.*, p. 46.

102 Cf. Allan Anderson, *An Introduction to Pentecostalism* (Cambridge: Cambridge University Press, 2004), pp. 243–9.

103 See Peter Gräbe, 'A Perspective from Regent University's Ph.D. Program in Renewal Studies: Theology in the Light of the Renewing Work of the Holy Spirit', *Pneuma* 27, no. 1 (2005), pp. 124–9.

104 Cf. Amos Yong (ed.), *The Spirit Renews the Face of the Earth: Pentecostal Forays in Science and Theology of Creation* (Eugene: Pickwick, 2009), pp. xvi–xx.

105 Cf. Yong, *Spirit-Word-Community*, p. 8.

106 Amos Yong, 'Finding the Holy Spirit at the Christian University: Renewal and the Future of Higher Education in the Pentecostal-Charismatic Tradition', in *Spirit-Empowered Christianity in the 21st Century: Insights, Analyses, and Future Trends*, (ed.) Vinson Synan (Lake Mary, FL: Charisma House, 2011), pp. 455–76.

107 Amos Yong, 'Poured Out on All Flesh: The Spirit, World Pentecostalism, and the Renewal of Theology and Praxis in the 21st Century', *PentecoStudies* 6, no. 1 (2007), pp. 16–46 (25).

108 Amos Yong, 'Finding the Holy Spirit at the Christian University', pp. 455–76 (466).

109 See J. Rodman Williams, *Renewal Theology: Systematic Theology from a Charismatic Perspective*, Three Volumes in One (Grand Rapids: Zondervan, 1996).

110 Cf. Vondey, *Beyond Pentecostalism*, pp. 192–6.

BIBLIOGRAPHY

Alexander, Paul. *Signs and Wonders: Why Pentecostalism is the World's Fastest Growing Faith* (San Francisco: Jossey-Bass, 2009).

Anderson, Allan H. *An Introduction to Pentecostalism* (Cambridge: Cambridge University Press, 2004).

Anderson, Allan H., Michael Bergunder, André Droogers, Cornelis van der Laan (eds). *Studying Global Pentecostalism: Theories and Methods*. Berkeley: University of California Press, 2010.

Hollenweger, Walter J. *Pentecostalism: Origins and Developments Worldwide* (Grand Rapids: Baker Academic Press, 1997; 2005).

Kay, William K. *Pentecostalism: A Very Short Introduction* (Oxford: Oxford University Press, 2011).

Synan, Vinson. *The Century of the Holy Spirit: 100 Years of Pentecostal and Charismatic Renewal, 1901–2001* (Nashville: Thomas Nelson, 2001).

Yong, Amos and Cecil M. Robeck, Jr. (eds). *The Cambridge Companion to Pentecostalism* (Cambridge: Cambridge University Press, 2012).

INDEX